Resisting Financialization with Deleuze and Guattari

Resisting Financialization with Deleuze and Guattari aims to provide a contribution in relation to three main areas: the understanding of contemporary capitalism and financialization from a critical perspective; the analysis of resistance to financialization; and the better understanding of the philosophy of Deleuze and Guattari.

Using a critical perspective, this book is informed by a Marxian literature in political economy and the poststructuralist works of Deleuze and Guattari, and Foucault. Through this, the author argues that it is relevant to combine Marxism and poststructuralism so as to better understand financialization. The analysis of resistance to financialization also provides a reflection on social democracy and Occupy Wall Street as contrasting ways to resist capitalism. Finally, this book will contribute to the analysis of Deleuze and Guattari through an analysis of their reception within political philosophy.

This book provides the intellectual tools needed by academics in order to articulate a critical and revolutionary interpretation of Deleuze and Guattari, as well as analyse their reception by political philosophy. It also offers these tools to a more general audience interested in political economy and capitalism.

Charles Barthold completed his PhD at the University of Leicester (2015) and is now a lecturer at the Open University, UK. He is interested in the intersection of financialization and the political and ethical responses to it. Similarly, he is interested in poststructuralist approaches, animal studies, corporate social responsibility and precarity.

Routledge Frontiers of Political Economy

For a full list of titles in this series, please visit www.routledge.com/books/series/SE0345

Resisting Financialization with Deleuze and Guattari

Charles Barthold

Routledge
Taylor & Francis Group

LONDON AND NEW YORK

First published 2018
by Routledge

2 Park Square, Milton Park, Abingdon, Oxfordshire OX14 4RN

52 Vanderbilt Avenue, New York, NY 10017

Routledge is an imprint of the Taylor & Francis Group, an informa business

First issued in paperback 2020

British Library Cataloguing-in-Publication Data
A catalogue record for this book is available from the British Library

Library of Congress Cataloging-in-Publication Data
Names: Barthold, Charles, 1985– author.
Title: Resisting financialization with Deleuze and Guattari /
   Charles Barthold.
Description: Abingdon, Oxon ; New York, NY : Routledge, 2018. |
   Series: Routledge frontiers of political economy ; 241 | Includes
   bibliographical references and index.
Identifiers: LCCN 2018001647 (print) | LCCN 2018002671 (ebook) |
   ISBN 9780203731727 | ISBN 9781138302723 (hardback : alk. paper)
Subjects: LCSH: Financialization. | Marxian economics. | Deleuze, Gilles,
   1925–1995. | Guattari, Fâelix, 1930–1992.
Classification: LCC HG173 (ebook) | LCC HG173 .B338 2018 (print) |
   DDC 332—dc23
LC record available at https://lccn.loc.gov/2018001647

ISBN: 978-1-138-30272-3 (hbk)
ISBN: 978-0-367-59014-7 (pbk)

Typeset in Bembo
by Apex CoVantage, LLC

Contents

Acknowledgements

I would like to thank my supervisors David Harvie and Stephen Dunne for their extraordinary intellectual generosity, their fantastic support and their incredible patience. Similarly, I would like to thank Campbell Jones for his essential help. I was very lucky to have the privilege to experience the marvellous ethos of the School of Management of the University of Leicester, in particular with Martin Parker, Gibson Burrell, Geoff Lightfoot, Simon Lilley, Keir Milburn, Dimitris Papadopoulos, Maria Puig de la Bellacasa, Steve Brown and many other wonderful people. Many thanks also to the members of the CPPE who always provided great discussions and ideas: in particular Nick Butler, Eleni Karamali, Sverre Spoelstra, Armin Beverungen, Matt Allen and Angus Cameron. Finally, I would like to express my gratitude to Kenneth Weir and Bent Meier Sørensen; as well as Andy Humphries and the editorial team of Routledge.

Many thanks as well to all the other PhD students of the programme for their help and their support. Finally, I would like to thank my family for their great support. Last but not least, many thanks to Nefertari Vanden Bulcke for her unconditional support as well as to Michael Whitburn for his precious time and incredible kindness.

Author's note

Some parts of this book have been published elsewhere as book reviews but have been substantially rewritten here. Some of Chapter 2 is based on a book review of *Badiou and Politic* by Bruno Bosteels (2005) published in *Ephemera: Theory & Politics in Organization*, 12(4), pp. 475–479, 2011. Some of Chapter 4 is based on a book review of *This Is Not a Program* by Tiqqun (2011) published in *Anarchist Studies*, 21(1), p. 125, 2013 and a book review of *The Guattari Effect* edited by Eric Alliez and Andrew Goffey (2013) published in *Organization*, 20(4), pp. 641–643, 2013. Finally, some of Chapter 6 is based on a book review of *Marketing Shares, Sharing Markets: Experts in Investment Banking* (2012) by Jesper Blomberg, Hans Kjellberg and Karin Winroth published in *Organization*, 21(5), pp. 746–748, 2014. Finally, 'Resisting financialisation with Deleuze and Guattari: the case of Occupy Wall Street' (with David Harvie and Stephen Dunne) in *Critical Perspectives on Accounting* (in press) is based on Chapter 7.

1 Introduction

Deleuze and Guattari and financialization

The French President François Hollande declared during the presidential campaign in 2012 that his main enemy was 'finance' (Hollande 2012a: 5; my translation). He therefore proposed to operate a series of measures to regulate finance, for example through means of a Tobin tax, and to separate investment banks and retail banks (Hollande 2012b). Hollande was not, however, able to implement such regulatory measures in particular because of the lobbying of French banks and the refusal of Chancellor Angela Merkel to implement Eurobonds (*The Economist* 2012a). The immediate context of the discussion was the extreme volatility of European sovereign debt markets, itself the result of widespread political, economic and social tensions and uncertainties (Haugh et al. 2009). In December 2017 – as I write this book – that is to say almost ten years after the 2007–2008 financial crisis, Hollande's attempt was the only one in any major country.

All this demonstrated a clear articulation between finance and politics. On the one hand, finance is a central problem for politics because financialization of the economy means any economic policy is directly faced with the fact that international flows of capital can cross borders (Bonefeld and Holloway 1995c). Dealing with finance is one of the major challenges of contemporary politics, even though politics seems powerless in front of finance, as Hollande's failure to regulate it made perfectly clear. Flows of finance operate at the global level, whereas politics attempts to confront it at the national level (Holloway 1994). Financialization of capital therefore seems to reinforce the feeling that there is no alternative and that the world of capital is the only world possible despite the financial crisis of 2007–2008. It would be 'easier to imagine the end of the world than to imagine the end of capitalism' (Jameson 2007: 199) which would lead to a 'capitalist realism' (Fisher 2009).

The situation is not new. As a young person living in a global city like Paris I was able to notice the financialization of my subjectivity. When I was ten years of age working-class people could afford to rent a decent flat in my neighbourhood and middle-class people could afford to own their flat. I remember that in the mid-1990s my maths teacher could afford to buy a flat which would now cost around 1 million euros, that is almost 70 years of the French minimum wage (SMIC 2014). I was able to feel the violence of finance capital on my subjectivity. The financialization of housing has implied for me the end of my 'right to the city' (Harvey 2012), meaning the opportunity to live where I was born. I am no longer able to afford to live in my neighbourhood because financial capital was massively invested in the Paris real estate market in the last 15 years, for instance from Qatar (Barret 2014). This brought about a trebling of Paris real estate prices in the 2000s (De Beaupuy 2013). The same story holds for anyone who does not come from a wealthy family and who was born in the 1980s in London, São Paulo or Moscow.

It became increasingly clear to me – because of real estate speculation in Paris – that resisting the power of capital on my life entailed resisting financialization and the power of flows of capital to cross borders and escape state regulation. It seemed to me that a 'resonance' (Thoburn 2003: 1) between a revolutionary understanding of Deleuze and Guattari and the Marxian literature on financialization would help elaborate a politics of resistance to financialization. My understanding was that Marxism provided the best political economy of capitalism and that Deleuze and Guattari provided the most effective political philosophy. Conversely, on the one hand, it seemed to me that a Marxist politics on its own was unable to elaborate a politics of resistance to financialization because of the crisis of Leninism and of social democracy, which failed to understand the struggles of the 1960s (Cleaver 2000: 74). On the other hand, it seemed to me that a Deleuzo-Guattarian politics, despite its remarkable understanding of the transformations of social subjectivity, required the framework of the Marxist political economy in order to fully understand the current centrality of finance for capital.

Objectives

My objective is to provide a critical reflection on financialization, which could assess how financialization operates and how it might be possible to resist it. I connect Deleuze and Guattari and Marx in order to provide a critique of financialization. My intention is to establish a 'resonance' between a revolutionary interpretation of Deleuze and Guattari and the Marxian literature on financialization (Thoburn 2003: 1). Against critics of poststructuralist philosophy and of Deleuze (Sokal and Bricmont 2004), I argue that the philosophy of Deleuze and Guattari[1] can bring about a relevant conceptualization of the complexity of the contemporary world through its processualist and materialist thought (Negri 2011).

The work of Deleuze and Guattari provides a very relevant political reflection on capital in the current situation because of its acknowledgement of the struggles that developed in the 1960s and 1970s (Deleuze and Guattari 1977, 1987). For example, Deleuze was involved in the struggles of French prisoners through the Prison Information Group in the aftermath of May '68 (Dosse 2010: 309–313). Guattari was directly involved in May '68 (Dosse 2010: 171). French orthodox Marxism was suspicious of the new struggles in the 1960s and 1970s including May '68 and the Prison Information Group.

Marx and the Marxian tradition generate a political economic thought that is extremely useful to understand the dynamic of capital, which is marked by financialization. Arguably, the academic tradition working on Marx provides a relevant critical reflection on capital not provided by mainstream economics and finance studies, which mainly argue that capital markets work and are grounded on the concept of *homo economicus* (for instance, Fama 1965). Finance studies tend to be practice-oriented as well. By contrast, Marxian concepts allow the operations and the transformations of capital to be historicized. I draw mainly on the Marxian literature on financialization, which seeks to understand the originality of this specific historical phenomenon that did not exist when Marx was writing *Capital* in the second half of the nineteenth century.

Financialization is a global and complex phenomenon. It has transformed the economy since the end of Fordism and the Bretton Woods financial system which was able to regulate international flows of capital (Bryan and Rafferty 2006: 112). International flows of capital are able to cross borders. Capital operates through debt, in particular mortgages for subprimes as collateralized debt obligations, but also student debt or private debt (Lazzarato 2012). Financialization implies an intensification of competition among capitals, and consequently an intensification of the exploitation of labour, in particular through derivatives (Bryan and Rafferty 2006) and the development of shareholder value governance (Froud and Williams 2000a, 2000b). Financialization also operates on the level of subjectivity (Martin 2002), the state (Martin 2007) and social reproduction, for instance through social impact bonds. The complex operations of financialization on the economy, social reproduction and subjectivity will be extensively explained further.[2]

My approach is not characterized by axiological neutrality because I wish to challenge financialization and the power of capital through a 'resonance' between the philosophy of Deleuze and Guatari, and a Marxian political economy (Thoburn 2003: 1). I study Deleuze and Guattari for political reasons. As a result, this book will try to respond to the following question: How can a revolutionary interpretation of Deleuze and Guattari politicize financialization?

In attempting to answer this question, in the first part I provide a study of the reception of the philosophy of Deleuze and Guattari, which allows me to articulate a non-naïve and situated revolutionary engagement with the philosophy of Deleuze and Guattari. Next, in the second part, I apply this revolutionary reading of Deleuze and Guattari to financialization. Finally, I seek to elaborate a Deleuzo-Guattarian politics of resistance to financialization drawing on the social democratic experience of President Hollande in France and of the Occupy Wall Street movement.

Reading Deleuze and Guattari

The first issue that arises is how to read Deleuze and Guattari. The work of Deleuze and Guattari is extremely diverse and complex. Deleuze and Guattari refer to the history of philosophy, musicology, linguistics, biology, physics, psychoanalysis, ethnology, the cinema, mathematics, geometry, literature, economics, political economy, geography and history (1977, 1986, 1987, 1994). Their work, however, arguably belongs to the field of philosophy because it is characterized by the 'creation of concepts' (Deleuze and Guattari 1994: 8). Different methodologies or methodological practices are operated in academia in relation to reading French contemporary continental philosophy. It is useful to briefly review the main methodological practices in relation to reading this philosophy in order to explain more clearly what would be a faithful interpretation of Deleuze and Guattari.

Such a review will not provide a thorough analysis of all the possible ways of reading philosophy, which would probably require a monograph in its own right. Similarly, a number of methodological French contemporary continental philosophy practices overlap. The idea is to confront and discuss the main methodological traditions of reading philosophy that are related to French contemporary continental philosophy. This should help contextualize and address the question of reading philosophy from the perspective of Deleuze and Guattari. Symptomatology (Althusser and Balibar 1997), archaeology (Foucault 1989, 2002), deconstruction (Derrida 1997) and genealogy (Foucault 1977a, 1998a: 369) will be discussed. Deleuze and Guattari were familiar with these methodologies because they were practised in their immediate environment.

A first approach is Althusserian symptomatology, which draws on psychoanalysis to produce an interpretation of a philosophical text. The idea is that a text is a symptom or a pathological effect of an id or other deeper causes. This methodology was designed by Althusser and his collaborators to provide a novel reading of *Capital* (Althusser and Balibar 1997). Symptomatology allows for a critical selection of texts and concepts within the framework of an oeuvre. It provides coherence to the reading of a philosophical text or oeuvre through a bird's eye view.

Accordingly, for Althusser and Balibar (1997), to provide a reading of a philosophical text would correspond to a psychoanalytic operation. The works of Deleuze and Guattari, however, strongly criticize the very notion of psychoanalysis and advocate the notion of schizoanalysis (1977, 1987). In particular, Deleuze and Guattari reject the interpretativist importance of the notion of Oedipus for psychoanalysis (1977, 1987). This form of symptomatology designed by Althusser and Balibar could produce a reading of Deleuze and Guattari. However, Althusserian symptomatology could not provide a Deleuzo-Guattarian methodology of reading Deleuze and Guattari because of the latter's rejection of psychoanalysis (Dosse 1997: 211; Holland 2012: 133; Schwab 2007). As a result, the current argument cannot use Althusserian symptomatology.

A second approach is structuralist-archaeological. Michel Foucault in *The Order of Things* (1989) and the *Archaeology of Knowledge* (2002) operated a structuralist- archaeological reading of philosophical texts. The idea was that a philosophical oeuvre is determined by a series of structures in the history of ideas, which Foucault defines as Renaissance, Classical and Modern 'epistemes' (Foucault 1989). For example, the philosophy of Descartes would have been determined by the Classical episteme which would have been marked by 'representation' (Foucault 1989: 77). The singularity of a specific philosophical oeuvre is not taken into account. It is possible to provide a structuralist archaeology of the oeuvre of Deleuze and Guattari.

Deleuze and Guattari criticize structuralism (1977, 1987). In particular, Deleuze and Guattari criticize the structuralist ethnology of Lévi-Strauss and its lack of consideration for change and 'disequilibrium' of primitive societies (1977: 187). Deleuze and Guattari reject structuralist linguistics and advocate the pragmatist linguistics of Hjelmslev (1987: 108). Deleuze and Guattari rejected structuralism (Dosse 1997: 210, 2012: 126). It would be impossible to operate a Deleuzo-Guattarian methodology of reading the philosophy of Deleuze and Guattari based on a structuralist methodology. Similarly, this book cannot use a structuralist methodology because the Deleuzo-Guattarian philosophy is post-structuralist as opposed to structuralist (Williams 2005: 53).

A third approach is genealogy. Genealogy was implemented by Foucault from the mid- 1970s, in particular in *Discipline and Punish* (1977a). Genealogy consists of a historical methodology that draws on Nietzsche's *On the Genealogy of Morality* (1994). From this perspective, philosophical texts could be interpreted within the specific power relations in which they are inserted. For example, the philosophy of Beccaria is interpreted by Foucault as constituting a specific power-knowledge apparatus connected to panopticism and disciplinary power (1977a: 9).

Genealogy resonates with the works of Deleuze and Guattari because of its poststructuralism (Williams 2005: 112). A reading of genealogy from the perspective of the ontology of Deleuze and Guattari can be provided (Colwell 1997). However, Deleuze and Guattari, on the one hand, and Foucault, on the other, have two separate projects which is illustrated by the fact that Deleuze's book on Foucault would be a 'metaphysical fiction' (Gros 1995). Deleuze and Guattari would have a different ontology of history than Foucault: 'Insofar as he sees the critique and creativity which characterize thinking the impossible (whether in terms of genealogy or a mode of living) as historical, it is clear that Foucault locates possibilities for social transformation within history as well. This . . . directly opposes Deleuze' (Taylor 2014: 129). This implies that the genealogical method does not seem compatible with the Deleuzo-Guattarian ontology.

More practically, a genealogy would imply extensive archival work on the oeuvre of Deleuze: 'Genealogy is gray, meticulous, and patiently documentary. It operates on a field of entangled and confused parchments, on documents that have been scratched over and recopied many times' (Foucault 1998a: 369). This methodology would correspond to a historiographic work, which does not fall within the scope of this work. An intellectual biography of Deleuze and Guattari already exists, even if it does not perform a genealogy (Dosse 2010).

A fourth approach is deconstructionist. It corresponds to an approach of reading philosophy inspired by the oeuvre of Jacques Derrida. It involves looking for contradictions in the sense of a specific text or oeuvre. For Derrida, there would always be 'textual ambivalences that remain unresolvable and prevent us from understanding fully "what the author really means"' which the oral language would not be able to clarify, as there would always be 'a difference between what is thought (or experienced or said or written) and the ideal of pure, self-identical meaning' (Gutting 2001: 292). In particular, in *Of Grammatology* Derrida operates a deconstructionist reading of Rousseau's *Essay on the Origin of Languages*: 'I have attempted to produce, often embarrassing myself in the process, the problems of critical reading' (Derrida 1997: 1).

There is a resonance between Derrida and Deleuze and Guattari because they share the same critique of representation and of structuralism since all three belong to poststructuralism (Williams 2005). Derrida, on the one hand, and Deleuze and Guattari, on the other, also share a critique of phenomenology (Lawlor 2012: 104). Derrida considers structuralism to be related to a metaphysics of presence (1997: 46). Patton argues that the Derridean deconstruction shares similarities with the Deleuzian philosophical practice, despite 'undeniable differences of style and method' (2003: 16).

Nevertheless, there seem to be broader differences between Derrida and Deleuze and Guattari. For instance, Deleuze and Guattari do not share Derrida's concept of 'logocentrism' (Gutting 2001: 294) and understanding of texts (Alliez 2003: 94). More generally, the approach of Deleuze and Guattari is more ontological, whereas Derrida operates a critique of metaphysics, that is to say of ontology (Patton and Protevi 2003: 6). Even though a deconstructionist reading of Deleuze and Guattari is possible, a Deleuzo-Guattarian reading of Deleuze cannot use a deconstructionist methodology.

Even though these four different approaches could be used to operate a specific reading of the oeuvre of Deleuze and Guattari or of its reception, none of these methodologies would be useful in providing a Deleuzo-Guattarian reading of Deleuze and Guattari, or a Deleuzo-Guattarian reading of the reception of Deleuze and Guattari. I shall examine below the Deleuzian theory of reading of 'buggery' and see if it is an operational methodology for my project (Deleuze 1995: 6).

Buggery by Deleuze and Guattari?

Deleuze wrote a number of history of philosophy works on Hume (1991), Nietzsche (1983), Bergson (1988a), Kant (1984), Lucretius (2004), Leibniz (1993a), Foucault (1988b) and Spinoza (1988c, 1990). Perhaps these works could provide a methodology that would generate a Deleuzo-Guattarian reading of the oeuvre of Deleuze and Guattari. This is how Deleuze talks about his understanding of a theory of reading philosophy:

> I myself "did" history of philosophy for a long time, read books on this or that author . . . But I suppose the main way I coped with it at the time was to see the history of philosophy as a sort of buggery or (it comes to the same thing) immaculate conception. I saw myself as taking an author

from behind and giving him a child that would be his own offspring, yet
monstrous . . . because it resulted from all sorts of shifting, slipping, disloca-
tions, and hidden emissions that I really enjoyed.

(1995: 6)

In other words, a Deleuzian reading of Deleuze could consist of 'buggery'. The
methodology of 'buggery' would not correspond to a truthful and faithful representation of the hypothetical meaning of the works of Deleuze and Guattari.
Deleuze and Guattari were particularly critical about a foundationalist linguistics that would try to ground a truth–correspondence theory: 'But for us, the
unconscious doesn't *mean* anything, nor does language' (1995: 22). Accordingly,
for Deleuze and Guattari, it is linguistically impossible to adequately represent
reality or the meaning of a text.

It would probably be possible to provide a reading of the oeuvre of Deleuze
and Guattari that would 'bugger' their philosophy (Deleuze 1995: 6). Arguably, applying the methodology of 'buggery' to Deleuze and Guattari has been
attempted, for instance by Brian Massumi (1992). However, this would entail
major difficulties because Deleuze did not provide a detailed explanation of
his methodology for reading texts within the framework of his history of
philosophy. Trying to 'bugger' Deleuze and Guattari would imply trying to
reproduce Deleuze's methodological practice of reading Kant, Hume, Bergson
or Nietzsche, but applying it to Deleuzo-Guattarian texts. Applying the methodology of 'buggery' to Deleuze and Guattari would be a very ambitious and
risky project, because 'a thought's logic isn't a stable rational system' that could be
easily reproduced by language, in particular in the case of Deleuze and Guattari
(Deleuze and Eribon 1995: 94).

The 'buggery' of the philosophy of Deleuze and Guattari is a very complex
project because Deleuze did not provide specific guidelines about it. Additionally, the notion of 'buggery' was developed by Deleuze in 1973 (1995: 12), that
is many years after he had written his first books on philosophy in the 1950s.
Perhaps the notion of 'buggery' corresponds more to a provocative definition,
as opposed to a systematic methodology. Therefore, this project will not use the
notion of 'buggery' as a methodological instrument.

There is another difficulty about reading the oeuvre of Deleuze and Guattari.
Concepts are used differently in the same book, to say nothing of the oeuvre
as a whole. For instance, in *A Thousand Plateaus* the concept of 'line of flight'
is used specifically and differently in relation to psychoanalysis (Deleuze and
Guattari 1987: 14), to biology (55), to linguistics (89), to faciality (124), to the
study of novels (186). Deleuze and Guattari refuse any essentialist understanding of concepts and philosophy: 'It's not a matter of bringing all sorts of things
together under one concept but rather of relating each concept to variables'
(Deleuze et al. 1995: 31). For Deleuze and Guattari a concept does not have an
essence, that is to say the same and identical meaning irrespective of the context.

There is a self-referentiality of the concepts of Deleuze and Guattari which
function dynamically and collectively, as opposed to individually. For instance,

the notion of rhizome is to be understood in relation to the concept of arborescence in the first plateau of *A Thousand Plateaus* (Deleuze and Guattari 1987).
There is an unavoidable 'pluralism' to the understanding of the concepts and of
the oeuvre of Deleuze and Guattari (Sibertin-Blanc 2006: 16). There are always
different possible understandings of a text by Deleuze and Guattari. According
to Deleuze and Guattari, concepts, texts and situations always have different
meaning because there is no transcendental or idealist construction of meaning
and truth. Writing a commentary on the oeuvre of Deleuze and Guattari that
would claim to provide the objective truth about it would not correspond to a
Deleuzo-Guattarian methodology of reading.

The existing literature is full of commentaries (Badiou 1999; Bogue 1989;
Buchanan 2008; Hallward 2006; Hughes 2009; Khalfa 2003; Sibertin-Blanc
2006; Stivale 2011; Williams 2003; Žižek 2004) and provides fewer studies of
the reception of Deleuze and Guattari. Therefore, the project of this work will
not consist of constructing a commentary on the oeuvre of Deleuze and Guattari, but rather it will provide a study of the reception of Deleuze and Guattari.

Studying the reception of an oeuvre as opposed to providing a commentary
on an oeuvre emphasizes the idea of context and pluralism. The latter implies
that there are always different and irreducible ways of reading a specific text or
a specific oeuvre. Studying the reception of an oeuvre entails an acknowledgement of the fact that different readings exist. Otherwise, analysing a reception
would not make any sense. The analysis of the reception therefore tries to understand why there are different ways of understanding a text, that is of constructing
the meaning of a specific text or oeuvre. Context is often important in order
to study the reception of a specific text or oeuvre. Analysing the reception of
an oeuvre means putting more emphasis on the context of the reception of a
text than providing a commentary, which implies being more concentrated on
the text.

To study the reception of Deleuze and Guattari will allow me to apply a
situated and non-naïve application of the philosophy of Deleuze to financialization, as I shall explain later. To study the reception of the oeuvre of Deleuze
and Guattari is a way of indicating from where I speak, from where I read and
understand Deleuze and Guattari. Similarly, it is a way of recognizing that my
own work is part of a broader tradition. To study the reception of an oeuvre
implies a form of modesty in relation to interpreting texts and as well a form
of non-naïve relationship with texts. Reading a text always implies a situated
construction of sense.

Analysis of the reception of Deleuze and Guattari

In this section, I shall explain how I shall perform the analysis of the reception
of Deleuze and Guattari. First, I shall explain why I decided to study a specific
reception of Deleuze and Guattari, as opposed to others. Next, I shall review
and then reject a number of reception studies methodologies that have already
been used on Deleuze and Guattari.

Since the 1990s, there has been a huge number of publications drawing on Deleuze in social sciences and humanities. On 25 November 2013, the entry 'Deleuze G*' in the Social Sciences Citation Index generated 2,174 results. In particular, 257 results were given for geography, 139 for sociology, 106 for cultural studies and 103 for anthropology. Similarly, on the same date, the entry 'Deleuze G*' in the Arts and Humanities Citation Index generated 5,132 results. In particular, 263 results were given for literature and 162 for 'humanities multidisciplinary'.

Consequently, for practical reasons it would be almost impossible to deal with all of these fields using a careful textual and qualitative analysis, as opposed to a quantitative study, which does not correspond to my project. I need to concentrate on a specific field, if I wish to operate a careful qualitative and textual analysis, which I shall explain later in this chapter. The field I have chosen is political philosophy. It can be arguably maintained that the philosophical reception of Deleuze and Guattari's oeuvre is the most relevant because both the authors produced primarily philosophical texts through a 'creation of concepts' (1994: 8). Deleuze and Guattari's books were directed primarily, but not exclusively, at a philosophical audience. After all, it is not by accident that Deleuze and Guattari decided to choose *What Is Philosophy?* as the title for their last book and not *What Is Psychoanalysis?*, *What Is Sociology?* or *What Is Literary Criticism?* It demonstrates the commitment of Deleuze and Guattari to define their theoretical practice as philosophical.

According to Deleuze and Guattari there is a strong connection between philosophy and politics. In a way, philosophy is always political because it creates concepts: 'A concept's full of a critical, political force of freedom' (Deleuze et al. 1995: 32). Similarly, Deleuze defines *Anti-Oedipus* as a 'book of political philosophy', even though it deals extensively with psychoanalysis, ethnology or history (Deleuze and Negri 1995: 170). According to Deleuze and Guattari, producing an ontology or concepts about being and becoming cannot be separated from a political understanding of the world. I will therefore mainly focus on the reception of the oeuvre of Deleuze and Guattari from the perspective of political philosophy. Studying the reception of Deleuze and Guattari by political philosophy seems relevant in being able to connect it to a critical approach of financialization, which I understand as being to a large extent a political issue. The reception of Deleuze and Guattari by aesthetic philosophy or the philosophy of science would have been less directly connected to the question of financialization than political philosophy.

Below, I shall discuss different methodologies of reception that have been applied to Deleuze and Guattari (Brott 2010; Cusset 2008; Dosse 2010; Lambert 2006; Sørensen 2005). These methodologies partly overlap. Next, I shall explain what type of methodology I use to provide a reception of Deleuze and Guattari. I shall not engage in a general discussion of reception studies, as this would require too much space.

A first type of analysis of the reception of Deleuze and Guattari focused on the field and institutions that produced a specific reading of Deleuze and Guattari

(Cusset 2008). Cusset tackled the question of the reception of the oeuvre of Deleuze and Guattari and more broadly of French theory in the United States (2008). Accordingly, his idea was to analyse the social construction of the analysis of Deleuze and Guattari in the American academy. This allowed him to understand the relations of power in the specific social field of American academy.

Cusset's analysis drew mainly on a methodology inspired by Pierre Bourdieu, which is positivistic and thus not compatible with the works of Deleuze and Guattari, which are critical about positivism (Cusset 2008: xiv). For instance, Bourdieu's notion of 'habitus' seems incompatible with the Deleuzo-Guattarian critique of structuralism (1977, 1987). Similarly, Simone Brott in an article focused on the importance of the reception of the oeuvre of Deleuze and Guattari in the field of architecture using an oral history methodoloy (2010). Even though this positivist type of work is useful, it does not provide a Deleuzo-Guattarian analysis of the reception of Deleuze and Guattari. In particular, Deleuze and Guattari provide a poststructuralist and critical analysis of language, which entails a critique of the truth-correspondence theory (Deleuze and Guattari 1987: 76). The current work will not operate this methodology of reception.

A second type of analysis of the reception of the oeuvre of Deleuze and Guattari consisted of analysing its effect on academia or society. This is what François Dosse performed at the end of his biography on Deleuze and Guattari (2010: 502). It was quite close to Cusset (2008) and Brott (2010), even though it did not take into account the power relations within the field that operated the reception. Dosse (2010) listed the academic journals and the scholars who were actively working on the works of Deleuze and Guattari in the early 2000s. The work was based on an empirical analysis of archives and interviews according to a methodology corresponding to history. Even though this work was useful, it corresponded to a form of historic positivism that is criticized by Deleuze and Guattari. In particular, Deleuze and Guattari have an ontological understanding of history which implies that subjective becomings are not reducible to historic causality (Taylor 2014). Therefore, I will not operate this methodology of reception.

A third type of analysis of the reception of Deleuze and Guattari consisted of the critique of other interpretations in order to defend a specific interpretation. Gregg Lambert provided a critique of the interpretations of *Capitalism and Schizophrenia* by Fredric Jameson, Hardt and Negri and Badiou in order to defend his own interpretation (2006: vii–viii). Lambert claimed that he had found 'three central propositions . . . at the basis of all of Deleuze and Guattari's works' (Lambert 2006: 12). Lambert implicitly argued that he had provided a truthful interpretation of the oeuvre of Deleuze and Guattari, which he opposed to other interpretations which he suggested were false. This position corresponded to a hermeneutic realism, which is in contradiction with the critique of the truth-correspondence theory operated by Deleuze and Guattari (1977, 1987). Therefore, I will not use the methodology of Lambert.

Cusset (2008), Brott (2010) or Lambert (2006) did not reflect on the problematics of writing a reception of Deleuze and Guattari within the framework of a Deleuzo-Guattarian methodology or within a framework that would be compatible with Deleuze and Guattari. By contrast, in an article Bent Maier Sørensen analysed the reception of Deleuze and Guattari in organization studies and tried to provide a Deleuzian methodology in order to produce a study of the reception of Deleuze and Guattari in this specific field (2005). Sørensen used the Deleuzian notions of 'territory' and 'abstract machine' to analyse the reception of Deleuzian organization studies (2005). Sørensen was aware that he needed a Deleuzo-Guattarian methodology to engage with the question of the reception of Deleuze and Guattari. My methodology is close to Sørensen's attitude, even though I shall not attempt to exactly reproduce his methodology, as I shall explain in the next section.

My methodology of reception will also be close to Deleuze and Guattari's notion of mapping, even though it will not exactly correspond to it. According to Deleuze and Guattari, the methodology of mapping is not only textual or geographical, but rather ontological. Any type of reality or process can be mapped. Cartography or mapping does not only constitute a theory of reading texts or philosophy, but also involves engaging with specific objects or material realities. Mapping means producing a cartography of a 'territory' and its assemblage (Stivale 1984: 31). This assemblage can be textual or material or a combination of both. Mapping constitutes an ontological methodology.

The map evaluates the 'coefficients' of intensity and of change of a specific reality in a rhizomatic fashion (Deleuze and Guattari 1987: 12). Producing a map entails being transformed by the map and not being a neutral observer with a bird's eye view, as a realist social scientist producing a representational tracing would be. Producing a map is related to operating a schizoanalysis: 'Cartography can only map out pathways and moves, along with their coefficients of probability and danger. That's what we call "schizoanalysis," this analysis of lines, spaces, becomings' (Deleuze et al. 1995: 34).

However, I shall not exactly use this methodology of mapping because Deleuze and Guattari do not provide specific guidelines about it. Second, my reading of the political philosophy reception of Deleuze and Guattari will prioritize a political interpretation of Deleuze and Guattari as well as an exegetical characterization combined with a political contextualization in relation to authors and texts. This approach is close to mapping and draws on the autonomist Marxist tradition of reception studies (Cleaver 2000).

The methodology of the reception of Deleuze and Guattari

The first part consists of a study of the reception of Deleuze and Guattati by political philosophy. This study will be close to Sørensen's analysis of the reception of Deleuze by organization studies (2005) and to the Deleuzo-Guattarian concept of mapping (Deleuze and Guattari 1977, 1987). These two methodologies provide poststructuralist approaches to an analysis of reception as they share the Deleuzo-Guattarian critique of the truth-correspondence theory. I did not exactly reproduce Sørensen's methodology because my study puts more emphasis on the notion of political reading of the reception of Deleuze and Guattari, whereas Sørensen's objective is to map the territory of the reception of Deleuze in organization studies. I did not exactly reproduce the Deleuzo-Guattarian methodology of mapping for reasons explained above.

My analysis of the reception of Deleuze and Guattari is strongly influenced by Harry Cleaver's autonomist Marxist analysis of the reception of *Capital* (2000). Cleaver operates a 'strategic' reading of the reception of *Capital*:

> The concept of a strategic reading here is very much in the military sense because it seeks in Marx's thought only weapons for use in the class war . . . To paraphrase Karl von Clausewitz's terms, strategy allows us to grasp the basic form of the class war, to situate the different struggles which compose it, to evaluate the opposing tactics in each of those struggles, and to see how the different tactics and different struggles can be better linked to achieve victory.
>
> (2000: 29)

Cleaver's analysis of the reception of *Capital* prioritizes political objectives, that is to say the struggle of the working class against capital:

> Yet I would monopolize the term "political" here to designate that strategic reading of Marx, which is done from the point of view of the working class. It is a reading that self-consciously and unilaterally structures its approach to determine the meaning and relevance of every concept to the immediate development of working-class struggle.
>
> (2000: 30)

My analysis of the reception of Deleuze and Guattari is both political and strategic, even though not in the exact sense of Cleaver (2000), because I shall prioritize an anti- capitalist and revolutionary reading of Deleuze and Guattari against other readings, which either depoliticize Deleuze and Guattari or associate their oeuvre with capitalism. My analysis of the reception of Deleuze prioritizes the idea that there is a 'resonance' between Deleuze and Guattari and Marx (Thoburn 2003: 1). This means that a series of creative connections can be operated between theses oeuvres. This does not mean that other interpretations of Deleuze and Guattari are epistemologically false and that I am right. This would not be compatible with the Deleuzo-Guattarian poststructuralist critique of realism and of truth-correspondence theory (1977, 1987). Some readers provide overtly realist interpretations of Deleuze and Guattari (De Landa 2004, 2010). I, however, would argue that there are a number of textual pieces of evidence of a Deleuzo-Guattarian poststructuralist critique of realism, for instance the plateau on 'the postulates of linguistic', which draws extensively on Hjemlsev (Deleuze and Guattari 1987: 75–110).

Cleaver criticizes the political economic and the philosophical readings of *Capital* on political grounds, not because they are epistemologically false, but because they are written 'from capital's perspective' (2000: 31). Althusser or Marcuse are criticized not for the lack of knowledge of their philosophical reading of Marx, but because of their lack of working-class political strategy (2000: 46). Similarly, I shall criticize the interpretation of Deleuze and Guattari provided by Badiou (1999) or Hallward (2006), because of their refusal to politicize the philosophy of Deleuze and Guattari, and not because they failed to understand it.

As argued above, I shall study the reception of Deleuze and Guattari by political philosophy because it would be almost impossible to operate a quantitative analysis of all the receptions of Deleuze and Guattari, because of the number of publications. More importantly, as my project is connected to contemporary politics, the political philosophy reception of Deleuze seems one of the most relevant fields to study, as opposed to ontology or literary criticism for instance.

I strategically organized my analysis of the reception of Deleuze and Guattari into three main interpretative positions: an elitist, a liberal and a revolutionary one. The elitist interpretation argues that the Deleuzo-Guattarian philosophy should be reserved for an elite of professional philosophers who would not be interested in transforming the world. The liberal interpretation argues that the Deleuzo-Guattarian philosophy is compatible with capitalism and the liberal tradition. Finally, the revolutionary interpretation, which I advocate seeks to use Deleuze and Guattari to transform the world.

These three positions are interpretative tendencies, as opposed to Platonist eternal Ideas. I do not argue that the interpretations provided by the authors that I analysed always corresponded to the three interpretative positions which I identified. My methodology to analyse the political philosophy reception of Deleuze and Guattari is qualitative. This means that it is not exhaustive and that not all authors will be covered. I selected the authors and the texts that seemed to me the most representative of the three main interpretative tendencies that I identified within the framework of my strategic reading.

I tried to provide a faithful analysis of these representative texts and authors through a careful textual exegesis. I strived as much as possible to be faithful to the arguments of the authors. I analysed, in particular, their philosophical projects and the concept that they operated. This implied providing quotes of the interpretative positions that I analysed. I tried to be descriptive in relation to the authors and the texts I analysed. Trying to provide a faithful exegesis of each philosophical interpretation of Deleuze entailed selecting a limited number of representative authors for each interpretative tendency because of lack of space. This specific qualitative approach implies a degree of arbitrariness in the choice of texts and authors.

At the same time, I tried to politically contextualize the description of the philosophical concepts which I provided. The political contextualization of a conceptual position contributes to its clarification and its understanding. This corresponds to the Marxist tradition of characterizing ideas prior to political contextualization. Cleaver's analysis of the reception of *Capital* provides a political contextualization of the readings of Marx; for example, Althusser's position is explained in relation with his role in the French Communist Party and orthodox Marxist politics in the 1960s (2000: 47).

My analysis of the political philosophy reception of Deleuze and Guattari is an analysis for practical reasons among many other possible analyses. In particular, and as Cleaver did for *Reading* Capital *Politically* (2000: 11), I only selected texts in English and French because I am not sufficiently acquainted with other languages. Obviously, there may be relevant untranslated work in Italian, German or Portuguese.

Applying my Deleuzo–Guattarian reception study to financialization

In the second part, I shall apply a revolutionary interpretation of the Deleuzo-Guattarian philosophy to the object of financialization as described in the Marxian literature. This analysis will be situated and contextualized by the analysis of the reception of Deleuze and Guattari. I do not claim any epistemological superiority and do not pretend that my own reading of Deleuze and Guattari is more truthful or more legitimate than others. Yet, studying the different possible readings of Deleuze and Guattari will allow me to grow aware of the situatedness of my own reading without the illusion of a bird's eye view.

Applying my revolutionary understanding of Deleuze and Guattari to the question of financialization will in the first part demonstrate the interest and originality of my analysis of the reception of Deleuze and Guattari. This will show that producing an analysis of the reception of Deleuze and Guattari can have direct and practical relevance in understanding a complex contemporary social phenomenon such as financialization.

It is necessary for historical and epistemological reasons to read the Marxian literature on financialization to understand this specific phenomenon. The Marxian literature on financialization was mainly written in the 2000s, which means it was able to fully integrate the development of financialization. By contrast, Deleuze died in 1995 and Guattari in 1992, and so could not possibly predict the future and witness the whole historical development of financialization.

A critic might question the relevance of the work of Deleuze and Guattari in relation to financialization. I would provide at least three responses to this objection. First, through a 'resonance' between Deleuze, Guattari and Marx, a Deleuzo-Guattarian approach can be connected to the Marxian literature on financialization, which provides a very specific engagement with the question of financialization. Second, the work of Deleuze anticipated some of the arguments made by the Marxian literature on financialization, through an analysis of the questions of credit and debt (Deleuze and Guattari 1977, 1987) and most of all through an understanding of the end of Fordism with concepts such as societies of control (Deleuze 1992a). Third, Deleuze and Guattari provide a social theory that allows for an understanding of the contemporary transformations of subjectivity within the framework of financialization.

A revolutionary reading of Deleuze and Guattari that aims at creating a 'resonance' with Marx (Thoburn 2003: 1) needs to agree with the helpful description of financialization provided by the Marxian literature. At the political level of a reflection on resistance to financialization, a fruitful dialogue can be established between a Deleuzo-Guattarian revolutionary reading and a Marxian political economy of financialization. In particular, my reflection informed by a revolutionary understanding of Deleuze and Guattari can help transcend the political shortcomings of the Marxian literature on financialization, which relies mainly on party and class politics (Bryan and Rafferty 2006; McNally 2009). This creative transcending of political impasses can be considered an example of resonance. The most interesting political insights in relation to resistance to financialization are connected to the question of debt and of 'debt struggle' (Caffentzis 2013a; Graeber 2011a; Lazzarato 2012).

I shall operate a discussion of Foucault's analyses of neoliberal governmentality (2007, 2008) as well as of his critique of orthodox Marxism, because it is connected to Deleuze and Guattari's own poststructuralist politics. Foucault as well as Deleuze and Guattari were able to understand the transformations of the struggles in the 1960s unlike orthodox Marxism. Foucault as well as Deleuze and Guattari tried to conceptualize what had happened in May '68 through a critique of orthodox Marxist politics (Deleuze and Foucault 1977; Deleuze and Guattari 1977, 1987; Foucault 1977b). By contrast, orthodox Marxism had been suspicious of May '68 and the new struggles in the 1960s (Cleaver 2000: 65; Dosse 2010).

The last chapter will elaborate on a Deleuzo-Guattarian politics of resistance to financialization drawing in particular on the question of debt, on the notion of event and on itinerant politics. I shall try to elaborate on a Deleuzo-Guattarian politics, which will draw on two recent attempts to resist financialization, namely President Hollande's social democratic politics in France and the Occupy Wall Street movement. This Deleuzo-Guattarian elaboration of a politics of resistance to financialization is a modest task, which is also exploratory as there is as yet no established field of research. It shall try to avoid two main problems of philosophical engagement with politics: 'speculative leftism' (Bosteels 2005) and the blueprint.

'Speculative leftism' implies that political philosophy cannot provide practical recommendations in relation to politics (Bosteels 2005). In other words, philosophy would not have anything to say to militants in terms of political strategy. This position is sometimes practised by French contemporary philosophy defending ideal principles such as 'democracy' (Rancière 2007) or the 'communist hypothesis' (Badiou 2010) without any clear practical and strategic recommendations. By contrast, the objective of the blueprint is to apply to politics a philosophical reflection as performed by Lenin in *What Is to Be Done?* (1969). The idea is that philosophy can provide a precise political methodology, for instance a vanguard party of professional activists that would lead the proletariat to revolution. By contrast, elaborating a Deleuzo-Guattarian politics of resistance to financialization implies a series of practical reflections on contemporary experiences such as Hollande's social democratic politics or the Occupy Wall Street movement.

In the second part of the book, I propose a specific reading of Deleuzo-Guattarian concepts such as event, itinerant politics (in the last chapter) or the Deleuzian engagement with orthodox Marxist politics. I also operate a reading of specific Foucauldian concepts such as governmentality. My reading of these texts is political and strategic, even though I try to provide a faithful exegetical engagement with texts. I select texts and interpretation to elaborate a Deleuzo-Guattarian politics of resistance to financialization. As the second part of the book is grounded on the first part, the application of the analysis of the reception of Deleuze and Guattari to financialization validates the first part.

I would argue that there is a Deleuzo-Guattarism that is not a closed system that would operate deductively. I see the work of Deleuze and Guattari as an 'open' body (Deleuze et al. 1995: 32) and with no definitive and systematic accounts of the world. The two joint books *Anti-Oedipus* (1977) and *A Thousand Plateaus* (1987) will be the most discussed and analysed, because they provide the most extensive analyses on capitalism and politics in the oeuvre of Deleuze and Guattari. Connecting Deleuze and Guattari and financialization implies an emphasis on *Anti-Oedipus* (1977) and *A Thousand Plateaus* (1987) and therefore on the joint works of Deleuze and Guattari.

Despite the argument of Stengers (2011: 141), it seems difficult to me to separate the concepts of Deleuze from the 'operative constructs' of Guattari in *Anti-Oedipus* (1977) and *A Thousand Plateaus* (1987). Deleuze and Guattari criticize the idea that it would be possible to differentiate individual authors in *A Thousand Plateaus*:

> Since each of us was several, there was already quite a crowd . . . To reach, not the point where one no longer says I, but the point where it is no longer of any importance whether one says I. We are no longer ourselves. Each will know his own. We have been aided, inspired, multiplied.
>
> (1987: 3)

As Genosko argues (2012: 166), the most fruitful interpretative strategy consists in operating rhizomatic connections between a series of texts written by Deleuze and Guattari (1977, 1986, 1987, 1994), but also by Deleuze writing alone (for example, 1992a, 2004), by Guattari writing alone (1996) and to a lesser extent by Deleuze and Foucault (1977) and by Guattari and Negri (1990).

List of chapters

The intended project is to explore how a revolutionary interpretation of Deleuze and Guattari can help politicize financialization. I shall seek to provide a study of the reception of Deleuze and Guattari by political philosophy in order to ground a non-naïve and situated revolutionary reading of Deleuze and Guattari, which I wish to bring into resonance with the Marxian literature on financialization.

Finally, I elaborate a Deleuzo-Guattarian politics of resistance to financialization which takes into account the Marxian reflections on financialization. In the second part of the book, I apply my revolutionary reading of Deleuze and Guattari to financialization. The application of my first part to financialization entails a practical validation of my study of the reception of Deleuze and Guattari.

The first part of this book consists of an analysis of the reception of Deleuze and Guattari by political philosophy. The field of political philosophy broadly construed is chosen because it seems relevant for a project that seeks to politicize financialization. I operate this study of the reception of Deleuze and Guattari with a specific methodology which is close to Sørensen's analysis of the reception of Deleuze and Guattari by organization studies, to the Deleuzo-Guattarian notion of mapping and to Cleaver's study of the reception of *Capital*. At the end of the first part, I am able to situate my revolutionary interpretation of Deleuze and Guattari.

In Chapter 2 ('The elitist interpretation of the philosophy of Deleuze and Guattari'), I examine a political interpretation of the oeuvre of Deleuze and Guattari that limits it to philosophy. This position argues that the oeuvre of Deleuze and Guattari operates a novel philosophical understanding of the world not connected to the idea of politically transforming the world. It is a depoliticizing understanding of Deleuze and Guattari. This position (Badiou 1999, 2004; Grosz 1993; Hallward 2006; Jardine 1984; Mengue 2003; Žižek 2004) is held either to dismiss the political relevance of the philosophy of Deleuze and Guattari or to dismiss the very idea of politics from the perspective of the philosophy of Deleuze and Guattari. According to this position, the philosophy of Deleuze and Guattari is essentially reserved for an elite of professional philosophers who are seen as disconnected from the political processes of collective decisions.

In Chapter 3 ('The liberal interpretation of Deleuze and Guattari'), I examine a political interpretation of the oeuvre of Deleuze and Guattari that associates their oeuvre with capitalism. According to this interpretative position (Boltanski and Chiapello 2005; De Landa 2010; Garo 2011a; Jameson 1997; Patton 2000; Tampio 2009), the oeuvre of Deleuze and Guattari is compatible with capitalism and the market. In fact, the oeuvre of Deleuze and Guattari could provide an efficacious philosophy of capitalism. It could complement the liberal philosophical tradition (Patton 2000; Tampio 2009). Otherwise, this interpretation is operated by anti-capitalist thinkers in order to criticize Deleuze and Guattari's alleged connection with capitalism (Boltanski and Chiapello 2005; Garo 2011a; Jameson 1997). This position associates the oeuvre of Deleuze and Guattari with capitalism either to praise it in order to say that it allows an interesting understanding of the market from a pro-capitalist perspective or to dismiss it from an anti-capitalist perspective.

Nevertheless, in Chapter 4 ('The revolutionary interpretation of Deleuze and Guattari'), I consider a third political interpretation of the oeuvre of Deleuze and Guattari that consists of a revolutionary reading. This third interpretative position is revolutionary (Massumi 1992; Negri 2011; Nunes 2010; Pignarre and

Stengers 2011; Read 2003; Sibertin-Blanc 2006, 2009; Thoburn 2003; Tiqqun 2011). In other words, this interpretative position maintains that the oeuvre of Deleuze and Guattari seeks to transform the world and existing dominant social relations. This interpretative position is anti-capitalist and aims at using Deleuze and Guattari in order to supersede capitalism. This interpretative position is held by authors coming from different revolutionary traditions such as anarchism, communism or the autonomist movement. My work corresponds to this position. However, my revolutionary interpretation of Deleuze and Guattari seeks to make it resonate with Marx because I wish to apply a Deleuzo-Guattarian politics of resistance to financialization. This contrasts with anti- Marxist revolutionary interpretations of Deleuze (Tiqqun 2011).

In the second part, I apply a non-naïve and situated revolutionary reading of Deleuze and Guattari to financialization. This implies engaging with the Marxian literature on financialization, because it provides the most relevant critical expertise on this topic. In fact, the works of Deleuze and Guattari were written before the full development of financialization unlike the Marxian literature on financialization. Nevertheless, the oeuvre of Deleuze and Guattari provides relevant concepts to reflect on resistance to financialization. It is useful to draw on Foucault as well as on Deleuze and Guattari because they shared many post-structuralist concerns in relation to orthodox Marxist politics.

In Chapter 5 ('Understanding financialization'), I shall engage with the Marxian literature on financialization. First, I shall explain how financialization replaced the Bretton Woods financial system and how it was linked to neoliberalism (Mirowski 2009, 2013). Next, I shall explain how financialization is connected to derivatives as a form of commensuration between capitals (Bryan and Rafferty 2006) which allows the exploitation of labour to be reinforced. Additionally, I shall show how financialization permeated social reproduction, subjectivity (Martin 2002) and the state (Martin 2007). Financialization is also connected to debt (Caffentzis 2013a, 2013b; Lazzarato 2012). The Marxian literature suggests that resistance to financialization can be brought about by class politics and a revolutionary subject.

In Chapter 6 ('Anticipating financialization'), I seek to show that Deleuze and Guattari were not able to predict financialization for historical reasons. The understanding of finance proposed by Deleuze and Guattari was rather limited. Some scholars use the philosophy of Deleuze and Guattari to provide non-critical account of finance. I disagree with them because of my revolutionary interpretation of Deleuze and Guattari (Armstrong et al. 2012; Hillier and Van Wezemael 2008; Lozano 2013a, 2013b; Vlcek 2010). By contrast, I sympathize with scholars who use Deleuzo-Guattarian concepts to provide a critical engagement with finance (Bay 2012; Bay and Schinckus 2012; Ertürk et al. 2010; Ertürk et al. 2013; Forslund and Bay 2009; Holland 2013; Lightfoot and Lilley 2007; Shaviro 2010). Deleuze and Guattari, however, were able to anticipate some of the aspects of financialization with concepts such as 'machinic enslavement' and 'societies of control'. Foucault was also able to anticipate some of the aspects of financialization through his reflection on neoliberal governmentality

(2007, 2008). Furthermore, the politics provided by Deleuze and Guattari and Foucault allow the shortcomings of the politics of the Marxian literature on financialization to be criticized.

Finally, in Chapter 7 ('Resisting financialization'), I seek to elaborate a Deleuzo–Guattarian revolutionary politics of resistance to financialization. This final chapter is practical and exploratory. Therefore, I draw mainly on two recent political experiences: French President Hollande's social democratic attempt and failure to regulate finance and the Occupy Wall Street movement. Debt seems the most practical strategic objective in relation to resisting financialization (Caffentzis 2013a; Graeber 2011b; Lazzarato 2012). I therefore draw on Occupy Wall Street to argue that a Deleuzian politics of resistance could try to confront financialization through an 'itinerant politics' and through an 'event'.

Notes

1 There are accounts of politics and subjectivity inspired by Marx, but I would argue that the poststructuralist approach of Deleuze and Guattari is more effective, in particular because of its materialist understanding of the question of difference. This point will be illustrated – *inter alia* – by the use of the concepts of 'event' and 'itinerant politics' in the final chapter. Overall, I would be more sympathetic with Marxian analyses that move away from the Hegelian teleology.
2 Therefore, contemporary finance is substantially different from the finance that existed at the time of Marx or Lenin and that was not as central in the accumulation of capital.

Part I

In the first part, I will provide an analysis of the reception of the Deleuzo-Guattarian oeuvre by political philosophy so as articulate a non-naïve and situated revolutionary interpretation of Deleuze and Guattari. This will allow me in the second part to engage with the question of financialization. Three interpretations will appear. First (Chapter 2), I will analyse the elitist interpretation which sought to reduce the oeuvre of Deleuze and Guattari to a contemplative philosophy refusing to be involved in politics. Second (Chapter 3), I will engage with the liberal interpretation that sought to relate Deleuze and Guattari to capitalism, either to criticize the Deleuzo-Guattarian philosophy or to celebrate it. Third (Chapter 4), I will study a revolutionary interpretation which sought to connect Deleuze and Guattari with revolutionary politics, either through a dialogue with Marxism or outside of Marxism. My own position will be close to the revolutionary reception which tries to create a 'resonance' with Marx (Thoburn 2003: 1).

2 The elitist interpretation of the philosophy of Deleuze and Guattari

Introduction

I shall start the analysis of the reception of the political philosophy of Deleuze and Guattari with an analysis of the elitist interpretation of their work. According to this interpretation, the Deleuzo-Guattarian philosophy is the concern of a limited number of professional, ivory tower philosophers. For Deleuze and Guattari, then, philosophy is an intellectual activity reserved for a small elite of privileged philosophers and the philosophy of Deleuze and Guattari could have no practical or political usefulness because of the very definition of philosophy that implies theoretical contemplation as opposed to practical engagement with the world. This elitist interpretation entails that there could not be any transformative and revolutionary Deleuzo-Guattarian philosophy. The main idea stems from considering the work of Deleuze and Guattari as a refined and meticulous ontology that rejects any engagement with power relationships within the 'real world'.

The role of Guattari in the construction of Deleuzian thought is underestimated and caricatured. Similarly, this implies from the textual point of view a denial of the theoretical importance of the works that Deleuze and Guattari wrote together, that is mainly *Capitalism and Schizophrenia* (1977, 1987), *Kafka: For a Minor Literature* (1986) and *What Is Philosophy?* (1994). According to the elitist interpretation, Guattari, the militant, corrupted Deleuze, the philosopher, with noxious and simplistic leftism, with notions such as disjunctive syntheses or desiring machines that lack philosophical rigour (Dosse 2010: 1).

Consequently, actual analysis of the politics of Deleuzian philosophy would be based on Deleuze's single authored books that were not written under the influence of Guattari. This elitist interpretation of Deleuze and Guattari tends to insist on a Deleuzian as opposed to a Deleuzo-Guattarian politics. The Deleuzian take on politics would be an aristocratic refusal of any mundane politics, including radical politics. This interpretative position is well represented in American, British and French philosophy departments. Badiou (1999, 2004), Žižek (2004), Hallward (2006), Mengue (2003) and a number of feminists (Butler 1987; Grosz 1985; Irigaray 1985; Jardine 1984, 1985) uphold this elitist interpretation of Deleuze and Guattari. Badiou, Žižek, Hallward and the feminists operate their reception of Deleuze and Guattari from a progressive political point of view, whereas Mengue's is liberal. Badiou, Žižek and Hallward are actually related to the Marxist tradition. All these authors assert that the Deleuzo-Guattarian philosophy tends to be apolitical and elitist and at the very least ineffective in relation to politics. I mean by elitist interpretation an interpretation that considers the philosophy of Deleuze and Guattari to be elitist.

I shall start by discussing Badiou's philosophy and his interpretation of Deleuze (and, implicitly, of Guattari), before analysing the position of Žižek. Žižek's interpretation of Deleuze and Guattari is more ambiguous as he argues that Deleuze's is the only interesting work and that it is characterized by apolitical philosophical elitism. In contrast, Žižek (2004) claims that the co-authored work of Deleuze and Guattari is not interesting. Next, I shall analyse the position of Hallward who argues more coherently that the whole oeuvre of Deleuze and Guattari is marked by apolitical philosophical elitism, which the author rejects from a leftist perspective, as does Badiou and Žižek.

I shall then discuss Mengue's interpretation of Deleuze and Guattari. Mengue argues that the philosophy of Deleuze and Guattari is an apolitical philosophical elitism that could inform a Postmodern ethic. Finally, I shall discuss the complex and challenging critiques of Deleuze and Guattari operated by a number of interesting feminist authors who essentially consider the work of Deleuze and Guattari as philosophical elitism disconnected from the feminist struggles and women's identity politics. This constitutes a relevant critique that was probably necessary in the 1980s and 1990s from the perspective of feminist struggles successfully grounded on identity politics.

The philosophy of Badiou

Badiou's elitist interpretation of Deleuze and Guattari is one of the most important. It is indispensable to explain from where Badiou speaks in order to understand his reception of Deleuze and Guattari. Badiou is in fact a very influential contemporary philosopher. His philosophy is closely connected to his politics. Both, however, are complex and have evolved since the 1970s (Bosteels 2011).

First, it is necessary to provide an account of the philosophy of Badiou in order to understand his reception of Deleuze and Guattari. The philosophy of Badiou claims to be inherently linked with ontology: 'Along with Heidegger, it will be maintained that philosophy as such can only be re-assigned on the basis of the ontological question' (2005: 2). Ontology can be defined as a discourse on being. The philosophical project of Badiou is different from the dominant contemporary schools of thought in departments of philosophy, that is to say phenomenology that is based on describing experience and analytic philosophy. The philosophy of Deleuze and Guattari reject phenomenology as well as analytic philosophy. Badiou defines conditions for any ontology:

> The a priori requirement imposed by this difficulty may be summarized in two theses, prerequisites for any possible ontology. 1. The multiple from

which ontology makes up its situation is composed solely of multiplicities. There is no one. In other words, every multiple is a multiple of multiples. 2. The count-as-one is no more than the system of conditions through which the multiples can be recognized as multiple.

(2005: 29)

For Badiou, being is constituted of multiples and multiples of multiples that can be described by Cantor's set theory: 'It is legitimate to say that ontology, the science of being qua being, is nothing other than mathematics itself' (2005: xiii). By contrast, Deleuze and Guattari do not confer an ontological privilege to mathematics (1994: 117). In other words, mathematics, in particular set theory, is for them not the language of being. According to Badiou, in addition to multiples and multiples of multiples the void has an ontological existence as well: 'The void of a situation is the suture to its being . . . the void is that unplaceable point which shows that the that-which-presents wanders throughout the presentation in the form of a subtraction from the count' (2005: 526). For Badiou there exist multiples and void. Additionally, there are events that are non-being: 'In ontology per se, the non-being of the event is a decision . . . The delimitation of non-being is the result of an explicit and inaugural statement' (2005: 304). According to Badiou, non-being has an ontological existence, even though this might seem paradoxical. Events are linked to the emergence of truths for subjects:

A subject is nothing other than an active fidelity to the event of truth. This means that a subject is a militant of truth. I philosophically founded the notion of "militant" at a time when the consensus was that any engagement of this type was archaic. Not only did I find this notion, but I considerably enlarged it. The militant of truth is not only the political militant working for the emancipation of humanity in its entirety. He or she is also the artist-creator, the scientist who opens up a new theoretical field, or the lover whose world is enchanted.

(Badiou 2005: xiii)

Similarly, Deleuze develops a theory of the event in *The Logic of Sense* (2004). The Deleuzian theory of the event is ontological because it corresponds to an incorporeal phenomenon (Deleuze 2004: 7). It is also linguistic because according to Deleuze the event is the condition of possibility of sense (2004: 22). Finally, the Deleuzian event is ethical: 'The eternal truth of the event is grasped only if the event is also inscribed in the flesh. But each time we must double this painful actualization by a counter-actualization, which limits, moves, and transfigures it' (Deleuze 2004: 182). The notion of event is present in *A Thousand Plateaus* (e.g., Deleuze and Guattari 1987: 15) and in *What Is Philosophy?* (e.g. Deleuze and Guattari 1994: 25). The event of Deleuze and Guattari, however, is not connected to a rationalist subject as is Badiou's event.

Finally, in *Being and Event*, Badiou affirms that his ontology is constructivist and nominalist, which confers a crucial role to language: 'The constructivist orientation of thought places itself under the jurisdiction of language' (2005: 504). It would mean that ontology can only exist through language, even though Badiou's philosophy advocates the notion of truth against relativistic conceptions. Nonetheless, in *Logics of Worlds* Badiou reformulates his philosophy. He uses the notion of 'materialist dialectic', which refutes the dualism of democratic materialism, affirming that not only material objects and languages exist but also truths (2009: 9).

Accordingly, the world would be constituted of bodies, languages and truths. This is compatible with *Being and Event* as long as bodies and languages are considered as multiples. Badiou refutes Postmodernism, which would argue that only differences exist and that truth is an illusion. Badiou also refutes a Postmodernist ethics grounded on suffering bodies:

> "Postmodern" is one of the possible names for contemporary democratic materialism. Negri is right about what the postmoderns "know": the body is the only concrete instance for productive individuals aspiring to enjoyment. Man, under the sway of the "power of life", is an animal convinced that the law of the body harbours the secret of his hope. In order to validate the equation "existence = individual = body", contemporary doxa must valiantly reduce humanity to an overstretched vision of animality. "Human rights" are the same as the rights of the living. The humanist protection of all living bodies: this is the norm of contemporary materialism.
>
> (2009: 2)

Even though Deleuze and Guattari are often classified as Postmodern thinkers, they have never claimed to be part of this movement. Additionally, Guattari wrote a very critical text about Postmodernism (1996: 114). In particular, Deleuze and Guattari do not specifically advocate an ethics based on difference.

Badiou's *Logics of Worlds* analyses how truths are inserted into worlds, as opposed to *Being and Event* which opposes being and truth. Therefore, in *Logics of Worlds* Badiou explains how a truth has the power to change a specific world:

> A truth presupposes an organically closed set of material traces; with respect to their consistency, these traces do not refer to the empirical uses of a world but to a frontal change, which has affected (at least) one object of this world. We can thus say that the trace presupposed by every truth is the trace of an event.
>
> (Badiou 2009: 35)

Logics of Worlds introduces the concept of world, which means a coherent milieu ontologically closed that can, however, be changed by the event of a truth (Badiou 2009: 582). Accordingly, truths are universal and not specific to a world. From the point of view of Badiou's ontology, there are multiples (bodies and languages are multiples as well), worlds (multiples and multiples of multiples ontologically closed), void and events (which are non-being). By contrast, for

Deleuze and Guattari there are rhizomatic and arborescent (molar and molecular, smooth and striated) phenomena that are interwoven (1987).

The politics of Badiou

It is also necessary to analyse the politics of Badiou in order to understand his reception of Deleuze and Guattari. At the beginning of his academic career, that is to say mainly in the 1960s and the 1970s, Badiou was a militant in one of the many French Maoist parties of that time. This implied strictly observing the discipline of a small party and referring to the Cultural Revolution, as well as criticizing the 'revisionists' of the French Communist Party or the 'hitlero-trotskyists'. Badiou's conception of communism was clear during this period:

> Before the realization of communism, the masses do not direct the histori-cal process, they do it. Direction is a function of class. For a fraction of the masses, direction signifies constitution as a revolutionary class, that is to say a class able to become a Statist class and to build the whole society accord-ing to its image.
>
> (Badiou and Balmès 1976: 91; my translation)

Bosteels demonstrates the importance of the Maoism of Badiou with respect to his oeuvre, because Badiou's 'post-Maoism' remains politically faithful to his 1970s ideals (2011: 110). The novel philosophy elaborated in *Being and Event* and *Logics of Worlds* would be a form of continuation of the Maoist issue. This entails that for Badiou constructing an ontology based on mathematics would be related to one of the main branches of the Marxist tradition.

Guattari was involved with Trotskyism during his youth (Dosse 2010: 29) as well as with the 22nd March Movement, which was instrumental in triggering the events of May '68 and is considered to be mainly anarchist (Dosse 2010: 170). However, after May '68 some Maoist militants of *Tout!*, *Vive La Révolution!* or the *Proletarian Left* would often refer to Deleuze and Guattari, in particular to *Anti-Oedipus* (Dosse 2010: 206–207). Interestingly, the spontaneist Maoists who sympathized with Deleuze and Guattari were criticized by the more orthodox Maoists of Badiou's political organization (Badiou 2004).

For the Maoist Badiou of the 1970s a communist society consisted of a spe-cific mode of production characterized by the rule of the working class, espe-cially through control of the state and its apparatuses. The role of the communist intellectual therefore was to obey and serve the Communist Party whose role was to direct the masses. Accordingly, the Marxist philosophy was supposed to be the philosophy of the party defending the interests of the proletariat, that is to say a Maoist communist party (Badiou and Balmès, 1976: 17). This Maoist conception of communism took into account a certain spontaneity of the masses inherited from the Cultural Revolution and from the movement of May '68. This specific Maoism therefore constituted to a certain extent a critique of the bureaucracy of really existing socialism.

At this point, Badiou was close to an orthodox Marxist vision of communism, which involved the building of a classless, egalitarian and proletarian society through the takeover of the state by a vanguard party and hopefully the subsequent withering away of both. Communism was at the same time the future emancipated society and the process of organizing the working class, which, accordingly, would inevitably have spawned a new world of equality. This was coherent with Lenin and Mao and corresponded to specific readings of Marx, in particular those focusing on the *Critique of the Gotha Program* (1970). In fact, in the *Critique of the Gotha Program*, there is a first stage of communism and a second, supposedly 'from each according to his ability, to each according to his needs' (Marx 1970).

Badiou abandoned 'party-state' politics and changed his vision of communism around 1984–1985 (2001: 100). Badiou needed an ontological account of the transition from capitalism to communism that did not exist in the *Critique of the Gotha Program*. This entailed that Badiou needed to produce an ontology in order to provide a novel and consistent radical politics that would remain faithful to Maoism (Bosteels 2011: 110).

In fact, the oeuvre of Badiou introduced the notion of event as pure emergence of newness and truth in *Being and Event*. This allowed Badiou to develop a rupturalist politics, that is to say a politics that implies a radical rupture with the present capitalist situation. Badiou departs from Marxist politics even though he does not reject Marx's analysis of capitalism:

> The part of Marxism that consists of scientific analysis of capital remains an absolutely valid background. After all the realization of the world as global market, the undivided reign of great financial conglomerates, and so forth – all this is an indisputable reality and one that conforms, essentially, to Marx's analysis. The question is: where does politics fit in with all this? . . . But everything suggests that on this point, such knowledge is useful, but provides no answer by itself. The position of politics relative to the economy must be rethought, in a dimension that isn't really transitive.
>
> (Badiou 2001: 105)

Badiou disconnects the economic infrastructure from the superstructure. Communism is no longer understood in terms of class relations within an orthodox Marxist paradigm, but in terms of human aspirations. Badiou disconnects what could be a radical political strategy from a political economic analysis. Badiou exits Marxism and constructs a whole metaphysics whose politics is grounded on the communist hypothesis. In a sense, however, he continues to be Marxist because he is faithful to a communist revolutionary project (Badiou 2011) and to what he defines as the 'materialist dialectic' in *Logics of Worlds*. Arguably, Deleuze and Guattari also remained faithful to a certain Marxism (Thoburn 2003).

A truth constitutes the fidelity to an event (Badiou 2005: 524). The fidelity to the event implies a rupture with the state of the situation that consists of a series of multiplicities (Badiou 2005: 522). For Badiou, there are four truths processes: art, love, science and politics. Politics constitutes a collective event, which has effects on society as a whole. He argues that the communist hypothesis is still relevant as an alternative to capitalism and constitutes a rupturalist politics. Further, he claims, drawing a comparison between the Fermat's theorem and the communist hypothesis, that the hypothesis should be tested until a solution is found.

Consequently, he refuses to consider that the failure of really existing socialism condemns a rupturalist communist project (Badiou 2009: 11). Failure is part of the process to reach truth. Badiou's conception of communism implies being faithful to the communist hypothesis, and then also to a series of communist events creating political truths, such as May '68 (Badiou 2009: 11). This corresponds to a radical communist politics.

In sum, Badiou's communism represents a total break with the state of the situation determined by the production and the reproduction of capital in Marxist terms (2001: 30). This implies a fidelity to the truths inaugurated by events. The political truth as event consists of the production of a rupturalist communist politics. It is possible to describe to a certain extent Badiou's concept as idealistic because it implies a break away from material reality. It is no mistake if he often refers to Plato (for instance, 2009: 9). Badiou's conception of communism is different from the Marxist or Leninist conceptions as he no longer endorses 'party-state' politics. Badiou, however, accepts the legacy of violent revolutions (1793, 1917, the Cuban Revolution and the Great Proletarian Cultural Revolution), which suggests that the usage of violent means is an essential part of the revolutionary event. In other words, Badiou affirms the necessity of terror.

Badiou's interpretation of Deleuze and Guattari

It should be noted that the processualist ontology of Deleuze and Guattari is radically different from Badiou's ontology, which is mainly inspired by set theory (2005). Additionally, the politics of Badiou differs from that of Deleuze and Guattari as the latter were never related to Leninist forms of party politics. In 1977, when Badiou was still an orthodox Maoist, he produced a pamphlet against Deleuze and Guattari (2004). More specifically, this pamphlet was related mainly to *Anti-Oedipus* (1977). In his text, Badiou accused Deleuze and Guattari of being fascist because of their lack of dialectical thinking (Badiou 2004).

The project of Badiou is different in *Deleuze: The Clamor of Being* (1999). Badiou no longer attacks Deleuze and Guattari politically and recognizes that Deleuze is a great elitist philosopher interested only in metaphysics in order to discard him as a thinker of a revolutionary alternative to capitalism. The aim is to negate the relevance of Deleuze and Guattari as revolutionary thinkers.

In fact, Deleuze and Guattari were politically radical. Guattari was Trotskyite and was then involved in the radical communist 22nd March Movement, which was connected to the triggering of May '68 (Dosse 2010). Guattari participated actively in May '68 and was involved in anti-psychiatry at the La Borde clinic.

Guattari was also involved with Italian autonomism in the 1970s and 1980s (Dosse 2010: 419). Deleuze was sympathetic to May '68 and claimed he was Marxist (Deleuze and Negri 1995: 171). Additionally, spontaneist Maoists in the 1970s (around *Tout!, Vive la Révolution* and even the proletarian left) were closed to his ideas. This does not mean that Badiou's elitist interpretation of Deleuze and Guattari is epistemologically wrong. Revolutionary intellectuals can produce theories that have rather conservative implications as Cleaver demonstrated in relation to specific philosophical and political economic interpretations of *Capital* (2000). Rather, this shows that he adopted a specific interpretative strategy to depict Deleuze and (more implicitly) Guattari as philosophers who would not be interested in politics.

Badiou's *Deleuze: The Clamor of Being* integrates the benefits of the long correspondence between Badiou and Deleuze at the beginning of the 1990s (1999: 1–6). The reception of Badiou's *Deleuze: The Clamor of Being* was mainly by the French academy. Badiou wrote his commentary on Deleuze and Guattari in 1997. The French political context in 1997 was marked by a slight recovery of anti-capitalism because of the 1995 huge social movement against the neoliberal reform of the pension system that was supported by many radical intellectuals, including Pierre Bourdieu. Consequently, Badiou's commentary on Deleuze and Guattari can be seen as a contribution to the French left-wing academic debates on politics.

The project of Badiou to counter Deleuze's influence on French revolutionary politics in a specific context marked by neoliberalism as a series of neoliberal measures had been systematically implemented since the end of the 1970s (Harvey 2005). Badiou interpreted Deleuze as an elitist philosopher in order to prevent the new generation of French revolutionary intellectuals from using the philosophy of Deleuze and Guattari. By contrast, Badiou wanted the new generation to use his philosophy in order to conceptualize neoliberalism and a political resistance to it. From the perspective of Badiou the philosophy of Deleuze and Guattari is a potential rival.

Badiou's commentary on Deleuze and Guattari is based on three hypotheses '1. This philosophy is organized around a metaphysics of the One. 2. It proposes an ethics of thought that requires dispossession and asceticism. 3. It is systematic and abstract' (1999: 17). This interpretation opposes the mainstream view asserting that Deleuze and Guattari are Postmodernist philosophers of the multiplicities. Badiou criticizes the idea that Deleuze and Guattari could be philosophers of 'planetary democratism', that is of multicultural liberalism (1999: 10). Accordingly, there would be an 'identity of thinking and dying' within Deleuze's thought (Badiou 1999: 13). According to Badiou, Deleuze's philosophy is 'aristocratic' and ascetic because thinking is a process of joining Being beyond the contingent singularity of the Self (1999: 11).

From the point of view of Badiou, the Stoic rather than the Spinozist ethics is the true source of inspiration of the philosophy of Deleuze and Guattari, and the reflection on sense in *The Logic of Sense* is more important than the developments of *Anti-Oedipus, A Thousand Plateaus* and *What Is Philosophy?* The relevance of Guattari is therefore downplayed by Badiou. The philosophy of Deleuze and Guattari is seen as marked by a duality between uncorporeal events and bodies as argued by the Stoics rather than by a metaphysics of the substance as claimed by Spinoza. When all is said, Deleuze could fundamentally be Bergsonian:

> This is to be attributed to his refined Bergsonism, for which in the final instance it is always what is that is right. Life makes the multiplicity of evaluations possible, but is itself impossible to evaluate. It can be said that there is nothing new under the sun because everything that happens is only an inflection of the One, the eternal return of the Same. It can also be said that everything is constantly new because it is only through the perpetual creation of its own folds that the One, in its absolute contingency, can indefinitely return. These two judgments are ultimately indiscernible. We must then wager.
>
> (Badiou 1999: 9)

Claiming that Deleuze and Guattari are Bergsonian rather than Marxist is a subtle way of discrediting the politics of Deleuze and Guattari within the framework of debates about revolutionary politics. In the French philosophical context, Bergsonism has been associated with spiritualism and a lack of engagement with politics, especially by Sartre and Marxism (Gutting 2001: 115). From this perspective, the argument of Badiou conceals left-wing thinkers that were influenced by Bergson, in particular Georges Sorel.

Badiou puts the emphasis on *The Logic of Sense* (2004), *Difference and Repetition* (1994), and the books on Leibniz (1993a) and on the cinema analysis, as opposed to *Capitalism and Schizophrenia* (1977, 1987). This demonstrates an underestimation of Guattari's role in relation to Deleuzian philosophy. In fact, dismissing Guattari is an adroit way of affirming that Deleuze's philosophy is elitist and therefore unable to inform radical politics. Otherwise, Badiou would have had to tackle the important militant experience of Guattari, who had been a Trotskyist, a member of the 22nd March Movement and very close to the Italian autonomists in the 1970s and the 1980s (Dosse 2010).

A number of substantial disagreements appeared in *Deleuze: The Clamor of Being* (1999). The first was Plato. Badiou argued that Plato was philosophically and politically central in order to defend the notion of truths against Postmodernism and the neoliberal ideology. Badiou blamed Deleuze for his critique of Plato: 'Plato has to be *restored*' (Badiou 1999: 101). The second disagreement related to psychoanalysis and particularly Lacan. Badiou used or prolonged Lacanian thought (Badiou 2005: 391) whereas Deleuze and Guattari criticized it, in particular in *Anti-Oedipus* (1977). Finally, Badiou proposed a politics entailing a theory of the subject whereas Deleuze and Guattari are critical about this arborescent notion, as opposed to rhizomatic multiplicities (1987: 3).

In sum, Badiou adopted an interpretative strategy in order to depoliticize the oeuvre of Deleuze and Guattari and prevent it from influencing the revolutionary political debate in France. In particular, Badiou downplayed the role of Guattari. This allowed Badiou to downplay the importance of the joint oeuvre of Deleuze and Guattari with in particular *Anti-Oedipus* and *A Thousand Plateaus*, which provide anti-capitalist and revolutionary analyses, and to operate an elitist interpretation of Deleuze and Guattari.

The next elitist interpretation I discuss also downplays Guattari's role in creating the Deleuzo-Guattarian oeuvre, or – if anything – treating Guattari as a 'bad influence' on Deleuze. I examine this interpretation, operated by Slavoj Žižek, in the next section.

The elitist interpretation of Žižek

The second important contemporary revolutionary philosopher who interprets the philosophy of Deleuze and Guattari as elitist is Žižek. Žižek is a very specific character in the context of contemporary philosophy. Žižek was philosophically trained in Slovenia, even though he had been in Paris to study Lacanianism. He participated in the dissent movement within the framework of communist Yugoslavia. Žižek was introduced to Western audiences with *The Sublime Object of Ideology* in 1989. Since then, he has been significantly influential in the English-speaking academy, in particular in the field of critical scholarship. Essentially, in *The Sublime Object of Ideology* Žižek combines Marxism and the psychoanalytical tradition in order to understand capitalism (1989). He emphasizes Marx's concept of the fetishism of the commodity (Marx 1976: 165) and the psychoanalytical notions of fantasy. Žižek engages at length with popular culture – in particular films and series – in his oeuvre.

Žižek (2004: 20) claims his interpretation of Deleuze and Guattari was influenced by Badiou's *Deleuze: The Clamor of Being*, which I discussed in the previous section. Accordingly, the most interesting part of Deleuze's oeuvre would be marked by an analysis of being (*Difference and Repetition* (1994), *The Logic of Sense* (2004), *Proust and Signs* (1972) and the *Introduction to Sacher-Masoch* (1989)), as opposed to the writings involving Guattari, in particular *Capitalism and Schizophrenia* (1977, 1987) and *What Is Philosophy?* (1994). The collaboration with Guattari is described as a 'bad influence' (Žižek 2004: 20). This is connected to the interpretative strategy of Žižek in relation to Deleuze and Guattari. Downplaying the role of Guattari is a means of avoiding discussing at length *Anti-Oedipus* and *A Thousand Plateaus*, which engage with anti-capitalist and revolutionary politics. Žižek's interpretative strategy seeks to depict the philosophy of Deleuze and Guattari as elitist in order to prevent it from influencing contemporary debates about revolutionary politics. Arguing that the philosophy of Deleuze is elitist and not revolutionary is a way for Žižek of promoting his own revolutionary philosophy. In other words, the philosophy produced by Deleuze (and Guattari) is presented as elitist and apolitical, whereas the texts that are more political and allegedly influenced by Guattari are said not to be interesting from an intellectual point of view.

The philosophy of Deleuze and Guattari would not primarily be a reflection on the One:

> One should therefore problematize the very basic *duality* of Deleuze's thought, that of Becoming versus Being, which appears in different versions (The Nomadic versus Being, the molecular versus the molar, the schizo versus the paranoiac, etc.). This duality is ultimately overdetermined as "the Good versus the Bad": the aim of Deleuze is to liberate the immanent force of Becoming from its self-enslavement to the order of Being.
>
> (Žižek 2004: 28)

Accordingly, this would be caused by Deleuze and Guattari's 'vitalism' (Žižek 2004: 28). The philosophy of Deleuze and Guattari would be a dualism for which being is one:

> The wager of Deleuze's concept of the "plane of consistency", which points in the direction of absolute immanence, is that of his insistence on the univocity of being. In his "flat ontology", all heterogeneous entities of an assemblage can be conceived at the same level, without any ontological exceptions or priorities.
>
> (Žižek 2004: 58)

The philosophy of Žižek

In this section, I shall argue that the two main differences between Deleuze and Guattari and Žižek are the usage of psychoanalysis, in particular Lacan, and the usage of Hegelian dialectic. In order to make these two points, I shall draw mainly on the joint oeuvre of Deleuze and Guattari, in particular *Anti-Oedipus* (1977), *A Thousand Plateaus* (1987) and *What Is Philosophy?* (1994). Žižek proclaims his loyalty to the Lacanian problematic:

> The key point here is that the subject is not the correlate of "thing" (or, more precisely, a "body"). The *person* dwells in a body while the subject is the correlate of *a* (partial object), of an organ without a body. And against the standard notion of person-thing as a life-world totality from which the subject- object couple is extrapolated, one should assert the couple subject-object (in Lacanese: $\$-a$, the barred subject coupled with the "object small a") as primordial – and the couple person-thing as its "domestication". What gets lost in the passage from subject-object to person-thing is the twisted relationship of the Moebius band: "persons" and "things" are part of the same reality, whereas the object is the impossible equivalent of the subject itself.
>
> (2004: 175)

The reasoning of Žižek borrows the Lacanian framework, in particular his understanding of the split subject. In this passage he explains the complex relationship between the split subject and the object little *a*. Similarly, he refers to the Lacanian triad of the Real, the Symbolic and the Imaginary (Žižek 2004: 102). This entails a Structuralist analysis of subjectivity. In contrast, Deleuze and Guattari extensively criticize the Oedipus triangle, the notion of familialism and Freudian psychoanalysis, which is associated with the reproduction of capitalism in *Anti-Oedipus*, even though they do not entirely reject Lacan's theory of the object little *a*:

> Lacan's admirable theory of desire however appears to us to have two poles: one related to "the object small *a*" as a desiring-machine, which defines desire in terms of a real production, thus going beyond both any idea of need and any idea of fantasy; and the other related to the "great Other" as a signifier, which reintroduces a certain notion of lack.
>
> (1977: 27)

Deleuze and Guattari's conceptualization of revolution within the framework of the structures of capitalism would be influenced by Lacanian thought (Watson 2009: 144). The notion of desiring machines and body without organs as anti-production seems akin to the Lacanian split subject and the object little *a* (Deleuze and Guattari 1977: 7). In the later works, hostility towards Lacan is more obvious, in particular in *A Thousand Plateaus* (Deleuze and Guattari 1987). In *A Thousand Plateaus*, Deleuze and Guattari associate Lacan with the rest of the history of psychoanalysis, which they strongly criticize (1987: 26). They criticize Lacan's supposed Structuralist understanding of subjectivity (Deleuze and Guattari 1987: 171). This is linked to development of the concept of assemblage in *Kafka: For a Minor Literature* (1986) and *A Thousand Plateaus* (1987) comprising not only desiring production, as in *Anti-Oedipus*, but also of linguistic elements. This implied the usage of the pragmatist linguistic theory of Hjelmslev and the final rejection of the Structuralist paradigm, which had already started with the notion of machine in *Anti-Oedipus* (1977). The second important philosophical disagreement between Žižek and Deleuze and Guattari resides in the place of the dialectic. Žižek criticizes Deleuzian hostility towards Hegel:

> For Deleuze, Hegelian negativity is precisely the way to subordinate difference to Identity, to reduce it to a sublated moment of identity's self-mediation ("identity of identity and difference"). The accusation against Hegel is thus double. Hegel introduces negativity in the pure positivity of Being, and Hegel introduces negativity in order to reduce differentiation to subordinated/sublatable moment of the positive One. What remains unthinkable for Deleuze is simply a negativity that is *not* just a detour on the path of the One's self-mediation. One is tempted to defend Hegel here: is what Hegel ultimately does to negativity not the unheard-of "*positivization*" *of negativity itself*?
>
> (2004: 52)

The philosophy of Žižek uses the Hegelian dialectic which he associates with the Lacanian approach. This implies a rational understanding of a dialectical totality functioning through negative moments. By contrast, Deleuze and Guattari have continuously rejected the Hegelian dialectic, for instance for Deleuze's single-authored work since *Nietzsche and Philosophy* (1983) and *Difference and Repetition* (1994), which were written in the 1960s. In *A Thousand Plateaus*, Deleuze and Guattari describe Hegel as a philosopher of a totalizing reason leading to the praising of state power (1987: 460). From the ontological point of view, there is a refusal of the notion of negativity in the philosophy of Deleuze and Guattari because of the centrality of notions such as production, expression or force. In *What Is Philosophy?*, Deleuze and Guattari reject the Hegel's dialectical philosophy of history in favour of a geographical account of history (1994: 90), which is influenced by the work of Braudel on the Mediterranean (1995).

The politics of Žižek

The dismissal of the philosophy of Deleuze and Guattari as being elitist is also based on the politics of Žižek. An important point resides in the notion of ideology. Deleuze and Guattari extensively criticize the notion of ideology: 'It has nothing to do with ideology. There is no ideology and never has been' (1987: 4). Deleuze and Guattari criticize the Marxist concepts of superstructure and infrastructure which are said to ground the notion of ideology (1977: 104).

In contrast to a conception of ideology grounded on the idea of superstructure, Deleuze and Guattari argue that the reproduction of power relations constitute the socius through a libidinal process: desiring production desires its own repression (1977). According to Deleuze and Guattari there is no ideological superstructure and economic infrastructure, but only a libidinal infrastructure. In *A Thousand Plateaus*, there are war machines that are captured by the state without any ideology and the violence of the master signifier imposes its sense through a regime of signs (1987: 175).

In other words, for Deleuze and Guattari there are no real power relations on the one side and their ideological legitimations on the other side. On the contrary, there are rhizomatic or molecular processes that are rigidified through a capture. Žižek insists on the notion of ideology. In particular, he argues that cynicism and 'interpassivity' have become the new form of ideology (2004: 179). Historically, ideology would function as structures producing 'interpellated' subjects through the school, the church or the press, according to Althusser's *Ideology and Ideological State Apparatuses* (1971). By contrast, neoliberalism would function through a creation of an apparent disbelief towards these traditional ideological modes:

> The outstanding mode of this "lying in the guise of truth" today is cynicism: with a disarming frankness one "admits everything", yet this full

acknowledgement of our power interests does not in any way prevent us from pursuing these interests – the formula of cynicism is no longer the classic Marxian "they do not know, but they are doing it".

(Žižek 1994: 8)

This model of ideological process is fetishistic disavowal. The patient, or groups of people deny knowing what they know; that is to say that capitalist power relations and liberal democracy are an illusion. Politically, this entails a number of differences with Deleuze and Guattari. Žižek characterizes Deleuze as an 'ideologist of late capitalism' (2004: 184) because his philosophy of multiplicities, of the connection and circulation of affects is said to correspond to the connection and circulation of capital and is linked to the biopolitical functioning of contemporary capitalism. Accordingly, this means that his ontological philosophy of multiplicity prevents him from conceptualizing a practical radical politics – taking into account class struggle, contradiction and resistance – and leads him to an elitist refusal of politics and, consequently, an implicit acceptance of the functioning of 'late capitalism'.

According to Žižek, contemporary capitalism functions through a production of ideology best described by the notion of fetishistic disavowal. Consequently, from the point of view of Žižek, a leftist political response to neoliberalism would involve preventing this ideological permeating through a cultural revolution, that is to say a transformation of daily life: 'in a radical revolution, people not only "realize their old (emancipatory, etc.) dreams"; rather, they have to reinvent their very modes of dreaming' (2004: 211). By contrast, the perspective of Deleuze and Guattari would describe the relationship between subjectivity and capitalism either in terms of machinic libidinal investment (1977) or in terms of assemblage (1987).

For Žižek, the notions of desiring machine or assemblage and the correlative rejection of psychoanalysis is not as efficient as Lacanianism in order to conceptualize the interpassive ideological characteristics of neoliberalism. Therefore, he combats the influence of the works of Deleuze and Guattari on the left:

> So, why Deleuze? In the past decade, Deleuze emerged as the central reference of contemporary philosophy: notions like "resisting multitude", "nomadic subjectivity", the "anti-Oedipal" critique of psychoanalysis, and so on are the common currency of today's academia – not to mention the fact that Deleuze more and more serves as the theoretical foundation of today's anti-globalist Left and its resistance to capitalism. *Organs without Bodies* goes "against the current": its starting premise is that, beneath this Deleuze (the popular image of Deleuze based on the reading of the books he co-authored with Guattari), there is another Deleuze.
>
> (Žižek 2004: xi)

In other words, Žižek dismisses the works that Deleuze and Guattari wrote together, even though these books, in particular *Anti-Oedipus* and *A Thousand*

Plateaus, provide a meticulous analysis of capitalism as well as an anti-capitalist politics. For Žižek, the only interesting part of the philosophy of Deleuze (and Guattari) is the elitist one, which provides a subtle ontology. This allows Žižek to avoid discussing the specific anti-capitalism of *Capitalism and Schizophrenia*. Similarly, this interpretation of Deleuze and Guaitari enables Žižek to avoid a justification of his own positions on psychoanalysis since Freudianism and (to a lesser extent) Lacanianism are criticized in *Capitalism and Schizophrenia*. For instance, Žižek's book does not engage at all with the question of anti-psychiatry or the problem of the Oedipus.

Organs without Bodies recognizes that the first part of the work of Deleuze, that is to say mainly *Difference and Repetition* and *The Logic of Sense*, has some philosophical interest, as opposed to the philosophical collaboration with Guattari (Deleuze and Guattari 1977, 1986, 1994). The interesting part of the oeuvre of Deleuze is considered an elitist and purely philosophical work that was unable to draw the philosophical and political conclusions of Žižek; that is to say an articulation of Hegelianism, Lacanianism and the question of ideology.

The interpretation of Deleuze and Guattari of Žižek is directed at the leftist audience. *Organs without Bodies* seeks to discredit the philosophy and politics of *Anti-Oedipus* and *A Thousand Plateaus* and to promote the politics of Žižek; that is to say a leftist Lacanianisn since the so-called elitism of Deleuze's single-authored books are presented as apolitical, and therefore cannot rival Žižek's in terms of political analysis.

Below, I will turn to Peter Hallaward's elitist interpretation of Deleuze and Guattari. It argues that the philosophy of Deleuze and Guattari is reserved for a depoliticized elite of professional philosophers. Accordingly, Deleuze and Guattari would not provide any effective revolutionary political philosophy.

The interpretation of Hallward

Peter Hallward is a relatively influential revolutionary philosopher as his presentation at the 2009 London-based conference on communism demonstrated[3] (Žižek and Douzinas 2010). He is a specialist of continental philosophy, in particular of Badiou. Hallward's book on Deleuze and Guattari, *Out of This World: Deleuze and the Philosophy of Creation*, dates from 2006, and is therefore informed by the works of Badiou and Žižek. To a certain extent, Badiou's project consisted of combating Deleuze and Guattari's influence on French revolutionary politics. By contrast, Žižek and Hallward direct criticism at the Anglophone academy and the alleged popularity of Deleuzo-Guattarian thought among left-wing academics, in particular the advocates of identity politics and Postmodernism. Žižek's and Hallward's contributions are probably more significant quantitatively than Badiou's, because the Anglophone academy has offered a better resistance to right-wing cultural hegemony than its French counterpart (Cusset 2008: xviii).

Hallward develops a specific reception of Deleuze's philosophy. His main interpretative hypothesis is that:

> Although, it may have some complicated implications the presumption is a very simple one. Deleuze presumes that being is creativity. Creativity is what there is and it creates all that there can be. Individual facets of being are differentiated as so many acts of creation. Every biological or social configuration, and so is every sensation, statement or concept. All these things are creations on their own right, immediately, and not merely on account of their interactions with other things. The merely relative differences that may exist or arise between created things stem from a deeper, more fundamental power of creative differing.
>
> (Hallward 2006: 1)

This differs from Badiou's hypothesis of the ascetic and systematic philosophy of the One and from Žižek's hypothesis of the ontological dualism between being and becoming, even though in the final analysis they all provide an elitist interpretation of Deleuze and Guattari. According to Hallward, Deleuze and Guattari can be seen as 'theophanic' thinkers in the tradition of Plotinus or Erigena:

> The essential point is that such individuation does not itself depend on mediation through the categories of representation, objectivity, history or the world. An individual is only truly unique according to this conception of things, if its individuation is the manifestation of an individuating power. More crudely, you are only really an individual if God (or something like God) makes you so.
>
> (Hallward 2006: 5)

Accordingly, every creature is an expression of an immanent God. The politics of Deleuze and Guattari is being incapable of thinking contradictions and social antagonisms because of its refusal of the dialectic (Hallward 2006: 167). This is crucial for Hallward because it would not be possible to conceptualize social relations without a dialectical thinking of the process and negativity, for instance resistance as the negativity of oppression. Therefore, not surprisingly, Hallward claims that the politics of Deleuze and Guattari lacks 'a decisive subject and strategy' (2006: 163). To a certain extent, Hallward negates the existence of a Deleuzo-Guattarian politics, because contemplation, as opposed to the Marxist transformative philosophy, would be its most important trait.

The philosophy and the politics of Hallward

First of all, it is clear that Hallward, like Badiou and Žižek, does not share the same philosophical approach as Deleuze and Guattari. Hallward's philosophical view consists of defending the notion of subject, which contradicts the concept of assemblage or multiplicity. For Hallward therefore the point of departure of any emancipatory politics or free activity resides in the constitution of a voluntary and free subject. Hence, according to Hallward, the most important philosophical question is to determine how a political subject can emerge from the diversity of the world. This corresponds to the subject of Rousseau's *The Social Contract* (2002) and of Robespierre as Hallward says in a discussion with other scholars:

> Well here we really do disagree, but it's an interesting disagreement. The kind of equality that I'm talking about is not the equality of liberal democracy. It's the equality that is implicit in something like the constitution of a general will or something like a Jacobin conception of politics – which takes shape in a very specific kind of conjuncture – or the equality that's implicit in a generic set, which is in my opinion a far more coherent way of talking about "anyone at all", because it provides a very clear conceptual analysis of what exactly that involves.
>
> (Alliez et al. 2010: 156)

The politics advocated by Hallward is a rationalist politics based on an abstract equality between citizens. It entails a form of discipline and rational strategy as the reference to Jacobinism demonstrates. Hallward is very critical of what a Deleuzian politics could be because it would be reserved to an elite, as he says in a discussion with other scholars:

> antithetical to a tradition which comes out of, say, Hume and Bergson (a slightly obscene combination), and which is based on "sympathy" and ultimately on a kind of mysticism. Who are they, these people who are capable of having sympathy for the people who are not part of their immediate situation? It's the Great Souls, the rare Great Souls – the elite. Much the same thing applies to Spinoza and in Nietzsche, two other key philosophical sources for Deleuze.
>
> (Alliez et al. 2010: 156)

The philosophy of Deleuze and Guattari is clearly opposed to a rationalist position which would posit subjects. From the political point of view, Deleuze and Guattari do not share the Rousseauist position of the general will that could be collectively and rationally constructed. The general will is supposed to be reached by the diversity of individuals through deliberation. In contrast, for Deleuze and Guattari, emancipation can only be the result of a politics of singularities. Hallward's standpoint is grounded on a rationalist politics implying subjects, freedom, decisions. From this point of view, Hallward connects this politics of the revolutionary subject with the tradition of communism, as he says in a discussion with other scholars:

> The thing is, though, that having made that assessment, what distinguishes the communist movement in the nineteenth century from, say, the anarchist

movement, which would agree on that point, is precisely the strategic conclusion that they draw. The communist conclusion is that we need, in response to this situation, an institution, an organisation, direction, and so on: precisely so that the proletariat can indeed dissolve itself as a *class* (within the historical constraints of a class-bound situation) but not as social existence, not as "emancipated labour".

(Alliez et al. 2010: 149)

Hallward opposes the discipline and strategy of communist politics to an anarchist refusal of organization and strategy. The communist politics would be a form of rationalist politics. Furthermore, Hallward associates his politics of the revolutionary subject with the Marxist tradition, as he says in a discussion with other scholars:

What is required, from this perspective, is the construction of a disciplined working-class political organisation that would be capable of *winning* the class struggle that takes shape around this time. Later, people will make roughly the same sort of argument in defence of the mobilisation of national liberation movements, for example. Both sorts of organisation emphasise things like discipline, unity, strategic purpose: certainly at the risk of problematic consequences, but the risk is unavoidable. This is the political legacy of Marxism, if you ask me. It's the combination of these two things: an assessment of historical tendencies and economic logics, articulated together with the formulation of political strategy.

(Alliez et al. 2010: 149)

The political philosophy of Hallward entails that the political revolutionary subject needs a strong political organization which enables a strategy to be implemented in order to take over power. In other words, the issue of the political subject is related to the question of strategy. The political subject needs to be a rational, conscious and reflexive agent in order to be able to apply a political strategy, that is to say a series of rational measures whose end is a revolutionary politics. The politics of Hallward clearly operates an implicit military analogy. The revolutionary subject – that is to say the working class or colonized people according to Hallward's examples (for instance in a discussion with other scholars, Alliez et al. 2010: 149) – should be constituted as a hierarchized army. Soldiers or militants should carry out the orders of the officers or the cadres. Consequently, this army needs a general (a political leader) who is able to take sensible strategic decisions such as when and where and with which forces it is necessary to attack the enemy. The space of politics is considered as the space of the battlefield.

Consequently, the main reproach that can be addressed to Deleuze and Guattari's politics is its 'anti-rationalist' refusal of the subject; that is to say the importance given to affects and to desire. Hallward therefore does not take into account Deleuze and Guattari's analysis of capitalism (axiomatic, society of control), or theory of the state (apparatus of capture, Asian mode of production), or social theory (for instance, socius):

> Like the nomads who invented it, this abstract machine operates at an "absolute speed, by being 'synonymous with speed'", as the incarnation of "a pure immeasurable multiplicity [...], an irruption of the ephemeral and of the power of metamorphosis" (TP, 386, 352). Like any creation, a war machine consists and "exists only in its own metamorphoses" (TP, 360). By posing the question of politics in the starkly dualistic terms of war machine *or* state – by posing it, in the end, in the apocalyptic terms of a new people and a new earth or else no people and no earth – the political aspect of Deleuze's philosophy amounts to little more than utopian distraction.
>
> (Hallward 2006: 162)

From Hallward's point of view, the subtle political economy of Deleuze and Guattari is not relevant because it is not articulated to an effective revolutionary politics. Hallward avoids the discussion of the political economy of Deleuze and Guattari because it corresponds to his interpretative strategy. Political economy and politics are interconnected, in particular in the Marxist tradition. Significantly, Hallward does not seriously criticize the notion of 'societies of control' (Deleuze 1992a). This allows him to formulate his politics of the rational and collective subject without tackling the issue of surveillance or the capturing of subjectivity by late capitalism.

Arguing that Deleuze and Guattari are elitist philosophers of the One, interested mainly in philosophy and philosophers that do not provide a consistent revolutionary politics, which implies from the point of view of Hallward a rational and disciplined organization, enables a conceptual confrontation to be avoided with the powerful political economy of Deleuze and Guattari. Hallward dismisses the political economy and the politics of Deleuze and Guattari with a general ontological claim about their philosophy, seen as a metaphysics of the One. Hallward therefore considers irrelevant a detailed discussion of the evolution of the philosophy of Deleuze and Guattari. Hallward reduces the Deleuzo-Guattarian oeuvre to philosophy so as to dismiss it politically.

This allows Hallward to be critical about the alleged Marxism of Deleuze and Guattari, as he says in a discussion with other scholars:

> The distinctive contribution of schizoanalysis to a logic of capital concerns how to get out of it, to reach this point where the body without organs is presented as a kind of apocalyptic explosion of any form of limit, where the decoded flows free to the end of the world, etc. There I think people who take some more conventional point of reference from Marx would be confused. They would think: "what is this for?"
>
> (Alliez et al. 2010: 144)

According to Hallward, Deleuze and Guattari use Marx without actually being legitimate Marxists. This is a clever interpretative strategy to position himself and the heirs of the politics of a collective and rational subject as the authentic owners of the legacy of Marx. This allows him to escape an explanation of the problematic relationship between his politics of a collective subject and the formulation of a political economy.

In other words, Badiou and Hallward's critique of Deleuze and Guattari's political philosophy derives from their rationalist and ontological presuppositions; that is an advocacy of the notions of truth and subject against an important fraction of continental philosophy: the epigones of Nietzsche, Heidegger and of Poststructualism. Hallward argues that the philosophy of Deleuze and Guattari lacks a conceptualization of relationality, for instance of resistance and oppression. Deleuze and Guattari, however, propose analyses of the connection between micro-processes involving affects, desire and language and macroprocesses (such as the social reproduction of class, gender and race) with concepts such as nomadism and apparatus of capture, or molecular and molar. According to Hallward this entails an elitist philosophy.

The critique of Hallward, like that of Badiou and Žižek, is purely philosophical and theoretical. This allows Hallward, as well as Badiou and Žižek, to dismiss the political activism of Deleuze and Guattari as irrelevant in terms of the deeper political significance of their philosophy. The philosophy of Deleuze and Guattari is regarded as consisting of philosophical elitism. Similarly, Hallward argues that Deleuze and Guattari's philosophy is 'theophanic' as are the writings of New Philosopher Christian Jambet. The New Philosophers are a group of French philosophers who operated a critique of Marxism from the perspective of anti-totalitarianism in the 1970s. The philosophy of Deleuze and Guattari are presented as being about contemplating the world for an elite of enlightened philosophers, as opposed to transforming the world for the majority.

Below, I will turn to Philippe Mengue's elitist interpretation of Deleuze and Guattari. In contrast with the previous interpretations, Mengue argued that the depoliticizing elitism of the philosophy of Deleuze and Guattari was a positive thing.

Mengue's elitist interpretation of the philosophy of Deleuze and Guattari

Mengue is a contemporary French philosopher. Mengue's interpretation of the philosophy of Deleuze and Guattari is elitist. The position of Mengue is different from that of Badiou, Žižek and Hallward. In fact, his politics is neither revolutionary nor Marxist, as is that of Badiou, Žižek and Hallward, because Mengue is liberal with a Postmodernist perspective:

> Indeed, there is a very strong link that is created between this creation and our relation to time (which is constitutive of postmodernity) and the "coming back" of democracy and of human rights from the political and juridical

point of view, as well as the autonomisation of ethics. It is very superficial to reduce postmodernity to an eclectism, to a simple "revivalism" and a coming back to what was once believed. This reduction is the reactive, vengeful idea of those who cannot console themselves with the loss of the historicist, revolutionary scheme associated with modernity. The resurgence of the democratic values is not the product of a rigid, conservative and reformist way back, to a refuge, out of necessity, to what had resisted with difficulty to the revolutionary flows and their immense failures.

(Mengue 2003: 16; my translation)

Mengue argues that the revolutionary politics of the 1960s and 1970s were based on a refusal of democracy and pluralism. His reasoning is in line with the New Philosophers of the 1970s (Ferry and Renaut 1990; Lévy 1979). The New Philosophers criticized the alleged totalitarianism of any revolutionary politics. Mengue therefore considers that the decline of revolutionary politics is a positive tendency because it is connected to the thriving of democracy:

On the contrary, it is essential to understand positively the strong and fruitful link that connects the abandonment of history and revolution to the re-evaluation and renewal of democracy and fundamental rights. The question of democracy and law is so central that it explains the impasses of the Deleuzian philosophy.

(Mengue 2003: 16; my translation)

Mengue defines democracy as a liberal system recognizing human rights, and most of all 'pluralism' (2003: 16; my translation). Consequently, democracy can be seen as characterized by the confrontation of different ideas within a capitalist society. For Mengue, capitalism is not contradictory with the functioning of democracy because this socio-economic system could 'reasonably' fulfil the needs of the people (2003: 193; my translation). Politics could then have a political domain not totally dominated by the capitalist logic of commodification.

Mengue criticizes the political philosophy of Deleuze and Guattari as being unable to properly articulate political liberalism (2003: 238). He argues that Deleuze and Guattari to a certain extent produced a Marxist revolutionary politics in the context of May '68:

I demonstrated that the refusal of democratic pluralism was connected to a heavy Marxist and historicist stratum, which was left uncriticised, and which constrains and fixes the Deleuzian thought in the preconceived thought of the Modernist intellectuals of the Ultra-Left, which prevents him from understanding the positivity of the politics and ethics of postmodernism.

(Mengue 2003: 204; my translation)

Mengue criticizes the Marxist influence on the oeuvre of Deleuze and Guattari. For him, this demonstrates that the philosophy of Deleuze and Guattari is partly dominated by a modernist and revolutionary logic grounded on an implicit unitary and historical subject. Even though Mengue defends the values of a liberal political system with representative democracy within the framework of a capitalism, he does not draw a liberal interpretation of Deleuze and Guattari. In fact, according to Mengue, the philosophy of Deleuze is more fundamentally a 'theory of multiplicities' opposed to analytic philosophy on the one hand and on the other hand the continental traditions of philosophy, mainly phenomenology, Hegelianism and Marxism (2003: 21). It is possible therefore to rescue the philosophy of Deleuze and Guattari from Marxism, according to Mengue.

Second, the philosophy of Deleuze and Guattarrri is presented as emphasizing the notion of becoming which should be opposed to a traditional idea of a logical progress in history (Mengue 2003: 22). Mengue produces an elitist interpretation of Deleuze and Guattari, which tries to formulate a kind of Postmodernist Deleuzo-Guattarian philosophy:

> The best lesson that can be drawn from Deleuzian thought is not *political* (even though Deleuze himself would probably not agree) and could not inform a political and efficient politics. Deleuzian philosophy should provide a number of bases for a postmodernist *ethics*, breaking with the historicist illusions of revolution and history. I could not have defended such a critical position without the opening created by Deleuze. The heterogeneity and incommensurability of the legal-political and the ethical (and hence the break between the "thinker" and the politician) in order to allow the Deleuzian concepts to bear fruit for Postmodernist thought.
>
> (2003: 206; my translation)

In sum, according to Mengue, the main interest of the philosophy of Deleuze and Guattari is to provide a Postmodernist ethics with an ontological framework including the notions of multiple and becoming. The revolutionary politics of Deleuze and Guattari are dismissed. The interpretation of Deleuze and Guattari provided by Mengue is depoliticized and elitist because it helps conceive of a postmodernity characterized by the plurality of values. This Postmodernist ethics is opposed to *ressentiment* (resentment) and negative affects despite the violence of capitalist accumulation. Only the happy few who are able to understand the subtle Deleuzo-Guattarian ontology of the multiple would be able to apply this ethics. The ethics proposed by Mengue (and his interpretation of Deleuze and Guattari) is elitist as it is reserved to a minority of philosophers who can ironically understand the vanity of the politicians who claim to actually be able to change the world beyond the liberal functioning of the routine of Western representative democracies. The interpretation of Mengue seeks to depoliticize Deleuze and Guattari in order to use their philosophy within the framework of a non- revolutionary and elitist project.

The challenging critique of Deleuze and Guattari from the perspective of feminist identity politics

Some Feminists (Grosz 1985; Irigaray 1985; Jardine 1984, 1985) provided challenging and relevant critiques of the philosophy of Deleuze and Guattari, in particular in the 1980s and 1990s. Feminism and women's studies are a very complex field that cannot possibly be covered here. Nevertheless, the interpretation of the philosophy of Deleuze and Guattari that was produced by these Feminist scholars was also elitist because Deleuze and Guattari were seen as elitist philosophers who would not be able to provide effective political tools for Feminism. This suspicion surrounding Deleuze and Guattari made sense from the perspective of Feminist struggles, which had been able to achieve a series of victories in the 1960s and 1970s in the United States as well as in France and elsewhere. Essentially, the philosophy of Deleuze and Guattari was considered a purely ontological and elitist endeavour:

> At the same time, while taking the United States as the ideal, D + G's work remains overwhelmingly Francocentric in its philosophical teleology. Their voyages to the outer continents of reason are firmly directed from their home front where they are at war with their own European heritages from Plato and Hegel to Sartre and Lacan. Impertinent, anarchical (without *archè*), philosophers of deterritorialized desire, D + G remain very much in the (European) tradition of the (male) *chevalier de la foi*: they are the faithful and vigilant keepers of the future.
>
> (Jardine 1984: 48)

Deleuze and Guattari would be interested in producing a purely philosophical reflection on the processes of becoming and being, including physical, geological and biological objects without confronting the issues of politics, in particular from the perspective of women. Jardine compared Deleuze and Guattari to knights *(chevaliers)*, that is to say an elite group in the context of a feudal society. Significantly, the political commitments of Deleuze and Guattari are ignored and not referred to, in particular Socialism or Barbarianism, the anti-psychiatry experience of the La Borde clinic, or the Prison Information Group (Dosse 2010). This makes sense within the framework of an interpretative strategy that seeks to reduce the oeuvre of Deleuze and Guattari to academic philosophy. At the same time, this interpretative strategy did not seem entirely unfair as Deleuze and Guattari were not directly involved in Feminist struggles (Dosse 2010).

The philosophy of Deleuze and Guattari was therefore considered as irrelevant from the perspective of the agenda of Feminist politics by certain Feminists, because of its purely philosophical content: 'For the American feminist theorist, D+G are perched precariously at the borders of France and the U.S. philosophy and feminism. They are awkwardly positioned on a complex and changing epistemological and political field of battle' (Jardine 1984: 48).

The purely philosophical approach of Deleuze and Guattari is seen as a covered phallocentric operation. Jardine drew on Deleuze's understanding of *Vendredi ou Les Limbes du Pacifique* (1972) (which is Michel Tournier's rewriting of *Robinson Crusoe*) in order to provide an account of the alleged masculinism of the philosophy of Deleuze. Robinson Crusoe in Michel Tournier's novel meets the non-European native Vendredi. Robinson Crusoe is then engaged in a process of becoming with the Speranza (the desert island) and with Vendredi (Jardine 1984: 58). The Other (Vendredi) is projected into a becoming process which involves the natural elements of the environment (the island, the sky, the sea) from which women are excluded:

> It would seem that the most radical promises offered by D + G's theory, as exemplarized in Tournier's fiction, are not to be kept – at least for now. For when enacted, when performed, they are promises to be kept only between bodies gendered male. There is no room for new becomings of women's bodies and their other desires in these creatively limited, mono-sexual, brotherly machines.
>
> (Jardine 1984: 59)

The concept of machine developed in *Anti-Oedipus* is held as particularly masculinist by such Feminists critical of Deleuze. By contrast, other Feminists like Donna Haraway consider the machine, in particular with the concept of cyborg, as an emancipatory paradigm for women (1991). The notion of becoming-woman is duly criticized by some Feminists:

> The metaphor of becoming woman is a male appropriation and recuperation of the positions and struggles of women. As such, it risks depoliticizing, and even aestheticizing struggles and political challenges that are crucial to the survival and self-definition of women.
>
> (Grosz 1993: 168)

The concept of becoming-woman is seen as masculinist and unable to help challenge the status quo from the perspective of Feminist struggles. The notion of becoming-woman could also be an intellectual tool to dispossess women of their identity and their gendered politics, because according to Deleuze and Guattari feminine processes could be universal because they involve men as well as non-human physical and biological processes. This is a relevant critique of the philosophy of Deleuze and Guattari which poses a challenging question to Deleuze and Guattari. After all, Deleuze and Guattari were males using the female imaginary in order to create a concept in a context characterized by patriarchy.

Grosz (1985), Jardine (1984, 1985) and Irigaray (1985) partly share this critical interpretation of the philosophy of Deleuze and Guattari. The thought of Deleuze and Guattari could be mainly philosophical and masculinist through its emphasis on heterogenesis. Providing an elitist philosophy would be inherently apolitical as far as women are concerned because it would not give them the political tool they used successfully in the 1960s and 1970s, namely identity politics. More recently, it should be noted that other Feminists including Grosz (1993, 2000) have produced a more positive interpretation of Deleuze and Guattari.

These Feminist interpretations of the philosophy of Deleuze and Guattari are elitist because they consider the Deleuzian project ultimately to be reserved for an elite group of male readers of philosophy. The philosophy of Deleuze could be embedded in the philosophical context that only a happy few can understand. The analysis of ontological molecular processes could then cast aside the Feminist molar struggles, which are arguably politically necessary.

Butler's historicist critique of Deleuze and Guattari

Judith Butler's Feminist interpretation of Deleuze and Guattari is also critical and elitist, although from a different perspective. Butler argues that Deleuze and Guattari are elitist philosophers seen as producing a depoliticized philosophy for academics. Butler blames Deleuze and Guattari for their anti-Hegelian conception of subjectivity which is said to be based on 'insupportable metaphysical speculation' (Butler 1987: 214 cited in Olkowski 2000: 87). Accordingly, the anti-Hegelianism of Deleuze and Guattari could well be the road to naturalism:

> Although Deleuze's critique of the Hegelian subject places him within the postmodern effort to describe a decentered affectivity, his appeal to Nietzsche's theory of forces suggests that he understands this decentered experience as an ontological rather than a culturally conditioned historical experience.
>
> (Butler, 1987: 215)

The understanding of desire as an ontological and natural process could prevent Deleuze and Guattari from understanding socio-historical processes. According to Butler, the philosophy of Deleuze and Guattari is unable to provide an intellectual framework for the Feminist struggles against masculinist power because it lacks a conceptual account of historical and political processes. In contrast, the oeuvre of Foucault is seen as much more helpful to understand the relations of powers and how they are gendered (Butler 1987: 215).

According to Butler, the philosophy of Deleuze and Guattari is elitist because it is only concerned with ontological issues and most of all because it lacks political utility. For Butler, Deleuze and Guattari thought constitutes an ontology of desire which is not able to foster a progressive and emancipatory politics, in particular from a Feminist perspective. The analysis of Butler unlike that of Grosz (1985), Jardine (1984, 1985) and Irigaray (1985) insists more on the political pointlessness of the philosophy of Deleuze and Guattari than on its phallocratism.

Grosz (1985), Jardine (1984, 1985) and Irigaray (1985) criticize the Deleuzo-Guattarian philosophy because it is seen as a subtle ontology reserved for an elite of masculinist philosophers. The elitist philosophy of Deleuze and Guattari is said not to be able to operate a Feminist identity politics that can defend women's rights. Butler also argues that the philosophy of Deleuze and Guattari is an elitist ontology that can inform a Feminist politics. Butler, however, insists more on the Deleuzo-Guattarian anti-Hegelianism.

The Feminists who criticize the philosophy of Deleuze and Guattari because of its elitism presented as irrelevant for women's struggles certainly have a point. I recognize that Feminist identity politics was successful in the 1960s and 1970s and that it did not correspond to Deleuze and Guattari's philosophy. However, it might be interesting in a financialized and post-Fordist context to articulate a Feminism that could enter into dialogue with Deleuze and Guattari.

Conclusion

The elitist interpretation of Deleuze and Guattari has been analysed in this chapter. Badiou, Hallward and Žižek produce an elitist interpretation of Deleuze and Guattari from a radical perspective. Their fundamental position is that the philosophy of Deleuze and Guattari does not confer an effective intellectual framework with respect to applying a revolutionary politics in the contemporary world. As a result, they argue that it is elitist and discredit it.

By contrast, Mengue provides an elitist interpretation of the philosophy of Deleuze and Guattari from the perspective of liberal politics. Mengue, however, does not think that Deleuze and Guattari advocate a liberal political philosophy. Instead, the author depoliticizes it through a systematic critique of the alleged noxious Marxist influence on Deleuze and Guattari. This allows him to operate an elitist interpretation of Deleuze and Guattari and develop a Postmodern ethics.

A number of Feminist authors connected to identity politics (Grosz 1985; Irigaray 1985; Jardine 1984, 1985) present an elitist interpretation of the philosophy of Deleuze and Guattari. Their project is to discredit the philosophy of Deleuze and Guattari from the point of view of a Feminist politics. Essentially, the philosophy of Deleuze and Guattari is seen as not being able to inform a progressive Feminist politics because of its lack of consideration for the molar politics of identity politics and its philosophical elitism. Butler (1987) argues that the philosophical elitism of Deleuze and Guattari is mainly interested in ontology and is unable to provide a philosophy of history that could inform a Feminist politics. Other Feminist thinkers (e.g. Haraway 1991) do not share this elitist interpretation of Deleuze and Guattari. In the next chapter, I shall provide an analysis of the liberal interpretation of Deleuze and Guattari. This interpretation of Deleuze and Guattari argues that their philosophy is compatible with capitalism and liberal thought.

Note

1 Other big names included Badiou, Žižek, Negri, Nancy and Rancière, among others.

3 The liberal interpretation of Deleuze and Guattari

Introduction

In this chapter, I shall continue the analysis of the reception of the oeuvre of Deleuze and Guattari by political philosophy. In the previous chapter, I tried to show that the elitist interpretation sought to reduce the Deleuzo-Guattarian oeuvre to academic philosophy. Deleuze and Guattari should be read by philosophers working in their ivory towers with no attempt being made to use Deleuzo-Guattarian philosophy to transform the world. Or rather, Deleuze should be read, for in this interpretation Guattari and his contribution tend to be marginalized. By contrast, the liberal interpretation of the politics of Deleuze and Guattari maintains that their oeuvre is compatible with liberal philosophy and capitalism.

This entails that the political philosophy of Deleuze and Guattari does not contradict notions such as private property, human rights, tolerance, the market and capitalism. More generally, as far as these scholars are concerned, Deleuze and Guattari's political philosophy corresponds to a poststructuralist understanding of liberalism.

First, I shall demonstrate that there is a liberal interpretation of the Deleuzo-Guattarian philosophy, which is operated by liberal philosophers who advocate capitalism and the market. Their project means incorporating the philosophy of Deleuze and Guattari as part of the tradition of liberal philosophy. The project is therefore mainly positive (Patton 2000, 2005; Tampio 2009). Second, I shall show that other scholars provide a liberal interpretation of the Deleuzian philosophy from a Marxist or critical position. They believe that Deleuze is liberal, even though they are critical about capitalism and the market (Boltanski and Chiapello 2005; Clouscard 1999; Garo 2011a, 2012; Jameson 1991). Finally, I shall analyse the position of De Landa who provides a liberal interpretation of Deleuze from the position of a flat ontology (2004, 2010).

The liberal interpretation of Deleuze and Guattari by liberal philosophy: Deleuze and Guattari the friends

There is an interpretative tradition within the Anglophone academy that asserts that liberal philosophy should be reformulated in poststructuralist terms, in particular with the philosophical vocabulary of Deleuze and Guattari. These scholars agree with the poststructuralist critiques of reference and realism unlike their positivist colleagues from political sciences departments and the advocates of analytic philosophy (Patton 2000, 2005; Tampio 2009). Their programme of research therefore maintains a poststructuralist approach within the framework of the values of the liberal tradition. This project is not limited to Deleuze and Guattari since it has also concerned Derrida, Lévinas, Lyotard and Foucault (Patton 2004, 2007).

The first author who clearly stated the compatibility of Deleuzo-Guattarism and liberalism was Paul Patton in *Deleuze and the Political* (2000). It will be therefore be useful to engage with the main arguments of Patton's *Deleuze and the Political* (2000). Paul Patton is a specialist of continental philosophy, post-structuralism and political philosophy. He is a professor at the department of humanities of the University of New South Wales. In his introduction, Patton makes a series of claims about the philosophy of Deleuze and Guattari (2000: 1). First, the work of Deleuze and Guattari is said to be characterized by a lack of engagement with the history of political philosophy and its important texts:

> Deleuze does not conform to the standard image of a political philosopher. He has not written about Machiavelli, Hobbes, Locke or Rousseau and when he has written on philosophers who rate as political thinkers, such as Spinoza or Kant, he has not engaged with their political writings.
>
> (Patton 2000: 1)

According to Patton, the oeuvre of Deleuze and Guattari never directly engages with the 'nature of justice, freedom or democracy' (2000: 1) and the writings of Deleuze and Guattari do not discuss the contemporary literature in political philosophy from the USA and the UK (Patton 2000: 1). From the point of view of Patton, the only two 'overtly political books' by Deleuze and Guattari are *Anti-Oedipus* and *A Thousand Plateaus*, even though Patton (2000: 1) also mentions 'Many Politics' (Deleuze and Parnet 1987) and 'Postscript on Control Societies' (Deleuze 1992a). All the same, for Patton the philosophy of Deleuze and Guattari is seen as 'profoundly political' because it links ontology and politics (Patton 2000: 1).

According to Patton, however, the political thought of Deleuze and Guattari is not incompatible with the 'Anglophone political theory' that is grounded on the liberal political philosophy (2000: 1). It follows that the writings of Deleuze and Guattari study how things constantly change and not how they tend to reproduce themselves: 'They appear to be more interested in ways in which society is differentiated or divided than in ways in which it is held together' (Patton 2000: 3). Patton recognizes that Deleuze and Guattari link philosophy and politics within the framework of a libertarian utopia (Patton 2000: 3). From this point of view *What Is Philosophy?* is particularly crucial to understand the authors' view on politics and utopia (Deleuze and Guattari, 1994: 99).

Patton mentions Deleuze and Guattari's involvement in a number of political actions – such as supporting the Prison Information Group – even though 'this public intellectual activity did not distinguish Deleuze from a variety of other neo-Marxist, existentialist, anarchist or left-wing liberal intellectuals who signed the same petitions and took part in the same demonstrations' (2000: 4). Nonetheless, Deleuze's theory of the political relevance of the intellectual constituted a singularity through his concept of theory as a 'relay' of practical activities: 'his conception of the political role of the intellectual and the relationship between his own political activity and his philosophy set him apart from many of his contemporaries' (Patton 2000: 4).

On the issue of Marxism, Patton claims that 'despite their adoption of aspects of Marx's social and economic theory, there are significant points at which Deleuze and Guattari abandon traditional Marxist views' (2000: 6). First, according to Patton, Deleuze and Guattari replace the 'Marxist philosophy of history in favour of a differential typology of the macro- and micro-assemblages which determine the character of social life' (2000: 6). This analysis strategically avoids mentioning that Deleuze and Guattari provide philosophical engagements with history, at least in *Anti-Oedipus*, *A Thousand Plateaus* and *What Is Philosophy?* In *Anti-Oedipus*, Deleuze and Guattari develop the notion of 'savages, barbarians, civilized men', which corresponds to primitive, imperial and capitalist societies (1977: 139).

In *A Thousand Plateaus*, Deleuze and Guattari used the notion of 'universal history' as they had previously done more extensively in *Anti-Oedipus*, in order to provide an analysis of the state in the *Treatise of Nomadology* (1987: 418). Finally, in *What Is Philosophy?* Deleuze and Guattari provided a 'history of philosophy' in the chapter 'What is a Concept?' and 'Geophilosophy' (1994: 32). The notion of geophilosophy insisted on geography and contingency to provide an alternative concept to the history of philosophy of Hegel and Heidegger. This was strongly influenced by Braudel's geohistory (Deleuze and Guattari, 1994: 98). I would argue that Deleuze and Guattari provided a philosophy of history that sought to understand capitalism. Arguably, Deleuze and Guattari had the same problematic as Marx, even though they did not share his exact theorization based on modes of production and class struggle (Deleuze and Negri, 1995: 171).

Second, according to Patton, Deleuze and Guattari replace the Marxist concept of contradiction with the notion of lines of flights. However, line of flight and contradiction have the same conceptual function; that is to display the fact that social formations are not eternal and that they are heterogeneous. Third, according to Patton, Deleuze and Guattari refute the Marxist 'internal or evolutionist account of the origins of the State in favour of a neo-Nietzschean view according to which the form of the State has always existed even if only as a virtual tendency resisted by other processes within a given social field' (Patton 2000: 6). I would argue that this specific point corresponds only partly to the analysis of the state by Deleuze and Guattari, because strictly speaking there is no state in savage societies as it emerges only with imperial societies (1977: 194). In fact, Deleuze and Guattari use the work of Pierre Clastres along with Nietzsche's to explain the emergence of the state in *Anti-Oedipus* (1977: 192).

Fourth, from the liberal perspective of Patton, Deleuze and Guattari disagree with the idea of 'economic determinism in favour of a "machinic determinism"' (Patton 2000: 6). Even though it is clear that the oeuvre of Deleuze and Guattari provides a strong criticism of the orthodox Marxist idea of base and superstructure that grounds economic determinism, the idea of machinic determinism is inaccurate (for instance, 1987: 68). Deleuze and Guattari extensively criticize the notion of determinism and advocate the concept of contingency (for instance, 1987: 431).

Patton, however, recognizes that the work of Deleuze and Guattari is influenced by the immanentist analysis of capitalism provided by Marx, which is linked to their view that capital operates in the manner of an '"axiomatic" system' (2000: 7). More importantly, Patton strategically argues that Deleuze and Guattari do not 'envisage global revolutionary change but rather a process of "active experimentation"'. It follows, then, that Deleuze and Guattari would consider minorities as politically relevant through their 'political potential of divergence from the norm' and not as revolutionary agents (Patton 2000: 7).

Patton considers *A Thousand Plateaus* to be a 'political ontology' in line with the Spinozist tradition linking the question of ontology to a formulation of a systematic ethics (Patton 2000: 9). This ontology endeavours to conceptualize the notion of multiplicity, 'which was a constant concern of Deleuze's earlier studies in the history of philosophy' (Patton 2000: 10). This is a rather inaccurate point as the notion of multiplicity is specifically related to Bergson (rather than Spinoza) and his distinction between qualitative and quantitative multiplicities in *Time and Free Will*:

> And in Bergson there is a distinction between numerical or extended multiplicities and qualitative or durational multiplicities. We are doing approximately the same thing when we distinguish between arborescent multiplicities and rhizomatic multiplicities. Between macro and micro-multiplicities.
>
> (Deleuze and Guattari, 1987: 33)

Deleuze and Guattari clearly relate their concepts of rhizomatic and arborescent to Bergson's distinction between quantitative multiplicities, for instance coins, and qualitative multiplicity. A qualitative multiplicity cannot be reduced and quantified. Therefore, it is rhizomatic. It corresponds for instance to an aesthetic experience. However, they also relate the notion of multiplicity to the scientific notions of molar and molecular entities:

> On the one hand, multiplicities that are extensive, divisible, and molar; unifiable, totalizable, organizable; conscious or preconscious – and on the other hand, libidinal, unconscious, molecular, intensive multiplicities composed of particles that do not divide without changing in nature, and distances that do not vary without entering another multiplicity and that constantly construct and dismantle themselves in the course of their communications,

as they cross over into each other at, beyond, or before a certain threshold. The elements of this second kind of multiplicity are particles; their relations are distances; their movements are Brownian; their quantities are intensities, differences in intensity.

(Deleuze and Guattari, 1987: 33)

Quoting *What Is Philosophy?*, Patton asserts that the definition of philosophy by Deleuze and Guattari consists of creating concepts that would bring about '"a new earth, a new people"' (2000: 12). According to Patton, a concept, strictly speaking, would be a 'singularity in thought' (2000: 12). By contrast, the dominant history of philosophy and its concepts can be described as the 'dogmatic image of thought', which corresponds to 'a pre-philosophical series of presuppositions which structures both the understanding of thinking and the character of the conceptual production which ensues on this basis' (Patton 2000: 18). The dominant history philosophy from Plato to Kant postulates the possibility for the subject to distinguish between falsehood and truth using a method that implies an 'underlying agreement between faculties upon an object which is supposed to be the same throughout its different representations' (Patton, 2000: 19). The image of thought amounts to a model of truth as recognition (Patton, 2000: 19).

By contrast, for Deleuze, the main danger lies in the inability to consider a problem and start a process of puzzlement and apprenticeship, that is to say stupidity (Patton 2000: 20). According to Patton, this also entails being aware of the 'real conditions which give rise to thought' (Patton 2000: 20). Patton uses mainly *What Is Philosophy?* to provide an account of the reflection by Deleuze and Guattari about philosophy. Patton seeks to connect the Deleuzo-Guattarian reflection on philosophy with the liberal tradition of anti-dogmatism.

The oeuvre of Deleuze and Guattari is described as a 'philosophy of difference' linked to a 'politics of difference' (Patton 2000: 29). Deleuze and Guattari are seen as constructing an anti-Hegelian ontology and an ethics of difference with the Nietzschean concept of will to power (Patton 2000: 30). For Patton, Deleuze and Guattari combine a reflection on difference and Nietzsche's analysis of forces: 'align the denial of difference with reactive force and the affirmation of difference with active force' (2000: 30). Accordingly, Deleuze and Guattari share with Derrida a rejection of Hegel, as he is described as representing the 'culmination of a metaphysical tradition which treated identity as primary and difference as the derivative or secondary term' (Patton 2000: 32). In actual fact, identities would then be produced by certain series of differences (Patton 2000: 35). This interpretative strategy allows Patton to connect the Deleuzo-Guattarian ontology of difference with a liberal multicultural politics of differences.

From the political point of view, Patton associates the notion of arborescence with 'the principles of organisation found in modern bureaucracies, factories, armies and schools, in other words, in all of the central social mechanisms of power' (2000: 43). According to Patton, Deleuze replaces the idea of class struggle with micropolitics and the dichotomy between the molar and the molecular

(2000: 43). Nonetheless, Patton does not take into account the fact that Deleuze and Guattari refer to the notion of proletariat in their analysis of minorities:

> Generally speaking, minorities do not receive a better solution of their problem by integration, even with axioms, statutes, autonomies, independences. Their tactics necessarily go that route. But if they are revolutionary, it is because they carry within them a deeper movement that challenges the worldwide axiomatic. The power of minority, of particularity, finds its figure or its universal consciousness in the proletariat.
>
> (1987: 83)

Abstract machines are 'virtual multiplicities that do not exist independently of the assemblages in which they are actualised or expressed' (Patton 2000: 44). According to Patton, the rhizome, and the micropolitical have an 'ontological primacy' on the arborescent and the macropolitical (Patton 2000: 45).

Patton also deals with the question of 'power' in the oeuvre of Deleuze and Guattari (Patton 2000: 49). Accordingly, Deleuze and Guattari, through Nietzsche's notion of will to power, consider 'reality as a field of quanta or quantities of force' (Patton 2000: 52). For Patton, Deleuze and Guattari complement this view with differential calculus: 'taking the differential calculus as his model, Deleuze argues that the will to power is the differential and genetic element which is realised in the encounter between forces' (Patton 2000: 52).

However, Deleuze and Guattari conceptualize 'double capture' phenomena (the example of the becoming-wasp of the orchid and the becoming-orchid of the wasp) through which two entities are transformed and produce a becoming without any domination (Patton 2000: 54). Double capture could be seen as corresponding to relationships disconnected from power relations, which liberal democracies should promote.

According to Patton, Deleuze and Guattari believe panopticism constitutes an abstract machine. By contrast, contemporary societies can be considered as marked by control rather than panoptic surveillance: 'control involves continuous modulation rather than discontinuous moulding of individuals and activities, competition rather than normalisation' (Patton 2000: 58). Therefore, Patton argues that 'unlike Foucault's analytic of power' the philosophy of Deleuze and Guattari 'does offer a surrogate for hope' (2000: 65), even within the framework of a liberal and capitalist society.

Furthermore, Patton confronts the ideas of 'desire, becoming and freedom' (2000: 68). According to Patton, the notion of 'politics of desire' is not rigorous enough to characterize the political thought of Deleuze and Guattari (2000: 68). From Patton's point of view, the political theory of Deleuze and Guattari is compatible with Foucault's microphysics of power, with power relations on the one side, and desire relations on the other (2000: 69). Patton insists that desire is revolutionary for Deleuze and Guattari (2000: 71). Patton associates the notion of becoming and the one of power: 'From the perspective of power, becomings may be regarded as processes of increase or enhancement in the powers of one body, carried out in relation to the powers of another, but without involving appropriation of those powers' (2000: 79). This would amount to an 'acquisition of affects' (Patton 2000: 82).

The argument of Patton on the microphysics of power does not take into account the fact that for Deleuze and Guattari desire or desiring machines have an ontological primacy because desire produces its own repression or recording (at least in *Anti-Oedipus*), whereas for Foucault power shapes subjectivity. *Discipline and Punish* explains how disciplinary subjects are produced by apparatuses of power knowledge whose best example is Bentham's panopticon (Foucault 1977a).

Patton argues that the concept of becoming is linked with the issue of minority (Patton, 2000: 80). Accordingly, for Patton the becoming of Deleuze relates to the 'social imaginary' and not reality; for instance becoming-woman refers to the imaginary of the woman and not real embodied women (2000: 81). Patton affirms that for Deleuze and Guattari 'a society without power relations' constitutes a mystification (2000: 82). It would then be impossible to destroy 'molarisation as such' (Patton 2000: 83). I would argue that this corresponds more to Patton's liberal politics than to the politics of Deleuze and Guattari since the latter advocate revolution in *What Is Philosophy?*, for instance with the notion of 'becoming revolutionary' (1994: 112). Furthermore, from the processualist perspective of Deleuze and Guattari desire is recorded or nomadic processes are captured. For Deleuze and Guattari power operates parasitically on creative processes. Consequently, I would argue that power is not an eternal fatality attached to the human condition as Patton implies.

According to Patton, Deleuze advocates a notion of 'critical freedom', as opposed to Charles Taylor's positive freedom and liberalism's negative freedom (2000: 87). Critical freedom is characterized by the ability to change one's values (Patton 2000: 87). The notion of critical freedom may not be adequate to characterize the philosophy of Deleuze and Guattari because *Kafka: For a Minor Literature* explicitly rejects the idea of critique:

> The assemblage appears not in a still encoded and territorial criticism but in a decoding, in a deterritorialization, and in the novelistic acceleration of this decoding and this deterritorialization (as was the case with the German language – to always go farther in this movement that takes over the whole social field). This method is much more intense than any critique.
>
> (1986: 48)

The questions of history and politics are dealt with as well (Patton 2000: 88). For Patton, unlike Marx, Deleuze and Guattari describe 'abstract machines of desire and power' as opposed to the theory of the modes of production (Patton 2000: 88). Accordingly, capital could constitute an example of socius: 'imagined surface upon which this control and coordination takes place' (Patton 2000: 89). The socius operates directly on bodies through a 'system of cruelty' (Patton 2000: 90). Accordingly, the primitive territorial machine functions primarily through kinship (lateral alliances) with a system of debt based on 'disequilibrium' on the body of the earth (Patton 2000: 90).

Second, the despotic machine organizes new systems of alliance and filiation that are vertical and connected to the despot and to God (Patton 2000: 91). According to Patton, the primitive and the despotic machines function with different types of overcoding, whereas the capitalist machine decodes; therefore capital 'becomes the new social full body' (Patton 2000: 92). This happens through a permanent 'conjunction' of decoded flows (Patton 2000: 92). Capitalism extracts a 'surplus of flux' as opposed to a code surplus (Patton 2000: 93). Consequently, for Patton, Deleuze and Guattari oppose the Marxist idea of surplus value because capital would extract a surplus coming from exchange and not a surplus value coming from living labour.

Additionally, there is a 'machinic surplus value' which Patton understands as 'flows of scientific and technological code' (2000: 93). Patton distinguishes capital as an axiomatic of decoded flows and capitalism as the social machine which includes both political and bureaucratic logics (2000: 95). The role of the state is to reterritorialize within capitalism, for instance through its bureaucracy (Patton 2000: 98). According to Patton, Deleuze and Guattari's universal history is 'anti-historicist' as the three types of social machines would virtually exist from the point of view of becoming (2000: 100). However, the primitive (or savage), the imperial (or barbarian) and the capitalist and the capitalist machines (or socius) also constitute a 'universal history', which Patton strategically avoids mentioning (Deleuze and Guattari, 1977: 140).

For Patton, revolutionary assemblages are connective and not conjugational or conjunctive (Patton 2000: 107). Patton equally qualifies as revolutionary events such as May '68, the end of Apartheid, the recognition of aboriginal right to land by the Australian High Court or the end of communism in Eastern Europe (2000: 108). However, he clearly makes no mention of revolutions, which belong to the imaginary of the left: the French, the Russian, the Cuban and the Chinese revolutions.

Patton also deals with the notion of state (Patton 2000: 109). Referring to *What Is Philosophy?*, Patton defines the philosophical activity as utopian (2000: 109). Patton therefore, tests the hypothesis that the jurisprudence on aboriginal title to land constitutes a war-machine against the apparatus of colonial capture in common-law countries (2000: 109). Accordingly, for Patton, the war-machine is a means of deterritorializing an assemblage (Patton 2000: 110). Any kind of opposition to the state represents a war-machine: 'revolution, riot, guerrilla warfare or civil disobedience' (Patton 2000: 111). As a result, within the framework of an implicit reformist politics, Patton contends that new rights are war-machines (Patton 2000: 127). This demonstrates that Patton endeavours to use the philosophy of Deleuze and Guattari in order to advocate a liberal politics.

Consequently, Patton insists on the notion of minorities which are seen as politically relevant through their 'political potential of divergence from the norm' (Patton 2000: 7). Patton places micropolitics within the liberal problematic of the recognition of the rights of minorities, which is legitimate within the framework of a liberal rule of law. Patton asserts that the jurisprudence on aboriginal title to land constitutes a war machine against the apparatus of colonial capture in common law countries (2000: 109). Minorities have the right to fight legally and non-violently (according to the model of the civil rights movement) in order to obtain new rights. This could function within the framework of a liberal identity politics. Deleuze and Guattari's political approach, however, provides a critique of human rights because of its refusal of the concept of universality (Alliez et al. 2010: 146).

Saving Deleuze and Guattari from the left

Nicholas Tampio is another representative of this liberal interpretation of Deleuze and Guattari (2009). First, the Tampio project affirms the fundamental difference between Hardt and Negri on the one hand and Deleuze on the other:

> Hardt and Negri, two key figures in this debate, claim that their concept of the multitude – a revolutionary, proletarian body that organizes singularities – integrates the insights of Deleuze and Lenin. I argue, however, that Deleuze anticipated and resisted a Leninist appropriation of his political theory. This essay challenges the widely accepted assumption that Hardt and Negri carry forth Deleuze's legacy.
>
> (2009: 383)

From the point of view of Tampio the work of Hardt and Negri – that is to say mainly *Empire, Mutltitude* and *Commonwealth* (2000, 2004, 2009) – is essentially characterized by their supposed Leninism:

> From his 1970s writings collected in *Books for Burning* . . . to his collaborative work with Hardt, Negri has maintained certain Marxist-Leninist assumptions: that the agent of political change is the proletariat; the means of political transformation is revolution; and the *telos* of politics is the end of sovereignty.
>
> (2009: 384)

Tampio defines Leninism as characterized by two features: the idea that the working class will bring about revolution and that it is necessary to fight for a communist society. This is very vague as it could apply to any socialist or communist politics which insists on the role of the proletariat. Strictly speaking, Tampio's definition of Leninism might also apply to the Social-Democratic parties of the Second International founded in 1889 or even to the Anarcho-Syndicalist movement. The Social-Democrats strongly opposed the Third International founded by Lenin and the Bolsheviks in 1920 because of the very specific conditions such as the centralization and the militarization that were imposed on the militants of the communist parties. In fact, in *What Is to Be Done?* (1969) and *The State and Revolution* (1937) Lenin had already advocated the organization of a more disciplined and centralized party in order to reinforce the struggle for communism. By contrast, Hardt and Negri invented the notion of multitude; that is to say a decentralized process of connection between singular resistances against capitalism in order to replace the centralism and supposed authoritarianism of the Leninist model (2000).

Consequently, it is clear that Tampio does not seriously discuss the notion of Leninism. He strategically uses this term in order to discredit the political theory of Hardt and Negri, and hence to discredit the possibility of a revolutionary interpretation of Deleuze and Guattari. Associating a revolutionary interpretation of Deleuze and Guattari with Leninism is a subtle way of implicitly connecting it to really existing socialism and Stalinism. This helps Tampio to discredit any revolutionary interpretation of Deleuze and Guattari and to promote a liberal interpretation of their oeuvre without discussing meticulously what could be a revolutionary interpretation of Deleuze and Guattari. Furthermore, Tampio argues that Deleuze departs from the notion of working class (2009: 390). So doing, Tampio strategically avoids mentioning that Deleuze and Guattari's writings refer to the notion of proletariat because it is a concept that belongs to the Marxist, as opposed to the liberal tradition:

> And if it is true that the tendency to a falling rate of profit or to its equalization asserts itself at least partially at the center, carrying the economy toward the most progressive and the most automated sectors, a veritable "development of underdevelopment" on the periphery ensures a rise in the rate of surplus value, in the form of an increasing exploitation of the peripheral proletariat in relation to that of the center.
>
> (Deleuze and Guattari, 1977: 231)

Tampio also argues that Deleuze rejects the notion of revolution in favour of a reformism that would be grounded on the notion of becoming revolutionary: 'Becoming revolutionary entails surveying the political landscape, attaining a certain degree of political power, inside or outside of the state, testing out new laws, policies, and rhetorics, and preserving the admirable elements of the society in which one lives' (2009: 390). This interpretation of the becoming revolutionary is contradictory because the term 'preserving' cannot define a becoming which is precisely supposed to designate movement and change. More importantly, Tampio strategically implies that the revolutionary becoming cannot be effectuated in an actual revolution so as to ground his liberal interpretation. This view does not, however, take into account the fact that for Deleuze a becoming can be effectuated ontologically (2004: 171). A becoming revolutionary can therefore be linked to a revolution, even though Tampio is right to distinguish history and becoming (Deleuze and Guattari, 1994: 110).

Additionally, Tampio argues that Deleuze rejects any idea of a communist social organization (2009: 390). This is not accurate as Deleuze and Guattari advocate the notion of utopia with reference to the socialist theorist Charles Fourier, which implies the creation of a free and egalitarian society (1994: 112).

This demonstrates that Deleuze and Guattari refer to the intellectual history of socialism and communism with Fourier and that they advocate a politics that is compatible with communism understood as a social community based on free and egalitarian self-development.

The interpretative strategy of Tampio minimizes the importance of Guattari because of his involvement in leftist activism. On the question of communism, this is essential from the point of view of the liberal interpretation of Deleuze, because Guattari refers to himself explicitly as a communist in *Communist Like Us*:

> Reuniting with the human roots of communism, we want to return to the sources of hope, that is, to a "being-for", to a collective intentionality, turned toward doing rather than toward a "being against", secured to impotent catchphrases of resentment.
>
> (Guattari and Negri, 1990: 131)

Tampio argues that Deleuzian thought provides concepts to reflect on the practices of the reformist left through the notion of 'left assemblages': 'Left assemblages are semi-coherent political entities that express and work for the ideals of liberty and equality' (2009: 394). Tampio however strategically avoids mentioning that Deleuze and Guattari were involved in radical militancy such as the Prison Information Group for Deleuze (Dosse 2010: 208), Socialism or Barbarism or the 22nd March movement for Guattari (Dosse 2010: 170). Additionally, Deleuze and Guattari continuously criticized liberal societies and even social democracy until the end of their lives (1977: 261, 1987: 468):

> Who but the police and armed forces that coexist with democracies can control and manage poverty and the deterritorialization–reterritorialization of shanty towns? What social democracy has not given the order to fire when the poor come out of their territory or ghetto? Rights save neither men nor a philosophy that is reterritorialized on the democratic State. *Human rights will not make us bless capitalism.*
>
> (1994: 107; my emphasis)

This liberal interpretation of the political philosophy of Deleuze and Guattari has been mainly developed in American and Australian universities. There are several reasons for this. First, even though the American critical academy has offered greater resistance than its French counterpart to the 1980s right-wing offensive, liberalism remains by far dominant in political philosophy (Cusset 2008). Consequently, liberalism ideologically permeates American and Australian universities. Thus, ironically, the liberal defence of minorities with a Deleuzian vocabulary is effectively a dominant and majoritarian interpretation that reproduces and reinforces the current relation of power within American and Australian universities threatening the very institutional existence of the scholarship's critical minority, most of all within the neoliberalization of higher education.

The liberal interpretation of Deleuze and Guattari by liberal philosophy, however, operates a strategic demarxization of Deleuzo-Guattarian texts. This strategic demarxization allows the liberal interpretation of Deleuze and Guattari to argue that is possible to integrate the Deleuzo-Guattarian philosophy within the framework of the liberal political philosophy. In particular, this entails avoiding putting an emphasis on the discussions on capitalism operated by *Anti-Oedipus* (1977) and *A Thousand Plateaus* (1987). Accepting the fact that the political philosophy of Deleuze and Guattari was strongly influenced by Marx would have meant the impossibility to associate it with a liberal political philosophy.

The liberal interpretation of Deleuze and Guattari by Marxism: Deleuze and Guattari the enemies

Paradoxically, another form of liberal interpretation of Deleuze and Guattari's political philosophy is its Marxist critique. From this perspective, Deleuze and Guattari are enemies because their philosophy allows for capitalism and the market to be advocated. According to this interpretation, it could be a form of postmodern or poststructuralist liberalism that should be criticized by critical scholars. I shall operate an analysis of their position below.

Deleuze and Guattari: enemies of the working class

According to French Marxist philosopher Isabelle Garo, Deleuze and Guattari reject Marxism and the idea of global and revolutionary change since their work does not retain crucial notions such as class struggle, relations of production, superstructure or infrastructure (2008, 2011a, 2011b, 2012). Deleuze and Guattari's philosophy of fluxes, which does not accept the dialectic, would function perfectly in a market economy with civil liberties. The Deleuzo-Guattarian political philosophy can be regarded as an avatar of political liberalism. At least, it can be seen as operating within the framework of liberal capitalism proposing only local changes. This interpretation is produced within a French academic context where there is very little room for radical and critical studies (Cusset 2008). There is fierce competition between the different forms of Marxism (which are connected to the political field) and other critical thoughts in the French context. As a result Garo, an orthodox Marxist, does not consider Deleuze and Guattari as legitimate radical thinkers, even though they were both theoretically and practically involved with radical politics.

This stems from the fact that the French Communist Party, with figures such as Sartre or Althusser, Trotskyist movements, with figures such as Daniel Bensaïd, or Maoist movements, with Badiou and Rancière, have had a history of direct influence on the academic and intellectual scene. Traditionally, radical academia has been linked to the influence of the organized political sphere. Garo's Marxist critique of Deleuze and Guattari, which claims that their political thought is, in the last resort, liberal can then be related to this fact. In other words, French orthodox Marxists seek to prevent Deleuzo-Guattarian philosophy from becoming a competitor within universities and the political field. There is a harsh orthodox Marxist tradition of critiquing Deleuze and Guattari as Michel Clouscard (1999) showed in the 1970s.

Garo operated a systematic critique of Deleuze and Guattari from a Marxist perspective. From her point of view, thinkers such as Althusser, Foucault, Castoriadis and Deleuze and Guattari developed singular philosophies that departed from Marxism and from any effective progressive politics (Garo 2011a, 2012). Consequently, according to Garo, these thinkers intellectually contributed to the neoliberal political agenda of the 1970s, 1980s and 1990s, because they weakened Marxist resistance. Accordingly, Althusser, Foucault, Castoriadis and Deleuze and Guattari participated in the destruction and discrediting of Marxism with the New Philosophers who were marked by anti-Marxism and anti-totalitarianism in the 1970s (Christofferson 2004), even though they were involved in this from a different perspective: 'Some specific intellectuals were characterised by the vicious and repetitive denunciation of the French Communist Party, balancing between the libertarian refusal of all oppressive powers and the liberal critique of the social State' (Garo 2011a: 66; my translation).

In reality, I would argue that the New Philosophers were critical of Deleuze and Guattari. Lévy, who is one of the prominent figures of the New Philosophers, produced a liberal critique of Marxism from the perspective of anti-totalitarianism, arguing that Marxism was essentially an authoritarian ideology that could not but lead to Stalinism and the gulag (1979). In the same book, Lévy criticized the oeuvre of Deleuze and Guattari. Conversely, Deleuze famously harshly criticized the New Philosophers. Having been asked what he thought about the New Philosophers he answered: 'Nothing. I think that their thought is worthless . . . This massive return to an author or to a vain empty subject as well as to stereotyped superficial concepts constitutes an unfortunate force of reaction' (Deleuze and Augst, 1998: 37).

Garo provided a meticulous orthodox Marxist refutation of Deleuze and Guattari. She argued that a politics inspired by Deleuze and Guattari was radically different from a Marxist one: 'But dealing with the relationship of Deleuze to Marx from a political perspective implies to conceptualise the Deleuzian political practice as an alternative to the Marxist politics, which would be assumed as defeated' (Garo, 2011a: 183; my translation). Additionally, Deleuzian politics could be regarded as an aporia for destroying any conceptualization of activism and any global anti-capitalism: 'Fundamentally, it is mainly the fierce critique of traditional political commitment and activism that accompanies it since the beginning, which in appearance would be still relevant, that leads to the abandonment of any perspective to transform capitalism as such' (Garo 2011a: 183; my translation).

Garo argued strategically that Deleuze as a scholar was not interested in Marx and suggested that he had had a poor knowledge of the oeuvre of Marx until the 1980s (2011a: 186–187). This does not seem accurate, however, as in *Difference and Repetition* (published in French in 1968), there is an important passage on the analysis of *Capital* (Deleuze, 1994: 186). Similarly, *Anti-Oedipus* (published in French in 1972) extensively engages with Marx and Marxism, in particular on the questions of the Asian mode of production (*Urstadt*) or the analysis of capitalism in *Capital*:

> In *Capital* Marx analyzes the true reason for the double movement: on the one hand, capitalism can proceed only by continually developing the subjective essence of abstract wealth or production for the sake of production, that is, "production as an end in itself, the absolute development of the social productivity of labor"; but on the other hand and at the same time, it can do so only in the framework of its own limited purpose, as a determinate mode of production, "production of capital", "the self-expansion of existing capital."
>
> (Deleuze and Guattari, 1977: 259)

Fundamentally, Deleuze and Guattari can be seen as disciples of Bergsonism rather than Marxism; this would represent a reactionary philosophy because of its insistence on duration as opposed to political struggles (Garo 2011a: 187). Additionally, for Garo the oeuvre of Deleuze harshly criticizes Hegelian dialectic affirming that is based on resentment (2011a: 194). This, according to Garo, leads Deleuzo-Guattarian philosophy to a rejection of Marxist problematic and of the politics of the French Communist Party, as the 'link between Hegel and Marxism is naturally evident' (2011a: 198–199; my translation).

Garo points out that Deleuzo-Guattarian politics is marked by the refusal of the concept of representation:

> Deleuze denounces in the Brechtian didactism a simple intention to explain and expose without taking into account the different periods of Brecht's oeuvre from this perspective. But it is as well a more topical issue that is dealt with and which concerns the relations of power within the theatrical institution. Deleuze associates what he calls "the seizure of power of the Brechtian" and the majoritarian democratic tradition. He rejects this way the "psychoanalytical, political, Marxist or Brechtian" conception of the conscious realisation because they converge politically and practically towards a seizure of power that is emancipatory.
>
> (Garo 2011a: 206–207; my translation)

Deleuze associates the idea of representation with a dominant power oppressing minorities though the imposition of a normalization. According to Garo, Deleuze borrows this critique of representation from the far left and its critique of the dominant parties and unions, that is to say mainly the French Communist Party and the General Confederation of Labour in the context of May '68 (2011a: 207).

Deleuze's aesthetic analyses of the cinema, in particular his dismissal of the Soviet and the Italian neorealist schools, demonstrate his critique of communism perceived as a politics of representation (Garo 2011a: 209). The interpretative strategy operated by Garo entails an identification between orthodox Soviet

Marxism and communism. Accordingly, all the left-wing communist groups that criticized Stalinism could be considered anti-communist.

From the point of view of Garo, the critique of representation is linked to a refusal of a politics that targets the capitalist system as such: 'The similar naive-ties of global representation and totalisable struggles are equally irrelevant for him. He refuses to produce a representation of reality which assists theoretically and practically in an understanding of the world. This corresponds to the old political cinema' (Garo 2011a: 210; my translation). In other words, Garo blames Deleuze for his rejection of Socialist Realism. She does not, however, take into account the meticulous critique of realism as an epistemology operated by Deleuze and Guattari and poststructuralism in general.

In reality, the theory of truth-correspondence, which is included in the criti-cal realism that Garo implicitly advocates, was criticized by the careful analysis of language in *The Logic of Sense*, or the critique of the category of subject, in particular in *Anti-Oedipus* and *A Thousand Plateaus*. Language cannot reproduce a faithful image of the world because it cannot duplicate the world. Therefore, Deleuze argues that sense is immaterial and linked to events (2004: 22). Similarly, the subject is not an external entity that observes the world from a distance like Laplace's demon that possesses a bird eye's view cognition of the world. Against this, Deleuze and Guattari argue that there are assemblages participating in the world and whose knowledge and actions are always situated in smooth or stri-ated spaces (1987: 377).

From the perspective of Garo, the two volumes of *Capitalism and Schizophrenia* (1977, 1987) develop a 'historical ontology' which is in contradiction with the Marxist project of political economy (2011a: 214; my translation). This onto-logical project is connected to an emphasis on the aesthetic aspect of the text which is seen as a means of subverting and discrediting Marxism rather than renovating it. For Garo, the Deleuzo- Guattarian refusal of the Marxist political economy is characterized by a Nietzschean analysis of society and economics:

> Marx describes capitalism as a mode of production. However, the definition proposed here avoids the analysis of the historical dialectic and replaces it with the vitalist theme of the fluxes taken from Nietzsche. These fluxes are more movements of commodities associated with monetary fluxes and combine with a diversity of other fluxes than a process of production as such, including relations of productions that are for Marx relations of exploitation between different social classes.
>
> (2011a: 219; my translation)

The interpretative strategy of Garo avoids discussing the extensive usage of the notion of desiring production in *Anti-Oedipus* (1977). This therefore sug-gests that their understanding of desire is inspired by a Marxist category, that is to say production, rather than other non-Marxist models to conceptualize desire such as the Freudian or the Lacanian models based on the notion of lack or even the Nietzschean will to power (marked by the eternal return and not by production). If I were to follow another interpretative strategy, I would argue that Deleuze and Guattari augmented rather than rejected the paradigm of Marxist political economy, because it was put to work in order to understand the psychology of the masses.

Additionally, Deleuze and Guattari developed concepts directly connected to the Marxist debates including the transition from feudalism to capitalism (Deleuze and Guattari, 1977: 225) or the question of the world market with the notions of 'Integrated World Capitalism' (Guattari and Negri, 1990: 77). I would argue that the notion of fluxes is totally compatible with Marx's analysis of capitalism, which insists on the immanence of the circulation and the accumulation of capital. Additionally, Garo contends that Deleuze and Guattari do not provide an analysis of class struggles and social classes (2011a: 228). Classes are theorized as forms of molar processes in the works of Deleuze and Guattari:

> As a general rule, State controls and regulations tend to disappear or diminish only in situations where there is an abundant labor supply and an unusual expansion of markets. That is, *when capitalism functions with a very small number of axioms within relative limits that are sufficiently wide.* This situation ceased to exist long ago, and one must regard as a decisive factor in this evolution the organization of a powerful working class that required a high and stable level of employment, and forced capitalism to multiply its axioms while having at the same time to reproduce its limits on an ever expanding scale (the axiom of displacement from the center to the periphery).
>
> (1977: 283)

This does not mean that molecular processes are not crucial for Deleuze and Guattari as molecular and molar processes are intertwined. In other words, social classes are the outcome of molecular processes in relation to molar processes.

In sum, according to Garo, Deleuze and Guattari participated in the movement of depoliticization and the subsequent critique of Marxism which was operated by neoliberalism (2011a: 230). For Garo, Deleuze and Guattari contributed to the triumph of capitalism and neoliberalism after the 1970s. Therefore, Garo produces a liberal interpretation of Deleuze and Guattari.

Jameson's ambiguous liberal interpretation: Deleuze and Guattari between the market and revolution

The position of the Marxist philosopher and literary critic Fredric Jameson is more complex. In *Postmodernism: The Cultural Logic of Late Capitalism* (1991), Fredric Jameson produces a critical analysis of postmodernism and describes the development and the transformations of contemporary capitalism as mainly cultural, as he says in an interview:

> In postmodernism, on the other hand, everyone has learned to consume culture through television and other mass media, so a rationale is no

longer necessary. You look at advertising billboards and collages of things because they are there in external reality. The whole matter of how you justify to yourself the time of consuming culture disappears: you are no longer even aware of consuming it. Everything is culture, the culture of the commodity.

(Stephanson and Jameson, 1989: 26)

Jameson is interested in poststructuralism, that is to say the theory that corresponds to the cultural logic of late capitalism. So doing, he provides an interpretation of Deleuze and Guattari, who are among the most prominent figures of poststructuralism. Essentially, according to Jameson, postmodern capitalism is marked by the spatialization of culture and the loss of historicity:

The distinction is between two forms of interrelationship between time and space rather than between these two inseparable categories themselves: even though the postmodern vision of the ideal or heroic schizophrenic (as in Deleuze) marks the impossible effort to imagine something like a pure experience of a spatial present beyond past history and future destiny or project. Yet the ideal schizophrenic's experience is still one of time, albeit of the eternal Nietzschean present. What one means by evoking its spatialization is rather the will to use and to subject time to the service of space, if that is now the right word for it.

(Jameson, 1991: 154)

The Deleuzo-Guattarian notion of schizophrenia is interpreted as a refusal of a historicist perspective. The schizophrenic would constantly forget everything: his personal identity and history. Schizophrenia bears the risk of being trapped in the permanent present of the circulation of capital. Interestingly, Jameson associates the modernist figure of the hero (1991: 154) with the supposedly postmodern figure of the schizophrenic. The philosophy of Deleuze and Guattari is considered an ideological theory that contributes to the capture of desire by late capitalism marked by mass consumption:

Continental ideologies of "desire" also get their share of attention in a critique by Leo Bersani that would apply, mutatis mutandis, to Kristeva as well as to Deleuze . . . It is not hard to show that the force of desire that is alleged to undermine the rigidities of late capitalism is in fact very precisely what keeps the consumer system going: "the 'disruptive' element in desire that Bersani finds attractive is for Dreiser not subversive of the capitalist economy, but constitutive of its power". This telling reversal can perhaps be read as the epitaph of one of the principal political positions of the 1960s, for which capitalism, by awakening needs and desires it was unable to fulfil, would somehow subvert itself; and it is certainly as part of a general systemic reaction against the 1960s that Michaels should be read.

(Jameson, 1991: 202)

Jameson apparently produces a harsh critique of the philosophy of Deleuze and Guattari, which entails that it is ultimately liberal and on the side of capitalism. In fact, the oeuvre of Deleuze and Guattari is presented as a postmodernist ideology that contributes to the eulogy of mass consumption. Liberating desire is regarded as contributing towards liberating more desire for consumption within the framework of symbolic power relations operated by marketing. The schizophrenic in this perspective corresponds to the spatialized and commodified consumer culture of neoliberalism.

In other texts Jameson produces a more positive analysis of the philosophy of Deleuze and Guattari. Instead of denouncing the anti-dialectical content of the oeuvre of Deleuze and Guattari, Jameson praises the political benefit of his dualism:

> It is a rehearsal of the distinction between the two great forms of time, the Aion and the Chronos, which will recur so productively in the Cinema books. But one might also conclude in another way, with the other postideological form of dualism as such. The latter has been argued to be omnipresent in Deleuze, not least in these materialist collaborations with Guattari, which some have set against, in a properly dualistic opposition, the more Bergsonian and idealistic tendencies of the works signed by Deleuze as an individual philosopher. In that case, a certain dualism might be the pretext and the occasion for the very "overcoming" of Deleuzian thought itself and its transformation into something else, something both profoundly related and profoundly different, as in Hegel's transcendence of what he took to be the dualism in Kant.
>
> (Jameson, 1997: 15)

Jameson argues that an aporetic dualism between the virtual and the actual or qualitative and quantitative multiplicities could be a productive contradiction. The tension produced by Deleuze and Guattari's dualism could be fruitful politically, as opposed to being a form of idealist refusal of the dialectic such as Garo would argue (2011a):

> Yet there is another way of grasping just such dualisms which has not been mentioned until now, and that is the form of the production of great prophecy. When indeed the ideological is lifted out of its everyday dualistic and ethical space and generalized into the cosmos, it undergoes a dialectical transformation and the unaccustomed voice of great prophecy emerges, in which ethics and ideology, along with dualism itself, are transfigured. Perhaps it is best to read the opposition between the Nomads and the State in that way: as reterritorialization by way of the archaic, and as the distant thunder, in the age of the axiomatic and global capitalism, of the return of myth and the call of utopian transfiguration.
>
> (Jameson, 1997: 15)

The usage of Kantian dualism would enable a revolutionary politics through grand opposite concepts and a form of prophetic utopianism. However, Jameson still tries to incorporate this dualism in his dialectical framework. Either the thought of Deleuze and Guattari is a dehistoricized and depoliticized ideology of postmodernism, or else it is a grand prophecy announcing some utopian future. In both cases, there is an underlying critique of the lack of dialectical thinking and historical contextualization of the thought of Deleuze and Guattari, which links it to the liberal hegemony.

Boltanski and Chiapello's ambiguous liberal interpretation: Deleuze and Guattari recuperated by capitalism

Another interpretation is close to the Marxist rejection of Deleuze and Guattari for being liberal. It is the interpretation operated by Luc Boltanski and Eve Chiapello in the *New Spirit of Capitalism* (2005). Boltanski and Chiapello come from different backgrounds within the French academy. Boltanski was in fact very close to Bourdieu in 1970, when they were working together at the School for Advanced Studies in Social Sciences (EHESS). Also, Boltanski contributed to the foundation of *Actes de la Recherche en Sciences Sociales*, which is the main journal to circulate Bourdieu's ideas. Nevertheless, he decided to abandon Bourdieu's methodology in the 1970s, because he did not agree with Bourdieu's structural critical realism. For Bourdieu, individuals are determined by social structures of which they are not conscious. For instance, in *The Inheritors* students' feelings and representations about their social situation is the product of the objective class relations reproduced in the French educational system (Bourdieu and Passeron 1979). In opposition to this, Boltanski insists on the individuals' agency.

Boltanski along with Eve Chiapello, an organization studies scholar, wrote an influential book about the recent transformations of capitalism (2005). *The New Spirit of Capitalism* addresses the question of the cultural and social transformation of capitalism, in particular through managerialism (2005). *The New Spirit of Capitalism* analyses 'the ideological changes that have accompanied recent transformations in capitalism' (Boltanski and Chiapello 2005: 3). Boltanski and Chiapello provide a liberal interpretation of Deleuze grounded on their critical sociology.

The New Spirit of Capitalism claims not to be Marxist (Boltanski and Chiapello 2005: xxiv) because the authors put the emphasis on pragmatic analyses focusing on personal meaning. The idea is to explain the changes capitalism has experienced since the 1960 shift from a Fordist and Taylorist organization marked by the Keynesian compromise to post-Fordism and neoliberalism. Boltanski and Chiapello use the Weberian concept of 'spirit' to explain how individuals and groups act and think within capitalism (2005: 8).

According to Boltanski and Chiapello, in the nineteenth century, the first characterization of the 'spirit of capitalism' centred around the 'bourgeois entrepreneur' and the description of bourgeois values (2005: 17). The second, between the 1930s and 1960s, insisted on rationalization (Boltanski and Chiapello 2005: 17). The 'third spirit of capitalism', however, was oriented towards a discourse about autonomy (Boltanski and Chiapello 2005: 19). For Boltanski and Chiapello, the transformation of the 'spirit of capitalism' is linked to its critique:

> The notion of the spirit of capitalism equally allows us to combine in one and the same dynamic the development of capitalism and the critiques that have been made of it. In fact, in our construction we are going to assign critique the role of a motor in changes in the spirit of capitalism.
>
> (2005: 27)

The 'new spirit of capitalism' incorporates the critique that has been levelled at it, in particular the critique by the May '68 movement in France. As a matter of fact, according to Boltanski and Chiapello, there are two major critiques of capitalism: the first is the 'artistic critique' and the second the 'social critique' (2005: 38). The 'artistic critique' emphasizes the loss of meaning, the 'disenchantment' and the unauthenticity of capitalism (Boltanski and Chiapello 2005: 40), whereas the 'social critique' insists on the selfishness of the bourgeoisie and the 'exploitation' of the working class (Boltanski and Chiapello 2005: 39). In sum, the 'artistic critique' focuses onto the issue of freedom whereas the 'social critique' is concerned with equality.

First, *The New Spirit of Capitalism* studied the shift in the managerial discourse between the 1960s and the 1990s. The new discourse gave executives some legitimization concerning their actions and opened up enthralling perspectives of self- development through the notion of projects (Boltanski and Chiapello 2005: 57). Boltanski and Chiapello analysed management texts destined to managers since they were supposedly the people whose consent was most important in the accumulation of capital, because they were in a position to refuse to participate in the capitalist process. Boltanski and Chiapello argued that this new managerialist discourse linked to the 'new spirit of capitalism' was a response to critiques, in particular the 'artistic critique' and its demand for authenticity and freedom (Boltanski and Chiapello 2005: 98). This entailed a new notion of 'justice' through the formation of 'networks' (Boltanski and Chiapello 2005: 122) and the emphasis on 'creativity' and 'innovation' (Boltanski and Chiapello 2005: 128). In this context of connections, managers were no longer concerned about traditional morality with its admonition to save money, but about the best possible allocation of their time within the network (Boltanski and Chiapello 2005: 152).

Second, Boltanski and Chiapello were interested in the historical process of the formation of the 'new spirit of capitalism'. Critique was the engine for the dynamics of capitalism. The origin of this phenomenon was linked to the fact that the May '68 critique was incorporated in the new spirit of capitalism. At the beginning, however, during May '68 'artistic' and 'social' critiques were associated (Boltanski and Chiapello, 2005: 169). Students were on the side of the 'artistic critique' whereas workers were on the side of the 'social critique'. Roughly, the former were fighting against the 'alienation' of their subjectivities (Boltanski and Chiapello 2005: 170), whereas the latter were fighting against 'exploitation' and the appropriation of their workforce (Boltanski and Chiapello 2005: 169). As a result, the critique of capitalism was soon divided.

This was increased by the fact that the capitalist system first responded to the 'social critique' by increasing the workers' wages after the Grenelle agreement in 1968, and only afterwards did it decide to deal with the 'artistic critique' after 1973 and the oil crisis. The decrease in the 'social critique' was influenced by the decline of the French Communist Party at the end of the 1970s (Boltanski and Chiapello 2005: 189). Subsequently, the working class and its practices were severely tackled, in particular through the numerous redundancies of industrial workers. Consequently, trade unions were weakened in the late 1970s, as a result of the loss of influence of the 'social critique' through managerial techniques such as the individualization of wages (Boltanski and Chiapello 2005: 188). The unions had also been set upon by the 'artistic critique' for increasing bureaucratization (Boltanski and Chiapello 2005: 178). This weakened the discourse on 'social classes' (Boltanski and Chiapello 2005: 273) and, generally speaking, led, in the 1980s, to a situation in which the critique of capitalism remained very limited since the appropriation of the artistic critique prevented an increase in the social critique (Boltanski and Chiapello 2005: 324).

Third, Boltanski and Chiapello analysed the state of the critique of capitalism in the 1990s and concluded that there had been a relative revival of the 'social critique of capitalism' with a legal discourse on 'exclusion' from the networks of society (Boltanski and Chiapello 2005: 346). Boltanski and Chiapello argued that the renewal of the artistic critique would benefit from an alliance with the 'ecological critique' (2005: 472). Finally, they claimed that both the 'social' and the 'artistic' critiques of capitalism should be encouraged (Boltanski and Chiapello 2005: 535).

Boltanski and Chiapello understand Deleuze and Guattari from a very specific perspective within the framework of their understanding of the new transformations of capitalism. On the one hand, they occasionally use Deleuzo-Guattarian concepts in their line of argumentation as the 'plane of immanence' (Boltanski and Chiapello 2005: 149). On the other hand, they argue that:

> The same philosopheme is also involved in less specific trends. At least in France after May 1968, it was placed in the service of a critique (particularly by Deleuze) of the "subject", in so far as the latter is defined with reference to a self-consciousness and an essence that could be anything but the trace of the relations in which it has been caught up in the course of its displacements. It was likewise deployed in a critique of anything that could be condemned as a "fixed point" capable of acting as referent. This comprised, for example, the state, the family, churches and, more generally, all institutions; but also master thinkers, bureaucracies and traditions (because they are turned towards an origin treated as a fixed point); and eschatologies, religious or political, because they make beings dependent upon an essence projected into the future.
>
> (Boltanski and Chiapello 2005: 145)

Deleuze and Guattari are associated with the artistic critique of capitalism and of stratified Fordist institutions. Specifically, Boltanski and Chiapello operate a connection between May '68 and the oeuvre of Deleuze and Guattari, which implies that their political philosophy was revolutionary in the 1960s and the 1970s:

> During the 1970s, this critique was almost naturally directed at capitalism, which was conflated in one and the same denunciation with the bourgeois family and the state. These were condemned as closed, fixed, ossified worlds, whether by attachment to tradition (the family), legalism and bureaucracy (the state), or calculation and planning (the firm), as opposed to mobility, fluidity and "nomads" able to circulate, at the cost of many metamorphoses, in open networks.
>
> (Boltanski and Chiapello 2005: 145)

The oeuvre of Deleuze and Guattari is assimilated into the artistic critique of capitalism, which contributed to the production of the new spirit of capitalism marked by the eulogy of change, movement and creation, as opposed to the conservative values of industrial capitalism. This means that the Deleuzo-Guattarian philosophy, which was radical in May '68, became a liberal philosophy that would be incorporated by neoliberal capitalism in the 1980s. This argument is based on a rather loose reading *of Anti-Oedipus* and *A Thousand Plateaus*. For instance, the critique of the family by Deleuze and Guattari is connected to a meticulous analysis of the role of psychoanalysis in capitalism, which Boltanski and Chiapello do not mention. I would argue, however, that Boltanski and Chiapello are right about the fact that the philosophy of Deleuze and Guattari provided a critique of the state, of the family and more generally of essences. Furthermore, Boltanski and Chiapello display another type of critique of Deleuze and Guattari:

> Finally, a third example is the Deleuzian enterprise developed in *Difference and Repetition* – published in 1968, and hence virtually at the same time as *Of Grammatology*. Deleuze develops a critique of representation in the sense of the correspondence between thing and concept, bound up with a metaphysics in which it is no longer possible to preserve the opposition between an original and a copy.
>
> (2005: 454)

Boltanski and Chiapello provide a critique of postmodern relativism seen as destroying values as well as the notion of truth. Accordingly, they associate Deleuze with Derrida. Their critique of Deleuzo-Guattarian philosophy however is also political:

> In the world of the "simulacrum", it is no longer possible to contrast a "copy" with a "model"; an existence orientated towards authenticity, as self-identity,

with an existence subjected by external forces to a mechanical repetition; an ontological difference, which would be that of the responsible subject, to its loss in the undifferentiated. The "plane of immanence" knows only differentials of force whose displacements produce (small) differences, continual variations between which there is no hierarchy, and "complex" forms of repetition.

(2005: 454)

From this perspective, the work of Deleuze and Guattari, in particular Deleuze's *Difference and Repetition*, is considered as a source for discrediting the artistic critique of capitalism. Boltanski and Chiapello contend that the ontological analyses of Deleuze in *Difference and Repetition* contribute to a negation of the aesthetic and an undermining of the rhetoric of authenticity. Accordingly, the world is presented as a series of illusions without room for an authentic subject. The Deleuzo-Guattarian philosophy, then, contributes to the capitalist status quo through an opposition to the artistic critique of capitalism and its correlative revolutionary and authentic subject. Boltanski and Chiapello avoid debating Deleuzo-Guattarian ideas about creation and newness, which would undermine their interpretative strategy.

A number of critiques can be levelled at the work of Boltanski and Chiapello. First, from the ontological point of view, their position is ambiguous since, on the one hand, they claim to take into account the individual's meanings and justifications – which corresponds to a constructionist perspective – and, on the other, their account of the sociological and historical changes of capitalism is realist (2005: xii), which concurs with their implicit claim that sociology can describe the world as it is. Not only is *The New Spirit of Capitalism* epistemologically realist, it is also positivist from the epistemological viewpoint despite its pragmatist claims (Boltanski and Chiapello 2005: 292).

Second, there is a problem with the historical narrative constructed by Boltanski and Chiapello. They claim to give an international account of the evolution of capitalism since the 1960s by only studying France. They base their study solely on the analysis of management discourse for managers. This does not meet contemporary historiography requirements, in particular in terms of archives and the exactitude of historical facts. This leads to some confusion, for instance in this passage:

But the order of response to the two critiques – the social critique in the first instance, then the artistic critique – derived not only from an evolution in employers' thinking and opportunities, but also from a transformation of critique itself. In fact, at the end of the 1960s and the beginning of the 1970s, social critique in its most classical form, articulated by the working-class movement (for instance, the wave of adhesions to the CGT in autumn 1968), but also in Trotskyist and Maoist far-left activism, underwent a revival to the point of eclipsing the artistic critique, which had unquestionably been more in evidence during the May events.

(Boltanski and Chiapello 2005: 178)

Maoist, Trotskyist and communist (from the General Confederation of Labour) militants are associated with the 'social critique'. Boltanski and Chiapello do not seem to be aware of the diversity of the Maoist movement, which encompassed spontaneist groups – around the papers *Vive la Révolution* (Long Live the Revolution), *Vive le Communisme* (Long Live Communism) or the Proletarian Left. The latter should in fact be associated with the 'artistic critique', since some members of the Proletarian Left were close to Deleuze and Guattari through the Prison Information Group (Dosse 2010: 170).

More seriously though, the dichotomy between an 'artistic critique' of capitalism and a 'social critique' lacks coherence. On the one hand, as argued by Lazzarato (2008: 30; my translation), 'the artistic professions (and not only the workers) have also been the victims of neoliberalism, exploitation and inequalities since the 1970s, in particular through the development of the casualization of employment contracts'; on the other hand, as Rancière explains, workers (and not only a separated class of artists) are also aesthetic subjects who are capable of feeling artistic emotions (2009). In other words, it is simplistic to divide the critique of capitalism into a 'social' stance – orientated towards equality – and an 'artistic' stance – orientated towards freedom. The progressive critique of capitalism demands emancipation, that is to say equality and freedom, and equality as a condition of freedom.

Finally, the work of Boltanski and Chiapello is both conceptually and politically ambiguous because of its usage of the notion of 'incorporation' of the critique of capitalism into the 'new spirit of capitalism' (for instance, Boltanski and Chiapello, 2005: 346). This concept of 'incorporation' is not pertinent to describe the relationship between an ideology and its critique because ideas or representations do not have bodies and are immaterial. Boltanski and Chiapello indirectly advocate the idea that it is impossible to resist capitalism because it systematically appropriates its critiques as Rancière argues (2009). This probably explains why Boltanski and Chiapello are not interested in practical resistance against capitalism and only in the 'new spirit of capitalism'.

In this context, the liberal reception of Deleuze and Guattari by Boltanski is essential and strategic. On the one hand, they argue that Deleuze and Guattari contributed to the artistic critique of capitalism, and that, as a result, their oeuvre was incorporated by the new spirit of capitalism. On the other hand, they contend that the works of Deleuze and Guattari (in particular *Difference and Repetition*) contributed to the rejection of the artistic critique. In both cases, the oeuvre of Deleuze and Guattari is presented as an objective ally of capitalism because it helped the process of emergence of the new spirit of capitalism. From this perspective, Boltanski and Chiapello operate a reception of Deleuze and Guattari that is similar to Garo's.

Essentially, according to Boltanski and Chiapello, Deleuze and Guattari contributed to the creation of a new form of capitalism. The interpretative strategy operated by Boltanski and Chiapello avoids discussion of the fact that Deleuze and Guattari were actively involved in anti-capitalist activism.

De Landa's liberal ambiguous interpretation: the flat ontology of Deleuze and Guattari

Finally, Manuel De Landa could be included in this interpretative tradition. De Landa develops his own philosophy based on a specific interpretation of Deleuze and Guattari. In fact, his project provides a demarxization of Deleuze and Guattari's work and hence neglects their views on capitalism, revolution or utopia. Monopolies are seen as the only problem with capitalism; that is to say a lack of implementation of liberal politics (De Landa 2010: 43).

The solution, then, would be to free multiplicities from monopolies: 'It appears that the problem with capitalism for De Landa is simply one of monopoly: so "small is beautiful", and all one needs to do is to abstract labour relations from monopoly formations, and that solves the problem that Deleuze and Guattari call capital', as Thoburn says in a discussion with other scholars (Alliez et al. 2010: 143–144). De Landa clearly says that he has no particular problems with notions such as the freedom of enterprise or private property per se: 'it's much much easier for a motivated, creative worker to start his/her own business' (De Landa 2004: 25). The rejection from the point of view of his 'flat ontology' of any interpretation of society as a coherent system implying relations of power demonstrates his 'objective' liberalism (De Landa 2004: 26). This amounts to a reformulation of political liberalism within a Deleuzo-Guattarian philosophy reduced to a 'theory of complexity', as Alliez argues in a discussion with other scholars (Alliez et al. 2010: 146).

De Landa develops his own philosophy based on a specific interpretation of Deleuze and Guattari. More particularly, De Landa insists on the notion of assemblages in order to understand social phenomena. He takes this concept from Deleuze and Guattari, but transforms it. All assemblages for De Landa are 'individual entities' (2010: 12). Large assemblages like social classes, countries or organizations result from an aggregation of local phenomena, even though the author distinguishes between rigid and molar large assemblages and fluid and molecular large assemblages (De Landa 2010: 12). Additionally, De Landa differentiates between the coding and the territorialization of the assemblage, because the code explicitly and exclusively refers to language (De Landa 2010: 13).

According to De Landa, it is not epistemologically possible to talk about society as an entity. Therefore, Deleuzo-Guattarian concepts such as socius are not trustworthy (2010: 25). De Landa denounces the conservative character of the linguistic turn (2010: 31), and argues that is necessary to provide a materialist politics based on Deleuze and Guattari. This implies producing an 'objective synthesis' that can explain the existence of a certain permanence of assemblages without using the Marxist dialectic that would remain too idealistic (De Landa 2010: 31).

The materialist politics that De Landa advocates is clearly critical of Marxism and the very notion of political economy. The project of De Landa explicitly entails dispensing with the Marxist influence on Deleuze and Guattari: 'Why are Deleuze and Guattari so deeply committed to this idea? Because as I said, they remained until the end of their lives under the spell of the bankrupt political economy of Marx' (De Landa 2010: 45). In particular, he rejects the Marxist Labour theory of value and the notion of the tendential fall of the rate of profit (De Landa 2010: 46).

According to De Landa, value is the product of exchange and not of the exploitation of human labour. Wealth is produced through the mechanisms of supply and demand as though it were a natural phenomenon. Therefore, 'trade and credit' can produce actual wealth (De Landa 2010: 46).

De Landa rejects most of the vocabulary used by the left:

> This is why locating assemblages at the right level of scale, a population of organizations that includes military ones, in this case, is so important. It is also necessary to stick to an ontology without reified generalities. Unfortunately, much of the academic left today has become prey to the double danger of abandoning materialism and of politically targeting reified generalities (Power, Resistance, Capital, Labor).
>
> (2010: 47)

De Landa (2010: 81) displays a realist understanding of Deleuze and Guattari whose philosophy, he claims, describes what really exists independently of our minds. Deleuze and Guattari are central philosophers for De Landa because they provide an innovative realist and materialist ontology: 'From the work of the philosopher Gilles Deleuze, we can derive such a novel ontology, an approach to the problem of existence that may be called a "neo-materialist metaphysics"' (2010: 83). De Landa's interpretation of the politics of Deleuze and Guattari is nevertheless liberal.

Conclusion

In this chapter I have analysed the liberal interpretation of the philosophy of Deleuze and Guattari. The liberal interpretation of the philosophy of Deleuze and Guattari entails that the Deleuzo-Guattarian philosophy is connected to private property, individualism and more generally capitalism. Patton (2000, 2005) and Tampio (2009) provide a poststructuralist reformulation of the main themes of the liberal political philosophy with Deleuze and Guattari. Their approach is therefore positive. Their interpretative strategy involves concealing or underestimating any texts that could be regarded as too critical of capitalism or liberalism.

By contrast, the liberal interpretation of Deleuze and Guattari operated by orthodox Marxism seeks to discredit the thought of Deleuze and Guattari because of their alleged liberalism (Clouscard 1999; Garo 2011a, 2012). The philosophy of Deleuze and Guattari is presented as providing a liberal politics that should be criticized. Usually, this is connected to broader critique about postmodernism and its role in critiquing orthodox Marxism in the 1960s and 1970s.

Finally, a third type of interpretation is more ambiguous. Jameson (1991, 1995) argues that the philosophy of Deleuze and Guattari corresponds to postmodern capitalism, but that its dualism can also be connected to a form of utopianism. Boltanski and Chiapello (2005) develop the idea that the oeuvre of Deleuze and Guattari was incorporated by the spirit of capitalism, and that Deleuzian thought undermines an artistic critique of capitalism. De Landa provides a liberal interpretation of Deleuze and Guattari within the framework of his ambitious neo-materialist novel ontology (2004, 2010). The liberal interpretation of Deleuze and Guattari seeks to associate the Deleuzo-Guattarian philosophy with capitalism.

In the third and final chapter of this part, I turn my attention to the scholars who have interpreted Deleuze (and Guattari) as revolutionary anti-capitalists.

4   The revolutionary interpretation of Deleuze and Guattari

Introduction

I analysed the elitist interpretation of Deleuze and Guattari, which reduces it to philosophy and depoliticizes it. I then analysed the liberal interpretation of Deleuze and Guattari, which seeks to associate Deleuze and Guattari with capitalism so as to laud or criticize their work. Below, I shall provide an analysis of the revolutionary interpretation of Deleuze and Guattari. I shall advocate this position and later apply it to the second part of this book to politicize financialization. I do not, however, claim epistemological superiority over the other two interpretations.

Several interpretative revolutionary traditions have opposed the elitist, anti-political and the liberal, capitalist receptions. This happened mainly in Britain, the United States and France. Generally speaking, this specific reception argues that the philosophy of Deleuze and Guattari informs a transformative and anti-capitalist politics. Some of these revolutionary interpretations have a number of points in common: they are sympathetic to Marxism and believe that a critique of the political economy is necessary. Other revolutionary interpretations of the philosophy of Deleuze and Guattari, however, are not linked to Marxism and reject any idea of political economy.

Additionally, a number of texts in these revolutionary interpretative traditions are published in the journal *Deleuze Studies*, in the Anglophone academic world and in the journal *Multitudes*, in the French academic world. *Deleuze Studies*, however, is pluralist and publishes articles both from the elitist and liberal perspective.

First, I shall analyse the revolutionary interpretations that are compatible with Marxism. I shall start with Massumi's interpretation (1992). I shall then deal with Thoburn's interpretation, which provides an extensive analysis of the relationship between Deleuze and Guattari and Marx (2003). I shall operate an analysis of specifically autonomist Marxist receptions of Deleuze and Guattari (Hardt and Negri 2000, 2004, 2009; Read 2003, 2009). By contrast, Sibertin-Blanc argues that Deleuze and Guattari provide a political thought that is different from Marxism, but compatible with it (2006, 2009). Rodrigo Nunes operates a specific articulation of the philosophy of Deleuze and Guattari with revolutionary activism (2010).

Second, I shall analyse interpretations that do not have the same relationship with Marxism. Stengers operates a novel revolutionary interpretation of Deleuze and Guattari that is not connected to a rigid idea of strategy (Pignarre and Stengers 2011). Finally, I shall analyse a series of overtly non-Marxist revolutionary interpretations of Deleuze and Guattari (The Invisible Committee 2007; Tiqqun 2011).

The revolutionary interpretation of Massumi

Brian Massumi proposes a revolutionary interpretation of the oeuvre of Deleuze and Guattari. He is a specialist of French philosophy and currently teaches at the University of Montréal. In *A User's Guide to Capitalism and Schizophrenia*, he provides an interpretation of *Anti-Oedipus* and *A Thousand Plateaus*, even though the two volumes are quite different (Massumi 1992: 1). Massumi translated *A Thousand Plateaus* into English (1987). His *A User's Guide to Capitalism and Schizophrenia* was quite influential in the Anglophone academy to introduce a revolutionary interpretation of Deleuze and Guattari in the early 1990s.

According to Massumi, then, schizophrenia consists in 'the enlargement of life's limits through the pragmatic proliferation of concepts' (Massumi 1992: 1). Massumi argues that for Deleuze and Guattari philosophy is one of the forms of schizophrenia, as opposed to state philosophy (Massumi 1992: 1). For him, *Anti-Oedipus* provides a 'typology of cultural formations' within the framework of a critique of 'pro-party versions of Marxism and school building strains of psychoanalysis' (1992: 3). By contrast, *A Thousand Plateaus* would be 'less a critique than a sustained, constructive experiment in schizophrenic, or "nomad", thought' (Massumi 1992: 4).

Massumi considered that *Capitalism and Schizophrenia* was a refusal of the 'representational thinking that had dominated Western metaphysics since Plato' (1992: 4). Accordingly, creative thought was not limited to philosophy: 'Filmmakers and painters are philosophical thinkers to the extent that they explore the potentials of their respective mediums and break away from beaten paths' (Massumi 1992: 6). The argument of Massumi implied that *Anti-Oedipus* and *A Thousand Plateaus* did not share the analysis of *What Is Philosophy?* with regard to the difference with the concepts produced by philosophy, the functions produced by science and the percepts and affects produced by art (1994).

According to Massumi, the notion of 'force' is central to the oeuvre of Deleuze and Guattari (1992: 10). Deleuze and Guattari reject the idea of metaphor because meaning would be 'more a meeting between forces than simply the forces behind the signs' (Massumi 1992: 11). In fact, content and expression are the dominated and dominating forces within a 'reversible' relationship in the works of Deleuze and Guattari (Massumi, 1992: 12).

Massumi argues that Deleuze and Guattari's thought is not systematic and that their concepts 'are heuristic devices to be adapted as the situation requires' (1992: 24). As a result, the definition of function would be 'dominating action' and the one of quality 'change of state' (1992: 24). This corresponds to an anti-realist epistemology. Accordingly, Massumi makes a political interpretation of the concepts of content and expression. The content of the school consists of its students, the 'substance of the content' are the actual students, the 'matter of the content' the bodies of the students, and the 'form of the content' the material disposition of the school, and eventually the essence of the school would be the '"making of a docile worker"' (Massumi 1992: 25).

Ordinary language aids the reproduction of power relations: 'Everyday language does not entirely straitjacket our potential, but it does restrict us to the lowest level of our virtuality. It limits the dynamism of our becoming to the stolid ways of being deemed productive by an exploitative society' (Massumi 1992: 40). According to Massumi, despite this power exercised by language through the mechanism of the 'order-word', the philosophy of Deleuze and Guattari provides the possibility of emancipatory breaks, for instance for marriage and school, which are described as two oppressive institutions (1992: 41). The order-word is the 'the funereal normality, the echoed refrain of the walking dead' (Massumi 1992: 41).

Against the rationalism of Chomsky and the structuralism of Saussure, for Deleuze and Guattari language is not primarily communicative, but an instrument of power through repetitive order-words. However, it can be a creative entity through dialects, which are 'deviation from a norm' (Massumi 1992: 42). This is well analysed, in particular in *Kafka: For a Minor Literature* with the creativity generated by the mixing of German, Yiddish and Czech (1986). The fundamental characteristic of language consists of 'incorporeal transformation' (Massumi 1992: 42). Fundamentally, the language is political, because 'all enunciation is collective' (Massumi 1992: 43).

Massumi also deals with the notion of habit. From the point of view of Massumi, '"abstract machine" is another word for synthesizer', and synthesis is the key concept to understand how inhuman processes can produce sensations (1992: 47). The connective synthesis is considered creative whereas the disjunctive synthesis operates a 'recording', imposing a normality, and consequently a political repression (Massumi 1992: 49). Identity and representation are the products of disjunctive syntheses. Consequently, they contribute to the reproduction of power relations. Disjunctive syntheses 'capture' connective ones (Massumi 1992: 49). Accordingly, a code is a 'pattern of repeated acts' operating in a milieu, that is to say a 'stable mixing of elements' (Massumi 1992: 51). The vision of theory provided by Deleuze and Guattari is therefore always incomplete and adverse to any systematization: 'No presentation envelops a complete knowledge of even the simplest system. This is not because information is lacking and needs to be found. Complete, predictive knowledge is a myth. The perpetual invention called "history" paces a void of objective indeterminacy' (Massumi 1992: 68).

Massumi understands the notion of 'socius' as a series of 'attractors proposed by a society for its individuals', which functions through binary social representation, reproducing family, economic exploitation, racism and religion within the capitalist logic: 'The whole system is an apparatus of capture of the vital potential of the many for the disproportionate and sometimes deadly satisfactions of the few' (Massumi 1992: 76). However, the line of argumentation of Massumi does not provide an account of the transformations of the socius throughout history. The recording operated by despotic societies is not the same as that which is operated by the immanent axiomatization of capitalism. The socius of capitalism is not only a passive capture, because it is a much more dynamic mode of production than previous ones.

According to Massumi, revolution within the thought of Deleuze and Guattari constitutes 'bifurcations on both global and local levels' (1992: 77). As he sees it, then, *Capitalism and Schizophrenia* does not refute the idea of a 're-becoming-active of the body politic' through a transformation of the social structures (1992: 77). In other words, for Massumi the Deleuzian politics provides a model for the understanding of large scale revolutionary and political change and not only limited political change, as opposed to the elitist and the liberal interpretations of Deleuze.

Psychoanalysis prevents revolution from happening by reproducing a neurotic self (Massumi 1992: 48). From this perspective, psychoanalysis is an indispensable instrument of capitalism. This explains the importance of the critique of psychoanalysis for Deleuze and Guattari (1977, 1987). According to Massumi, Deleuze and Guattari's politics can be characterized as a permanent overcoming of identities:

> The end of gender politics, for Deleuze and Guattari, is the destruction of gender (of the molar organization of the sexes under patriarchy) – just as in their view the end of class politics is the destruction of class (of the molar organization of work under capitalism. The goal would be for every body to ungender itself, creating a nonmolarizing socius.
>
> (1992: 89)

A revolutionary Deleuzo-Guattarian politics would not be compatible with a purely molar politics based on abstract identities such as gender, class or race. Gender, class or race, however, could obviously be involved in a revolutionary becoming that would provide a transcending of identities.

Massumi defines the concept of becoming as 'a tension between modes of desire plotting a vector of transformation between two molar coordinates' (1992, 94). In fact, becomings 'counteractualize' molar entities, for instance an animal for the becoming-animal (Massumi 1992: 95). Rather than a reproduction, the becoming is a connection (Massumi 1992: 89). Massumi operates an analogy between the image-thought and neurosis, which consists of the imposition of a molar ordering on the becoming (1992: 97). Accordingly, the becoming as line of flight provides a translation of the body into 'an autonomous zone effectively enveloping infinite degrees of freedom' (Massumi, 1992: 102). The becoming-other is mostly political and could be a collective rather than individualistic counter-actualization of some social oppression: 'The social movements of Blacks, aboriginals, feminists, gays and lesbians – of groups relegated to sub-Standard conditions – provide far better frames of reference than Standard

Man alone at home with his dog, embarking on anti–Oedipal adventure' (Massumi,1992: 103).

The thought of Deleuze and Guattari against utopias would constitute a striation of spaces of freedom (Massumi 1992: 103). However, this does not correspond to what Deleuze and Guattari argue about utopia in *What Is Philosophy?* (1994: 110). Massumi describes mapping of becoming as strategic thinking (1992: 103). Politically speaking, becoming might be favoured by refusing (1) the 'molar order' of the 'habit', turn (2) zones lacking molar control into 'autonomous zones' (Massumi 1992: 104). The main idea of Massumi is to transform a zone of power relations into an autonomous zone. 'Camouflage' (3) might be another form of fostering becoming (Massumi 1992: 105). Plural political tactics (4) using reformism and radicalism as well as the desire for activism ('come out' (5)) would constitute another form of becoming (Massumi 1992: 106).

By contrast, the logic of transcendence produces social and political oppression (Massumi 1992: 11). Massumi defines becoming-other as 'anarchy' as the two poles of society there would be paranoia and fascism on the one hand, and on the other schizophrenia and anarchy (1992: 116): 'May 1968 in France and the initial phases of most modern revolutions can therefore be considered super-molecular becoming-other' (Massumi 1992: 120–121). Massumi also mentions the Situationists, radical ecologists, hippies, radical feminists and the Spanish National Confederation of Labour (Massumi 1992: 121). Massumi's interpretation of Deleuze is clearly revolutionary. As far as he is concerned, micropolitics can also correspond to historical changes.

Against this, liberal democracies only 'represent the "Other"' in order to control society, in particular with the mass media (Massumi 1992: 122). Massumi talks about 'minidespotisms' taking place within contemporary Western and democratic institutions whose ultimate source is the unity of the subjectivity (1992: 125). Recently, however, the most political sensitive conflict is seen as having moved from class antagonism to 'subjectivity battles' as was demonstrated by the New Right discourse defending the neurotic subject against drugs, abortion or pornography (Massumi 1992: 127).

Likewise, molarity is 'phallocentric' (Massumi 1992: 127). For Massumi, neoconservative politics corresponds to postmodernism (1992: 128). The 'operative categories of capital' are 'worker/capitalist and commodity/consumer' (Massumi, 1992: 128). These operative categories, however, are said to be actualized through 'incorporeal traditions' (Massumi 1992: 128). For Massumi, capitalism is operating a '"real subsumption" of society' (1992: 132). Capitalism functions as a quasi-cause, which nevertheless still requires 'disciplinary and liberal institutions (armies, schools, churches, malls,. . .)' (1992: 133). Consequently, Massumi argues that the Foucauldian microphysics of power is compatible with the philosophy of Deleuze and Guattari. Massumi does not draw on the notion of societies of control, which entails a post-Fordist and post-disciplinary society (Deleuze 1992a).

Capitalism recodes within the Fordist liberal nation-state, as opposed to the neoconservative 'transnational-state' and its post-Fordism (Massumi 1992: 134).

Accordingly, in the context of postmodern capitalism molar oedipalized individuals are transformed into fluid consumers:'Life as a succession of soap operas. Postnormality' (Massumi 1992: 135). This creates 'a situation of structural cynicism (as opposed to personal hypocrisy)' (Massumi 1992: 136). Consequently, there is no need to pretend to believe in molar institutions as 'all a body needs do is desire – and subordinate its desiring to earning and consuming' (Massumi 1992: 136).

Against the elitist and the liberal interpretations of the philosophy of Deleuze and Guattari, Massumi links Deleuze and Guattari's oeuvre to actual collective revolutionary politics such as the French Situationists or the Spanish National Confederation of Labour against the elitist or liberal interpretations of other commentators who reject any association between Deleuze and Guattari and radical politics.

Even though he uses the thesis of the real subsumption of society by capital held by the autonomist Marxists, Massumi's revolutionary interpretation of Deleuze and Guattari seems more anarchist, in particular with the notion of autonomous zones. In his revolutionary interpretation of Deleuze and Guattari, Massumi combines the philosophy of Deleuze and Guattari with the apparatuses of power/knowledge of Foucault.

The revolutionary interpretation of Thoburn

Thoburn has shown more determination than most to provide a revolutionary interpretation of the works of Deleuze and Guattari. Thoburn deals specifically with the issue of the relationship between Deleuze and Marx. Thoburn mentions that Deleuze, at the end of his life, wanted to write a book specifically on Marx whose title would have been 'The grandeur of Marx' (2003: 1). Accordingly, Thoburn argues that Marx is essential for Deleuze and Guattari, in particular in *Capitalism and Schizophrenia* (Thoburn 2003: 2). The idea of the functioning of society as 'a continuous process of production' is a direct legacy of Marx (Thoburn 2003: 2). In fact, the project of Thoburn is to create a dialogue between Deleuze and Marx to contribute to a Deleuzian revolutionary politics:

> This book seeks to contribute to a Deleuze–Marx resonance through a foregrounding of the question of politics immanent to capitalist relations. It is, in a sense, a Deleuzian engagement with Marx's communism. It explores a series of milieux and conceptual territories – from the question of the proletariat, to the problem of value, control, and the critique of work – to see how Deleuze's engagement with Marx and with Marxian concerns can develop useful and innovative political figures.
>
> (2003: 4)

From this perspective, a Deleuzian considers that life is political (2003: 5). Nevertheless, this takes into account the dynamic of capitalism: 'I would argue that Deleuze's project is precisely concerned to develop a politics of invention that is adequate to capital' (Thoburn 2003: 6). In other words, Thoburn connects a Deleuzian revolutionary interpretation to the problematic of a political economy.

Thoburn argues that Deleuze and Guattari 'align their privileged political category of the minor with the proletariat', which implies a connection between 'communism' and 'minor politics' (2003: 3). According to Thoburn, a revolutionary Deleuzian politics is necessarily linked to an anti-capitalist approach. Deleuze and Guattari reject a politics based on identities and representation, namely molar entities, because it lacks the creativity of processes (Thoburn 2003: 8). Therefore, the leftist discourse of '"becoming conscious"' of an identity – based on class, gender or race – is criticized (Thoburn 2003: 8).

Thoburn insists on the critique of post-Marxism, which he defines as 'neo-Gramscian thought', in particular Ernesto Laclau and Chantal Mouffe:'Certainly it marked a movement from the politics of *production* to the politics of *democracy* and civil society' (2003: 11). By contrast, for Thoburn, the politics of Deleuze and Guattari is marked by an emphasis on production since: 'the plane of all processes, flows, and constraints of politics, ideas, culture, desire and so on' (2003: 11). This productive political philosophy opposes the over-simplistic notions of base and superstructure, in favour of an 'intensification of Marx' (Thoburn 2003: 11). Additionally, insisting on production implies a continuation of the Marxist project of political economy, whereas the post-Marxists seem to be interested only in politics and not in political economy.

Thoburn's project connects his reading of Deleuze and Guattari and the question of his relationship with Marx, from the point of view of the operaist and autonomist perspectives (Thoburn 2003: 12). Thoburn provides an extensive discussion of the notion of 'minor politics'. Minor politics exists through 'continual engagement with molar stratifications' (Thoburn 2003: 15). The condition of the possibility of minor politics is the fact that the 'people are missing', as argued in Deleuze and Guattari's book on Kafka (Thoburn 2003: 16). Accordingly, the two main 'historical models' of people are the American and the Soviet models (Thoburn 2003: 16). These two models constitute failures:

> For Deleuze, both the social democratic model of the "citizen" and the orthodox Marxist model of "becoming conscious" are hence over. Politics, thus, does not become a process of the representation of the people, but of the invention of a "new world and a people to come".
>
> (Thoburn 2003: 17)

Minor literature – as exemplified by Kafka's oeuvre, which refuses the artificial opposition between art and life – constitutes a model for minor politics (Thoburn 2003: 18). This process has nothing to do with communication (Thoburn 2003: 20). Accordingly, the notion of line of flight is not substantially different from the Marxist notion of contradiction as they both emphasize the transformation of social formations (Thoburn 2003: 29). Thoburn argues that Marx is a 'minor author', who produces the literature of the proletariat (2003: 32). Minor politics rejects both 'anarchist spontaneity' and the Leninist party, even though Deleuze and Guattari are not per se against the idea of party (Thoburn 2003: 41). Thoburn, then, opposes the politics of creation' of Deleuze and Guattari and the postmodernist and Foucauldian concept of resistance (2003: 41). This implies that desire is ontologically more fundamental than resistance (Thoburn 2003: 42).

Thoburn also takes on the issue of the proletariat: 'The lumpenproletariat and the proletarian unnamable' (2003: 47). Thoburn mentions *The Eighteenth Brumaire of Louis Bonaparte* in which the concept of proletariat does not correspond to 'an authentic historical subject', but rather to a social group engaged in a situated and innovative historical process (Thoburn 2003: 48). Thoburn argues that Marx's concept of proletariat does not refuse differences, unlike some poststructuralist critics of Marx maintain. Orthodox Marxists however have consistently rejected the lumpenproletariat and the idea that outcasts and marginals could contribute to the revolution. In fact, Marx's texts do not give a 'scientific definition' of the lumpenproletariat (Thoburn, 2003: 53).

The lumpenproletariat is presented as 'a tendency toward the maintenance of identity' (Thoburn 2003: 54). Lumpenproletariat support to Louis Bonaparte, for instance, is a 'farcical' and reactionary repetition of history (Thoburn 2003: 56). The lumpenproletariat represents a parasite since it does not take part in production (Thoburn 2003: 57). Bakunin's anarchism is said to be based on the revolutionary and anti-authoritarian identity of the lumpenproletariat (Thoburn 2003: 60). Following Balibar (1994: 149), Thoburn asserts that the proletariat 'is almost completely absent' from *Capital* (2003: 61). This would be the consequence of the political and conceptual hesitations of Marx's political environment: 'As Balibar argues, the vacillations in Marx's more overtly politically engaged works between the oppositions of economic/politics, statism/ anarchy, compulsion/freedom, hierarchy/equality [...] these are the essences of the conceptual and political milieu of Marx's time' (Thoburn 2003: 61).

The proletariat is not reducible to an identity and constitutes an 'unnamable' and a 'political autonomous subject' (Thoburn 2003: 62). In fact, according to Thoburn – following the analyses of the *Grundrisse* – the milieu of the proletariat is the 'real subsumption' of society and life by capital:

> Marx's theory of capital is a theory of the composition of life as a complex and mutating social system – an "organism" that assembles not distinct entities – say, workers, machines, and natural objects – but relations and forces across and within apparent entities.
>
> (2003: 63)

Accordingly, society functions as an 'automaton' producing 'constant change' (Thoburn 2003: 63). Thoburn argues that 'the essence of the proletariat is the abolition of work' (2003: 64).

Accordingly, he opposes the tragic historical (and hence more meaningful) repetition of the proletariat to the farcical historical repetition of the lumpenproletariat (Thoburn, 2003: 65). This ties in with the *Anti-Oedipus'* idea that 'the proletariat is the universal plane of minor politics' (Thoburn 2003: 66).

Thoburn also extensively engages with the issue of production. Thoburn uses the analyses of Italian 'workerism' and 'autonomy' (2003: 69). Likewise, he discusses Hardt and Negri's *Empire.* Thoburn, however, opposes Negri's concept of 'autonomy-in- production' to autonomy, Workerism and Deleuze's politics (2003: 70). Deleuze and Guattari's view on capitalism actually corresponds to Raniero Panzieri and Mario Tronti's concept of 'social factory' (Thoburn 2003: 71). For Panzieri, 'the relations of productions are within the productive forces' (Thoburn 2003: 77). Workerism and autonomy have rejected the social-democratic and neo-Gramscian Eurocommunism, which was very influential in Britain around *Marxism Today.* Fundamentally, in the *Red Notebooks,* in *Working Class* or in *Workers' Power* an emphasis is put on technological change and 'political struggle' (Thoburn 2003: 73).

For Thoburn, the concept of abstract machine in the works of Deleuze and Guattari is the analogical equivalent of the mode of production for Marx (2003: 75). Returning to the issue of Workerism, Tronti's oeuvre advocates the notion of 'capitalist communism', which means that profit is the distribution among capitalists of the total 'social surpus-value' (Thoburn 2003: 78). The true sense of Marx's concept of general intellect would be 'the greater expansion of life that can count as work' (Thoburn 2003: 85).

Nonetheless, Negri proposes the concept of 'socialized worker', which emphasizes communication (borrowing from Habermas's theories), that is to say 'intellectual cooperation' (Thoburn 2003, 86). Furthermore, the socialized worker of Hardt and Negri is described as a 'cyborg' – in line with Donna Haraway's theories – and a biopower entity (Thoburn 2003: 87). For Thoburn, Deleuze and Guattari's analysis of capitalism is not coherent with the ideas of Hardt and Negri.

Accordingly, for Deleuze and Guattari, money as a general equivalent deterritorializes through the extraction of surplus-value and wage – 'impotent money' reterritorializes (Thoburn 2003: 93). Deleuze and Guattari distinguish two modes of oppression. First the 'machinic enslavement' where the worker is straightforwardly the passive slave of a machine within the domain of production, and 'social subjection' where the individual is separated and dominated by the machine within the domain of subjectivity, through consumption for instance (Thoburn 2003: 94). Finally, there is the notion of societies of control that mainly correspond to a transformation of capitalism – and an abstract machine as any social machine – characterized by '"social business"' (Thoburn 2003: 96). Additionally, Deleuze and Guattari describe a 'machinic surplus-value', which is the product of 'intellectual labour' and is therefore different from material labour and 'regular' surplus-value (1977: 232 cited in Thoburn 2003: 96). In *Anti-Oedipus,* the addition of the two surplus-values is the 'surplus value of flux'. By contrast, according to *A Thousand Plateaus,* 'machinic surplus value' corresponds to 'the break between the two planes of capital – the flow

of the full BwO and the axiomatized identities that are its reterritorialization'
(Thoburn 2003: 97).

Thoburn confronts the question of 'the refusal of work' within workerism and
autonomy (2003: 103). Thoburn describes workerism (*operaismo*) and autonomy
(*autonomia*) as two parts of a plural, radical stream of the Italian extra-parliamen-
tary left 'expressing a double flux' between the far left and the transformation
of production (2003: 104). Thoburn however recognizes that workerism and
autonomy can be assimilated into minor politics, except the militarization processes that took place during the end of the 1970s in Italy (2003: 105). Actually,
workerism and autonomy did not only oppose orthodox communism and social
democracy but councilism, self-management (Lip in France for instance) and
anarcho-syndicalism as well (Thoburn, 2003: 110). Actually, for Tronti, work per
se constitutes the experience of alienation (Thoburn 2003: 111).

However, for Negri and other workerists and autonomists, class is not defined
through the sociological class structure or through the Leninist dichotomy –
'"class in itself" and "for itself"' (Thoburn 2003: 114) – but relatively to a series
of dynamic technological, political, social and economic phenomena, for which
practical working class is the main trait: 'At the level of socially developed capital,
capitalist development becomes subordinated to working class struggles' (Tronti
1979 cited in Thoburn 2003: 115). This corresponds to the concept of class
composition, which refutes any structuralism or realism and most of all posits
the necessity to 'continually find mechanisms and sites of political invention,
alliance, and resistance' (Thoburn 2003: 115).

In fact, this could be manifested through the process of 'autovalorization',
which are autonomous practices (for instance squatting in 1970s Italy) freed from
capitalist valorization and state control (Thoburn 2003: 119) Thoburn, however,
acknowledges the relative historical failure of the experiences of autovalorization because: 'state oppression of autonomia induced a self-defeating increasingly
militarized defence of marginal spaces' (2003: 120). Thoburn assumes that the
link between the minorities and the autonomist movement can be described as
'inclusive disjunction' (2003: 123). The *emarginati* – contemptuously regarded
by the Italian Communist Party as members of the lumpenproletariat – refused
work in the 1970s and played a crucial part in the Movement of '77 (Thoburn
2003: 126). Similarly, the Metropolitan Indians (*Indiani Metropolitani*) are an
interesting illustration of minoritarian and autonomist politics and artistic creation (Thoburn 2003: 132).

In conclusion, Thoburn contends that Deleuze and Guattari try to answer
the question 'What is to be done?' in 'resonance' with Marxism and away from
orthodoxies (2003: 140). Fundamentally, Deleuze's politics should be seen as 'a
return (with differences, of course) to core Marxian problematics' (Thoburn
2003: 140). Accordingly, the proletariat is a 'plane of composition immanent
to, and against the flows of axioms of capitalist production' (Thoburn 2003:
142). Finally, Deleuze proposes a communist critique of democracy, rejecting
a molar liberal and juridical majority (Thoburn 2003: 142–143). Clearly, he
opposes any liberal or social-democratic interpretation of the politics of Deleuze

and Guattari, which he connects with the problematization of workerism and autonomia (rather than with other types of radical politics such as anarchism or Maoism for instance). Thoburn's approach does not correspond to Massumi's reception, which is characterized by anarchism and Foucault's microphysics of power.

Autonomist readings of Deleuze and Guattari

Toni Negri is a very influential political philosopher. He has developed his own stream of autonomist Marxism along with Michael Hardt (2000, 2004, 2009). Negri draws extensively on the philosophy of Deleuze and Guattari as well as on other philosophers such as Spinoza, Marx and Foucault. In an article (2011) on the thought of Deleuze and Guattari which was written in 1997, that is to say when he was working on *Empire* (2000), Negri operates his political interpretation of Deleuze and Guattari. Negri contends that Deleuze had not been able to overcome structuralism before meeting Guattari (2011: 157).

Accordingly, Deleuze and Guattari within *Capitalism and Schizophrenia* (1977, 1987) are very much influenced by the revolutionary atmosphere of 1968 (Negri 2011: 158). This implied a substantial engagement with Marxism from the theoretical and practical points of view. *Anti-Oedipus* (1977) is presented as a book allowing for an understanding of contemporary phenomena such as globalization or the real subsumption of society by capital (Negri 2011: 159). Negri argues that the oeuvre of Deleuze and Guattari is compatible with his analysis on the multitude 'The shifting of the revolutionary apparatus from centrality to multiplicity is proposed through the theory of the rhizome and of networks' (2011: 163). It is not clear, however, how the multitude can articulate the singularities that compose it. It seems that Negri's argument is mainly based on a political economic study of post-Fordism and class composition. *A Thousand Plateaus* (1987) can be seen as redefining contemporary materialist philosophy (Negri 2011: 165).

Jason Read, currently professor of philosophy at the University of Southern Maine, provides another influential revolutionary interpretation of Deleuze and Guattari connected to autonomist Marxism. The context of his reading of Deleuze and Guattari is the American academy. He provides a revolutionary interpretation of the philosophy of Deleuze and Guattari, which combines a Deleuzo-Guattarian reading of Marx and a Marxist reading of Deleuze and Guattari:

> Deleuze and Guattari's two-volume *Capitalism and Schizophrenia* remains a significant exception to thinking in terms of any such division between Marxism and poststructuralism. Deleuze and Guattari maintain a complex relation with a version of Marx's concepts of the mode of production and labor (or living labor) as well as the Marxist problematic in general. As Deleuze states in a conversation with Negri, "I think Felix Guattari and I have remained Marxists in our two different ways perhaps, but both of

us. You see, we think any political philosophy must turn on the analysis of
capitalism and the ways it has developed."

(Read 2003: 164–165)

According to Read, the problematic of Deleuze and Guattari is closely connected to the general approach of Marx and Marxism. This implies that the
notions of revolution and political economy are linked to the oeuvre of Deleuze
and Guattari and their understanding of society and politics. Nevertheless, he
uses the philosophy of Deleuze and Guattari to update the thinking of Marx
and confront it with transformations of capitalism such as post-Fordism or the
development of immaterial labour: 'My point being in part that in each of these
cases a new "Marx" is produced to responds to the exigencies of the present'
(Read 2003: 158).

Drawing on Althusser's reading of *Capital*, Read provides a 'symptomatic reading' of the oeuvre of Marx with the help of the theoretical innovations of poststructuralist thinkers (Foucault, Derrida, Deleuze and Guattari) and autonomist
Marxism (2003: 12). Deleuze and Guattari are particularly important because
they are both an important reference in the poststructuralist and autonomist
literature. This entails insisting on the notion of immanence:

> Deleuze places Foucault's statements regarding power within a general his-
> tory of the problem of immanent causality, a history that includes Althusser's
> Spinozistic interpretation of Marx. Deleuze's understanding of immanence
> in many ways complements Althusser's understanding of immanent causal-
> ity in that in each case it is a matter of recognizing the differences internal
> to immanent causality and not the identity.
>
> (Read 2003: 164)

The philosophy of Deleuze and Guattari provides a conceptualization of
immanence that allows Read to operate a novel reading of Marx through the
notion of 'micro-politics of capital' (2003). Read, however, reads both Deleuze
and Guattari within Marxism:

> For Deleuze and Guattari a quasi-cause is a paradoxical entity because it
> involves the retroactive causality and effectivity of what is itself an effect.
> This effect, the appearance or attitude toward that which appears as the pre-
> supposition of a mode of production, or more generally that which appears
> to be outside the historicity and history of practice and production, is itself
> a cause in that it shapes and affects the attitudes of those who live within
> that particular mode of production.
>
> (2003: 42)

In fact, Read contends that it is possible to understand the notion of quasi-
cause within the framework of the notion of mode of production. However,
the concept of mode of production is rejected in *Anti-Oedipus* (1977: 11). This

means that Read operates a symptomatic reading of Deleuze and Guattari as well, because he seeks a convergence between the philosophy of Deleuze and Guattari and Marxism rather than the contrary, as advocated by the proponents of the elitist and liberal interpretations. Read's interpretation of Deleuze and Guattari is therefore guided by how best to formulate the version of Deleuze and Guattari in order to understand the current functioning of contemporary capitalism and how it can be politically opposed.

In the *Micropolitics of Capital*, Read mainly quotes *Anti-Oedipus* and more generally the two volumes of *Capitalism and Schizophrenia*. In another text, however, the interpretation provided by Read of Deleuze and Guattari is more extensive. Read claims that the entire work of Deleuze is revolutionary and coherent with the Marxist problematic. In particular, Read insists on the revolutionary approach to the issue of the critique of the image of thought in *Difference and Repetition* (Read 2009). Read argues that, from the beginning, the philosophy of Deleuze is characterized by a critique of the ideological mystifications that legitimize the reproduction of the relations of power and by the desire to produce a revolutionary transformation of social relations (Read 2003: 79). Deleuze is said to propose the concept of image of thought in order to respond to the Marxist problematic of ideology.

The conceptualization of this problem continues with the notion of socius, which records the desiring production in *Anti-Oedipus*. Deleuze and Guattari later articulate the opposition between 'state thought and nomadic thought' in *A Thousand Plateaus* (Read 2009: 97). This demonstrates that the works of Deleuze and Guattari consistently deal with thought and the existing relations of power in a specific moment of history.

Accordingly, capitalism ontologically transforms subjectivity. This highlights the limitations of the traditional categories of subject, dialectic or even for understanding the immanent functioning of subjectivity:

> It is not a matter of a dialectical negation, or a historical telos, of labour-power taking the subjective form of the proletariat as that class with nothing to lose but its chains. Production in Deleuze and Guattari is not the act of a subject at all, it is an abstract subjective activity, an activity that exceeds subjectivity and constitutes it. It even exceeds any attempt to delimit it to a specific type of activity, to designate it as labour.
>
> (Read 2009: 99)

Consequently, according to Read, revolution should not be conceptualized in terms of proletariat, historical subject or historical telos, but rather through an ontological thinking. In other words, revolution should be thought as a 'virtuality':

> As Deleuze and Guattari argue, capitalism entails a fundamental, almost ontological transformation of what constitutes subjectivity and objectivity: an unqualified and global subjectivity encounters an unspecified object, or,

in more conventional terms, labour-power confronts the commodity. The connection between this activity and revolution does not pass through a subject of history, but rather passes through the relationship between the virtual and the actual, the creative activity constitutive of society and its actual articulation and concealment within a specific society.

(2009: 99–100)

From this point of view, Read does not agree with Thoburn on the question of the proletariat. In fact, according to Thoburn, the concept of proletariat is compatible with the oeuvre of Deleuze and Guattari. By contrast, according to Read the revolution in the oeuvre of Deleuze and Guattari is a virtuality. Read's conception of revolution departs from a purely Marxist conception grounded on class politics and a historical telos, for instance.

The Marxist revolutionary interpretation of Sibertin-Blanc

Sibertin-Blanc provides another revolutionary interpretation of the oeuvre of Deleuze and Guattari, which is connected to Marxism but not directly to autonomist Marxism. Sibertin-Blanc was trained as a French academic in philosophy. He is currently professor of philosophy at the university of Toulouse-Mirail. His PHD thesis was about the political philosophy of Deleuze and Guattari. Sibertin-Blanc associates the works of Deleuze and Guattari to a vitalist thought characterized by a 'clinic' approach to phenomena (own translation) (Sibertin-Blanc 2006: 1). The philosophy of Deleuze and Guattari is seen as a kind of medicine that tries to determine what the diseases of societies are. This, then, is a Nietzschean project (Sibertin-Blanc 2006: 2). According to Sibertin-Blanc, the thought of Deleuze and Guattari is also 'critical', because it opposes the dominant social patterns (own translation) (2006: 2).

Even though Deleuze and Guattari oppose capitalism and different dominant discourses in psychoanalysis, politics and literature, for instance, they produce an extensive and profound rejection of the notion of critique in *Kafka: For a Minor Literature*. The notion of deterritorialization is presented as an explicit substitute and improvement of the project of critique (Deleuze and Guattari 1986: 47). Deleuze and Guattari, however, perform a critique of psychoanalysis, in particular in *Anti-Oedipus* (1977).

According to Sibertin-Blanc, there is a clear continuity between *Anti-Oedipus* and *A Thousand Plateaus* (2006: 27). In other words, the explicitly Marxist vocabulary of *Anti-Oedipus* is not a regrettable exception in the oeuvre of Deleuze and Guattari. There could be a clear Marxist or Marxian problematic in both volumes of *Capitalism and Schizophrenia*. In particular the notion of assemblage developed by *A Thousand Plateaus* is to be understood in combination with the concept of group-subject in *Anti-Oedipus*.

Sibertin-Blanc argues that Deleuze and Guattari were influenced by Foucault's microphysics of power and his apparatuses of power/knowledge theorized in

Discipline and Punish and *The Will to Power* (2006: 32). This could have helped Deleuze and Guattari to conceptualize the connection between relations of power and the production of knowledge. This does not take into account the opposite conceptions of subjectivity of Deleuze and Guattari on the one hand, and Foucault on the other. For Deleuze and Guattari there is creativity and production at the heart of subjectivity or the functioning of the assemblages. The power, the striated space, the socius, the arborescent structure therefore strive to capture the creative processes of the desiring machines or the rhizomatic processes.

By contrast, the Foucauldian apparatus of power/knowledge entails that power configures subjectivity, even though it is possible to resist discipline or biopower. In other words, for Deleuze and Guattari, creativity or resistance possesses and ontological and chronological precedence over power, whereas for Foucault it is the opposite. Additionally, on the specific issue of the relationship between power and knowledge, Foucault is not the only reference of Deleuze and Guattari. In fact, the Marxist notion of ideology, the Nietzschean will to power, and the Lacanian master signifier are alternative problematizations to Foucault of the link between power and knowledge that were extensively reflected on by Deleuze and Guattari.

Sibertin-Blanc provides a specific reading of the politics of Deleuze and its articulation with Marxism:

> Actually these ostensibly different aspects are intimately linked together. At any rate, they must be, for the overlapping of a "becoming minoritarian" and a "becoming-revolutionary" not to be illusory, for the affirmation of a "becoming-minoritarian of everyone" not to be reduced to a speculative formula empty of all effective content, and for the very term "revolutionary" not to conceal a political vacuity. Bearing this in mind, we will put forward the hypothesis that the emergence of the multiplication of minoritarian struggles, in the analysis of the conjuncture which Deleuze carries out, takes over from class struggle. This does not mean that it simply supplants class struggles, but rather that it prolongs them while complicating their coordinates and transforming their modes of realisation, but also interiorising certain of their presuppositions and difficulties.
>
> (2009: 124)

For Sibertin-Blanc minority politics is different from the Marxist notion of class struggle and the minorities are not the Marxist proletariat. Consequently, his interpretation is different from Thoburn's for whom the minor and Deleuzo-Guattarian politics is connected to the proletariat. Sibertin-Blanc, however, argues that there is some connivance between the minority politics and the politics of the Marxist class struggle, as opposed to some antagonism in line with what orthodox Marxists like Garo (2011a) would argue.

Sibertin-Blanc argues that the Deleuzian politics of the minority and of the becoming revolutionary is compatible with the notion of universalism:

Then we must consider a universality of a process of relational inventions, and not of an identity of subsumption; a universality which is not projected forward in a maximum of identitary integration . . . In short, no longer an extensive and quantifiable universality, but on the contrary an intensive and unquantifiable universality, in the sense that subjects become in common in a process where their identitary anchorages are dissipated, to the advantage of that conception and radically constructivist practice of autonomy required by a new minoritarian internationalism. "Minorities from all countries . . ."

(2009: 134–135)

The argument of Sibertin-Blanc on universalism is very attractive because it allows the Deleuzo-Guattarian politics to dialogue with the universalist political philosophy and its tradition since the Enlightenment, with famous figures such as Rousseau, Kant and Hegel. There is, however, an epistemological problem. Deleuze and Guattari criticize the notion of human rights (1994: 107), the tradition of natural law and the notion of contractualism. Furthermore, the concept of universalism needs a subject, probably even a historical subject. However, Deleuze and Guattari extensively reject the notion of subject, for instance in the first plateau of *A Thousand Plateaus* (1987: 3–4).

The Marxist revolutionary interpretation of Nunes

Nunes provides another Marxist and revolutionary interpretation. He is professor of philosophy at the Pontificia Universidade Católica do Rio Grande do Sul in Brazil. Unlike Žižek (2004), for instance, he harshly criticizes the idea that the philosophy of Deleuze and Guattari could be understood as a dualism. According to Nunes absolute dualism does not exist in the works of Deleuze and Guattari because they are always relative.

For Nunes, there are three main interpretations of Deleuze. First an 'activist' interpretation represented by Hardt and Negri in works such as *Empire* (2010: 107). A second reception with Hallward and Badiou consider Deleuze and Guattari as dangerous 'depoliticizing' thinkers (Nunes 2010: 107). For Nunes, a third reception sees Deleuze and Guattari as advocates of capitalism, because of their reflection on the desiring machines. Fundamentally, these three receptions have the same understanding of dualism in the work of Deleuze and Guattari, which would ultimately consist of the opposition between the virtual and the actual (Nunes 2010: 108). Nunes provides a specific interpretation of the politics of Deleuze and Guattari:

If it is true that Deleuze and Guattari place a higher value on deterritorialization, this value is subordinated to the practical problem of resisting the conservatism that reduces the real to the given and turns the latter into necessity. That this error should be opposed *in act* entails that it is never a matter of saying that *everything is possible*, which is practically vacuous, but of saying that, in every *here* and *now*, there are *potentials* that can be *acted upon*. If the political practice to be derived from this attitude can be given a name, it is *intervention* . . . An intervention singularises a situation as the contingent production of certain conditions, decomposes it into different levels and registers (macro- and micropolitical, molar and molecular, etc.).

(Nunes 2010: 121)

Accordingly, the virtual might correspond to relative deterritorialization, which would allow the performing of activism and political strategy within the framework of an intervention. Deterritorialization would amount to saying that any political situation is not entirely determined and that resistance is always possible, to a certain extent at least. Strategy would imply understanding and following the lines of deterritorialization. Furthermore, according to Nunes, Deleuzo-Guattarian politics does not contradict large scale political transformations:

Yet we have already seen how there is nothing in Deleuze and Guattari that is *contrary* as such to the scalability, mass mobilisations or forms of organisation that more radical transformations may demand; the front is always both micro- and macropolitical.

(2010: 123)

Nunes does not, however, agree with the idea that an emancipatory politics could be generated by an absolute deterritorialization, which is always linked to destruction and death in the last instance (2010: 121). Nunes describes Deleuzo-Guattarian politics as an intervention, that is to say an informed planned action on a specific political conjuncture. In other words, he reintroduces the orthodox Marxist intellectual apparatus of military metaphor of the strategy within the Deleuzo-Guattarian thought. A political intervention is always to be meticulously planned. The idea is to contribute to the general political situation, which is conceptualized in terms of opposed armies on a battlefield, using different arms including ideas and different methods of activism.

It may seem attractive to combine the traditional Marxist political analysis within the Deleuzo-Guattarian ontology. It is not clear though how it is possible to plan and implement a strategy for a molecular politics. In reality, it is impossible to master desires and passions like the disciplined militants of a Marxist-Leninist party.

The effort of Nunes to solve the metaphysical problem of dualism in Deleuze and Guattari is certainly remarkable. It might, however, be argued that the series of dualisms that appear in the oeuvre of Deleuze and Guattari (territorialization/deterritorialization, smooth/striated, rhizomatic/arborescent, actual/virtual) are a necessary – even though linguistically imperfect – condition to express the idea of becoming, which is asignifying and hence beyond language.

Stengers's interpretation of Deleuze and Guattari

Isabelle Stengers is an influential contemporary philosopher. She provides another revolutionary interpretation of Deleuze and Guattari, which is connected more loosely to Marxism. Isabelle Stengers is mainly a philosopher of sciences. She is professor of philosophy at the Université Libre of Brussels and worked with Ilya Prigogine, the Belgian Nobel Prize winner for physics. She developed a critique of epistemological realism within the framework of the Deleuzian thought. She was notably involved in the controversy that followed the publication of Sokal and Bricmont's *Intellectual Impostures* (2004). Stengers defended poststructuralism against the claims of Sokal and Bricmont.

The works of Stengers are also connected to anti-capitalist activism and the alter- globalization movement. Along with the activist and publisher Philippe Pignarre she contributed reflections on the demonstrations in Seattle in 1999 (2011). The demonstrations of Seattle in 1999 demonstrated that capitalism was not the end of history, and that anti-capitalist activism was still possible. Being an anti-capitalist in the 2000s therefore implied 'inheriting from Seattle' (Pignarre and Stengers 2011: 3).

Stengers is opposed to any depoliticized interpretation of Deleuze and Guattari:

> Let us not assume that the figure of the schizo (I am not speaking about dealing with schizos, as he did) is bound to be a deterritorializing one. It may as well be reterritorialized as a *nec plus ultra* academic reference for debunking the illusions of normality of the modern Subject again and again. And as such it will be a subject for innumerable academic dissertations by precocious students, just like Artaud or Nietzsche or . . . For those of us who teach and breathe the academic air, reclaiming the machinic freedom of cartography, which Guattari's operative constructs require, may well mean learning the signature of the black hole that threatens any (academic) relaying, and transforms relayers into sophisticated, spinning babblers: it is the fear of exposing oneself to the accusation of being duped, to compromise oneself with what others may be able to debunk.
>
> (Stengers 2011: 153)

Stengers insists that the philosophy of Deleuze and Guattari is to be used in the 'real world' in order to inform a real revolutionary politics. This politics is regarded as minoritarian and deterritorialized as opposed to a majoritarian and molar politics. The philosophy of Deleuze and Guattari can be captured by some careerist academics keen to get rid of its 'dangerous' politics. The oeuvre of Deleuze and Guattari would be reduced to a commodity used by academics to reproduce their power in higher education institutions through the construction of an expertise materialized in publications, conferences and edited books. It is arguably what happens with some advocates of the elitist and the liberal interpretation of Deleuze and Guattari.

Stengers draws a distinction between the works of Deleuze and the works of Guattari. In fact, she argues that Guattari produces 'operative constructs' as opposed to Deleuze's concepts (2011: 146). In other words, unlike Deleuze, Guattari is not a philosopher. It is true that of Guattari's main activity was the La Borde clinic and that he was not a full- time academic in a department of philosophy. Second, he never wrote anything alone on the history of philosophy. Third, when he met Deleuze at the end of the 1960s, he was mainly associated with the Lacanian milieu. Stengers's argument is therefore valid up to a certain point as Guattari cannot be described as a traditional academic philosopher.

I would argue, however, that it is impossible to distinguish between Deleuze and Guattari in *Anti-Oedipus* (1977), *A Thousand Plateaus* (1987) and *What Is Philosophy?* (1994), which are doubtless major works of post-war French philosophy. If Stengers was to be followed, it would be quite impossible to define the 'socius', 'desiring machines', 'rhizomatic' or 'arborescent' processes, 'striated' or 'smooth' spaces, which would be either concepts or operative constructs. It is probably safer to argue that both Deleuze and Guattari were philosophers and that they produced a series of concepts, in particular in their joint work. To be fair, Stengers presents her point as a hypothesis and refers mainly to Guattari single-authored work (2011: 138).

In *Capitalist Sorcery: Breaking the Spell*, Stengers provides a specific account of her understanding of the politics of Deleuze and Guattari (Pignarre and Stengers 2011). Stengers develops an analysis of capitalism:

> If the singularity of capitalism is to be a "system of sorcery without sorcerers", struggling against such a system imposes the need to make its procedures visible, sensible. And never to relinquish what it has captured, as if the operation of capture constituted a judgement of truth.
>
> (Pignarre and Stengers 2011: 135)

It means that capitalism is a machine that is able to have people act and do things through influences that can be compared to spells. In other words, in a capitalist mode of production, people tend to act and think according to specific patterns that contribute to the dynamic of the accumulation of capital. Talking about the sorcery of capitalism is a means to circumvent the notion of ideology and its supposed realist epistemology (Pignarre and Stengers 2011: 42). Stengers, however, distinguishes 'minions' from the rest of the people. These 'minions' contribute more or less consciously to the actual functioning of the capitalist system and oppose anti-capitalism (Pignarre and Stengers 2011: 32). This is a way of confronting views by claiming that everyone is an incapable cog in the invincible capitalist machine.

The relationship of Stengers to Marxism and the left wing is complex. Stengers rejects orthodox Marxism and advocates a Marx who should be read in 'pragmatic' fashion:

> We are inheritors of Marx in the sense that, for us, capitalism exists. Yet we have just characterised its mode of existence in a manner that many of his

other inheritors would characterise as "symptomatic". Politics, according to many Marxist readings, is simply a translation of relations of force. On this count there is nothing to kill, only ectoplasm "finally" dismissed to the kingdom of appearances to which it belongs. We do not want to pose the question of knowing if such an objection is authorised by Marx, or if it is the fruit of a "false reading". What is important, for us, is that the thesis by which it is authorised, the thesis that results in the disqualification of politics, is a poison. Whoever has been poisoned is doomed to define others as "misguided", lacking the correct perspective and not as a protagonist with whom it is a matter of learning to coexist politically.

(Pignarre and Stengers 2011: 16)

According to Pignarre, who is an activist and publisher, and Stengers, capitalism functions as a social and economic formation that is systematically connected. Stengers, however, refuses grand politics and its global and molar strategies within the framework of the understanding of the politics of Deleuze and Guattari. Pignarre and Stengers seem to be reluctant to accept the very idea of political strategy:

In *A Thousand Plateaus*, Deleuze and Guattari evoked "an itinerant creation" implying an ambulant people of "relayers" in explicit contrast with a model society but perhaps also, implicitly, with absolute nomadism, hacker style . . . For the relay to be taken, it must be given, even if those who give know that they are not masters of what they give, that when a relay is taken it is not a matter of simple translation but of a new creation.

(2011: 123)

According to Pignarre and Stengers, the politics of Deleuze and Guattari is characterized mainly by the notion of relays that provide a functioning dynamic for a molecular politics; that is to say a politics opposed to oppressive and molar majorities, as advocated by the West, the male or the white, but also by grand left-wing politics. It is a politics of small groups that are able to become 'group-subjects' and to create together. There must, however, be circulation of creativity between these specific groups with their situated experiences.

This itinerant politics is not reduced to a series of marginal groups that would be condemned to remain in the periphery of society without ever being able to actually transform capitalism through a revolution or some other kind of process. This would correspond to the notion of lumpenproletariat. In fact, the critical reply to Stengers from an orthodox Marxist perspective might be that her Deleuzian itinerant politics is actually a eulogy of the lumpenproletariat and that it contributes to a depoliticization and deorganization of the radical left, in particular in the context of the alter-globalization movement.

Stengers would first argue, however, that the proletariat is a molar and majoritarian figure that is no longer needed by a Deleuzo-Guattarian politics. Second, a molecular politics of relays can provide a revolution and a destruction of the capitalist system through the generalization of the creation of spaces of creation and freedom that would weaken the structure of capitalism and finally cause it to collapse (Pignarre and Stengers 2011: 111). I would argue therefore that the itinerant politics is a credible instrument to elaborate a Deleuzo-Guattarian revolutionary politics. I will come to this point in the final chapter.

Consequently, this interpretation of the philosophy of Deleuze and Guattari is really revolutionary, because it is not only about local changes and improvements to reform capitalism (as contended in some versions of the liberal interpretation of Deleuze and Guattari); it is about creating a new world, liberated from capitalism, even if this happens through the multiplication of the creation of small new worlds.

Stengers refuses both the orthodox Marxist perspective of the planned strategy of the working class and its party, which would eventually lead to the destruction of capitalism, and the anarchist spontaneity, which argues that the masses will get rid of capitalism without the assistance of any kind of organization (Pignarre and Stengers, 2011: 122). From this perspective, she follows Guattari's line of argumentation in *Communists Like Us* that rejects the notion of political party and the spontaneist perspective (Guattari and Negri 1990). Stengers tries to articulate a global transformation of society and the autonomy of the groups of activists.

I would argue that Stengers, along with Pignarre, provide a novel and convincing articulation of a Deleuzo-Guattarian politics and Marxism. In particular, I shall draw on the notion of itinerant politics in the second part of this book.

Non-Marxist revolutionary interpretations of Deleuze and Guattari

Massumi, Thoburn, Alliez, Negri, Read or Sibertin-Blanc's works are examples of revolutionary interpretations of the political philosophy of Deleuze within the framework of Marxism (against Garo's liberal interpretation of Deleuze and Guattari from a Marxist perspective). There is also, however, a non-Marxist revolutionary interpretation of Deleuze and Guattari's political philosophy. In fact, the Invisible Committee in the *Coming Insurrection* (2007) develops a revolutionary politics based not on a Marxist politics, but on a problematic of communization and insurrection. They demonstrate how the 'becoming revolutionary' is striated by the different codes of the social milieus (2007: 89).

This revolutionary interpretation of Deleuze and Guattari's political philosophy by the French autonomist movement is not represented in the French academy. The Invisible Committee opposes the analyses of *Multitudes* (closer to the Italian Autonomist Marxism) as their harsh criticism of the decentralized political model constituted by the coordinations demonstrates: 'the parabureaucrats have invented since twenty years the coordinations' (2007: 111). According to the The Invisible Committee, the collapse of the existing political system through the insurrectional 'multiplication of communes' is inevitable (2007: 107). The main problem of the interpretation of the political philosophy of

Deleuze and Guattari by The Invisible Committee is its refusal to consider any political economy.

Deleuze and Guattari's political economy and analysis of capitalism is therefore not used to understand the dynamics of 'late capitalism'. This could be explained by the fact that the *Coming Insurrection* was written before the systemic crisis of capitalism in 2008, notwithstanding the obvious romanticist spontaneism of The Invisible Committee. This implies that my own application of Deleuze to the question of financialization will not be related to this specific revolutionary interpretation of Deleuze because of its lack of engagement with political economic questions.

Tiqqun's *This Is Not a Program* develops the same perspective with concepts such as 'revolutionary deterritorialization' (2011: 16). Tiqqun is a French collective that has published several journal issues since the end of the 1990s and developed concepts such as 'Bloom' or the 'Imaginary party'. Tiqqun is usually considered as an autonomist collective. In fact, it belongs to the French *autonome* or autonomist movement and engages with the Italian autonomist tradition. It refers to Deleuze and Guattari, to Foucault, to Heidegger, or to Guy-Ernest Debord. *This Is Not a Program* also publishes photos according to an aesthetic device invented by the Surrealists, for instance in *Nadja* (Breton 1988).

First, Tiqqun rejects most Marxist class analyses, even though open Marxism might provide close reasonings (for instance, Holloway 2010):

> Historical conflict no longer opposes two massive molar heaps, two classes – the exploited and the exploiters, the dominant and dominated, managers and workers – among which, in each individual case, one could differentiate . . . It is thus in each of us that war is being waged between imperial socialization and that which already eludes it.
>
> (2011: 12)

Tiqqun claims that domination and control is produced through apparatuses of power/knowledge that capture our subjectivity, as opposed to only exploiting the working class. Consequently, domination is based not on economic exploitation, but political control:

> THE POLITICAL NOW DOMINATES THE ECONOMIC. What is ultimately at stake is no longer the extraction of surplus value, but *Control*. Now the level of surplus value extracted solely indicates the level of Control, which is the local condition of extraction. Capital is no longer but a *means* to generalized control.
>
> (Tiqqun 2011: 155)

In order to resist this political domination, Tiqqun claims it is necessary to construct political activity within an immanent process: 'We have called this plane of consistency the Imaginary Party' (2011: 13). This liberating political process is opposed to the conception of the political party either in its Leninist or its reformist form. It corresponds to local activities within the framework of an enhanced 'circulation' of affects (Tiqqun 2011: 13). Tiqqun is very critical of the ideology of citizenship of the French left wing, especially the anti-globalization movement and the French critical left (New Anticapitalist Party, French Communist Party, *Le Monde Diplomatique*) (2011: 17). Accordingly, this would represent 'Bloom', that is to say the political endeavour to amend the system rather than to destroy it (Tiqqun 2011: 143).

Finally, Tiqqun advocates a revolutionary break with the 'Empire' and its apparatuses through 'diffuse guerrilla' (2011: 84). Having analysed the practices of the 1970s Italian autonomist movement Tiqqun believes direct and armed confrontation with the state should be avoided to prevent any repetition of the political and military failure of the Red Brigades (2011: 74). Revolutionary processes are to be understood as autonomous 'desubjectivation' beyond representation (Tiqqun 2011: 55).

This Is Not a Program provides a very ambitious philosophical account of the contemporary processes of domination as well as a revolutionary political theory grounded on Deleuze and Guattari, which is not to say that some issues cannot be raised. *This Is Not a Program* does not feature a reflection on political economy; that is to say an account of the transformations of contemporary capitalism. No analysis of the global crisis of capitalism is therefore included. More importantly, this prevents Tiqqun from articulating its revolutionary politics with the situation created by the crisis.

The notion of emancipatory desubjectivation is particularly relevant, if one agrees with Foucault's argument on the apparatuses of power/knowledge. In other words, if control and oppression function through the production of subjects within the framework of techniques of power, freedom resides on the destruction of the subject. However, the concept of desubjectivation prevents Tiqqun from precisely describing what would be a free society. *This Is Not a Program* therefore includes no discussion at all of authors such as Fourier, who tried to think up and realize a utopia or even contemporary experiences of anti-capitalist struggles such as the Zapatista movement in Chiapas.

Finally, the Situationist notion of 'spectacle' based on Hegelian dialectics is used, whereas most of the analyses are grounded on Deleuze and Foucault whose oeuvres harshly criticize the very notion of dialectics. It is clear that The Invisible Committee and Tiqqun provide an anarchist interpretation of Deleuze and Guattari, which contradicts the Marxist interpretation of Massumi, Thoburn, Alliez, Negri, Read and Sibertin-Blanc. The Invisible Committee and Tiqqun are spontaneist in contrast with the anarchist reception of Deleuze and Guattari provided by Massumi, which was connected to Marxism and to political economy.

Conclusion

The revolutionary analysis of Deleuze and Guattari's politics does in fact hinge on the question of the status of political economy and the question of political organization. Whereas the heterodox-Marxist position (Massumi 1992; Negri

2011; Nunes 2010; Pignarre and Stengers 2011; Read 2003; Sibertin-Blanc 2006; Thoburn 2003) advocates a political economy, the anarchist position does not (The Invisible Committee 2007; Tiqqun 2011).

Additionally, although Thoburn, Negri, Read, Sibertin-Blanc and The Invisible Committee, as well as Tiqqun, agree on the rejection of the Leninist party, their different revolutionary interpretations vary on the question of political organization. The Invisible Committee is the most adamant in rejecting any form of political organization except small groups (2007: 96). This can be explained by the French autonomist movement's refusal to be connected with any form of institutional organization (political, academic or social organizations). As a matter of fact, the political parties, the associations and the trade unions of the French left (socialist, communist and even left-wing communists from the perspective of the French autonomist) are largely discredited either because of their collaboration with the neoliberalization of France (the French Communist Party has supported and participated in two socialist cabinets since 1981) or for their inability to influence this process. Their lack of reference to political economy, however, prevents them from understanding the neoliberal processes.

In sum, the revolutionary interpretations of Deleuze and Guattari are quite diverse. First, there are the thinkers who connect the philosophy of Deleuze and Guattari with the Marxist problematic, even though they clearly reject orthodox Marxism. Proponents of this position include Thoburn, Negri, Read and Sibertin-Blanc. They could be described as heterodox Marxists who try to understand the Deleuzo-Guattarian politics in connivance with Marx; that is to say a political economy and a strategic politics. Nunes can be added to this group because of his strategist interpretation of the philosophy of Deleuze and Guattari.

Thoburn, Negri and Read specifically connect the Deleuzian politics with autonomist Marxism. There are some differences and debates among them, even though they share the same problematic. The analysis of Thoburn, for instance, refuses the notion of multitude advocated by Hardt and Negri (2000, 2004, 2009). Then, there are those who provide an anarchist revolutionary interpretation of the philosophy of Deleuze and Guattari with thinkers like The Invisible Committee, Tiqqun and Massumi for whom the Deleuzian politics is to be understood as an absolute deterritorialization and desubjectivation. They are spontaneist, and therefore they are not particularly interested in understanding politics in terms of military strategy as is the case with the heterodox Marxists or the autonomists.

Stengers advocates a specific revolutionary interpretation of Deleuze which is neither Marxist, strategist nor anarchist, spontaneist. In fact, she defends an itinerant politics that implies organizing in small groups through relays without agreeing to a strategist conception of politics. I shall use the concept of itinerant politics in the second part. Generally, I sympathize with all the authors who try to create a resonance between a Deleuzo-Guattarian revolutionary politics and a Marxian problematic of financialization.

Part II

The question that this book tries to respond to is the following: 'How can a revolutionary interpretation of Deleuze and Guattari politicize financialization?' In the first part, I have provided an analysis of the reception of the Deleuzo-Guattarian oeuvre by political philosophy so as to articulate a non-naïve and situated revolutionary interpretation of Deleuze and Guattari. Three interpretations appeared. First (Chapter 2), an elitist interpretation sought to reduce the oeuvre of Deleuze and Guattari to a contemplative philosophy refusing to be involved in politics. Second (Chapter 3), a liberal interpretation sought to relate Deleuze and Guattari to capitalism and the markets, either to criticize the Deleuzo-Guattarian philosophy or to celebrate it. Third (Chapter 4), a revolutionary interpretation sought to connect Deleuze and Guattari with revolutionary politics, either through a dialogue with Marxism or outside of Marxism. My own position belongs to the revolutionary reception which tries to create a 'resonance' with Marx (Thoburn 2003: 1). Therefore, in the second part of this book, I shall apply my revolutionary interpretation of Deleuze and Guattari to the question of financialization, as it is understood by Marxian literature (Chapter 5). Conversely, applying a situated revolutionary interpretation of Deleuze and Guattari demonstrates the relevance of the first part of the book; that is to say the analysis of the reception of Deleuze and Guattari.

As I have already noted above, at the end of his life Deleuze stated in a conversation with Negri: 'I think Felix Guattari and I have remained Marxists, in our two different ways, perhaps, but both of us. You see, we think any political philosophy must turn on the analysis of capitalism and the ways it has developed' (Deleuze and Negri, 1995: 171).

For Deleuze and Guattari, philosophy or the creation of concepts was inseparable from a reflection on the capitalist system. In the quotation above, Deleuze put an emphasis on studying the recent transformations of capitalism: 'capitalism and the ways it has developed' (Deleuze and Negri 1995: 171). Therefore, he was aware that capitalism was not as some orthodox Marxists would maintain a monolithic system with an unchanging functioning and organization since the industrial revolution. Arguably, the analysis of the effect of finance on capitalism since the 1970s is a project that coheres with the Marxist problematic of Deleuze and Guattari and their intention to seriously analyse capitalism.

Financialization is a complex phenomenon that Deleuze and Guattari were not fully able to understand, despite their efforts to invent concepts like 'Integrated World Capitalism' (Guattari 2000: 105), 'machinic surplus value' (1987: 453) and 'societies of control' (Deleuze 1992a), which anticipated some of the arguments of the Marxian literature on financialization. I shall therefore engage with the contemporary Marxian literature on financialization in order to understand the role of finance in our world (Chapter 5). Next, I shall show how Deleuze and Guattari as well as Foucault were able to anticipate some of the transformations of financialization and how they disagree with most of the Marxian politics of the literature on financialization (Chapter 6).

Finally, I shall elaborate a Deleuzo-Guattarian politics of resistance to financialization that will seek to provide a practical reflection on combatting the power of finance (Chapter 7). In order to perform this task, I shall draw on the failure of the French social-democratic attempt to regulate finance with President Hollande and the Occupy Wall Street movement. I shall argue that financialization needs to be resisted through a horizontal politics grounded on an itinerant politics and the notion of event. This Deleuzo-Guattarian politics will avoid two opposite problems: 'speculative leftism' (Bosteels 2005) and providing a blueprint (Lenin 1969).

5   Understanding financialization

Introduction

It was during the financial crisis of 2007–2008 that people in the Global North realized the extent of the power of finance upon the world and the lives of individuals. I shall draw on a critical, interdisciplinary and Marxian literature to analyse the phenomenon of financialization (Bonefeld and Holloway 1995b; Bryan and Rafferty 2006; Bryan et al. 2009; Duménil and Lévy 2011; Epstein 2005; Harvey 2005; Lazzarato 2009, 2012; McNally 2009; Martin et al. 2008; Martin 2002, 2007; Mirowski 2009, 2013).

In fact, there is a historical gap between the development of financialization and the analyses by Deleuze and Guattari on capitalism. Financialization developed gradually from the 1970s to the financial crisis of 2007–2008, while Deleuze and Guattari produced their analyses of capitalism mainly in the 1970s in *Anti-Oedipus* (1977) and *A Thousand Plateaus* (1987). In particular, at the time of the 2007–2008 crisis, Deleuze and Guattari had been dead for more than a decade. Deleuze died in 1995 and Guattari in 1992.

Social and economic processes are not eternal essences that can be discovered by philosophers, social scientists or economists. This means that social and economic processes do not have immutable laws embedded in a hypothetical human nature. Social and economic processes are produced by history, as argued by Marx and Engels, for instance in the *Communist Manifesto*: 'History of all hitherto existing societies is the history of class struggle' (1969: 14). It is not possible to study social and economic processes before they actually take place historically. It is therefore necessary to consider contemporary literature rather than the works of Deleuze and Guattari for an analysis of financialization. I shall, however, confront contemporary literature on financialization with the works of Deleuze and Guattari in the next chapter (Chapter 6).

Financialization has substantially changed the role of finance within the framework of the economy and of society. Finance no longer mainly consists of providing credit and investment to the economy used to be the case in the context of a Fordist capitalism (Bryan and Rafferty 2006). Finance permeates all the spheres of the economy and of life. To use a Marxist vocabulary, the production as well as the reproduction of capitalism are directly connected to finance or financial logics. They are therefore financialized. In other words, the domain of the production of commodities as well as its cultural, social and subjective conditions are financialized.

The aim of this chapter, however, is to provide an engagement with the Marxian and multidisciplinary literature on financialization. I shall perform three tasks in this chapter.

First, I shall provide a brief history of finance and its transformations since 1945. This will allow me to historicize and contextualize the phenomenon of financialization, which will entail an explanation of how the Bretton Woods financial system was ended. In order to do this, I shall draw on a Marxian literature to demonstrate that financialization is connected to the historical phenomenon of neoliberalism (Harvey 2005; Mirowski 2009, 2013). In the next chapter, I shall discuss neoliberalism drawing on Foucault (2008).

Second, I shall review the contemporary Marxian literature on financialization. This will allow me to provide an account of financialization and its functioning, and to show how financialization is related to derivatives (Bryan and Rafferty 2006), to social reproduction (Dowling and Harvie 2014), to debt (Lazzarato 2012) and even to the state and public policies (Martin 2007) as well as to subjectivity (Martin 2002). Additionally, I shall criticize the social studies of finance approach.

Third, I shall assess the politics of this Marxian literature on financialization. The Marxian literature on financialization argues that class politics and of the notion of revolutionary subject should be operated to resist financialization.

A brief history of finance: from 1945 till the present day

In this section, I shall provide a brief history of finance since 1945 to contextualize the phenomenon of financialization. I shall first operate an analysis of the Bretton Woods financial system, and I shall then explain why it was ended. To be able to perform this task, I shall draw on a Marxian political economic literature.

The Bretton Woods financial system, 1945–1971

At the end of the Second World War the world financial system and the world economy were transformed with a regulative line (Hobsbawm 1994: 274). The Bretton Woods financial system provided a 'reconstitution of the global financial system' which had been broken by the Great Depression and the Second World War (Bryan and Rafferty, 2006: 112). Generally speaking, the Bretton Woods financial system was connected to the implementation of Keynesian macroeconomic policies:

> the new goal was economic certainty and stability and the asserted agenda was nation-centred accumulation, with open international trade being re-established. This regime allowed for the privileging of social programmes and full employment, funded by high (and managed) levels of

economic growth. In simple terms, we can associate this with the rise of "Keynesianism".

(Bryan and Rafferty 2006: 112)

The Bretton Woods agreements wanted to facilitate international trade in a context characterized by regulated finance. International finance was regulated with the Bretton Woods system because international financial flows were the 'swing mechanism', as opposed to wages (Bryan and Rafferty 2006: 113). This was operated in order to facilitate international trade as there was a consensus that increased trade would restore prosperity. International financial flows of capital were strictly controlled. It was decided that the dollar was the 'global trading currency, with the dollar convertible to gold at a rate of $35 per ounce' (Bryan and Rafferty 2006: 113). Problems appeared because the amount of dollars became gradually disconnected from the gold reserves of the United States. Furthermore, some financial problems appeared through international flows of capital:

> Within the policy trilemma, the Bretton Woods Agreement worked in providing national social policy agendas and stable exchange rates only so long as the proclivity of capital to expand could be contained mainly to within national borders or directed though international trade. Yet the momentum of capital to expand internationally had not evaporated in 1944, and there was continual pressure on nation states, especially from financial institutions, to facilitate this expansion.
>
> (Bryan and Rafferty 2006: 114)

In the 1950s, the Bretton Woods financial system was first tested with the Eurodollar markets (Obstfeld and Taylor 2004: 159). These financial markets did not provide the identity of their clients. The Eurodollar markets were used by Western corporations and communist countries to escape the national legislations of the United States and other countries of the Bretton Woods system. The Eurodollar markets represented $20 billion in the middle of the 1960s (Bryan and Rafferty 2006: 114). They were constituted by financial operations between banks, as opposed to the spot market. Typically, large corporations could find an 'alternative source of cheap and large volume finance, offering interest rates and exchange rates that differed from those under national regulation' (Bryan and Rafferty 2006: 115). Even though the Eurodollar markets had started in the 1950s, it was in the 1960s that they developed dramatically. This was an important source of tension for the Bretton Woods financial system.

From finance to financialization: from 1971 till the present day

The Bretton Woods financial system was ended by Nixon's devaluation of the dollar in September 1971, which gradually brought about free-floating rates between currencies (Bryan and Rafferty 2006: 118). Nevertheless, the US dollar remained the most important currency. This provided a deregulation of finance and an explosion of international financial flows. Finance became increasingly important in the world economy, which produced a financialization; that is, 'the increasing role of financial motives, financial markets, financial actors and financial institutions in the operation of the domestic and international economies' (Epstein 2005: 3).

In particular, there was a surge in the profit rate of US financial corporations in 1974 and a profit rate of US financial corporations in excess of US industrial corporations in 1982 (Duménil and Lévy 2005: 38, Figure 2.11). This brought about an increase of the US ratio of the net worth of financial corporations to that of non-financial corporations from around 10 per cent in the early 1970s to 30 per cent in 2000 (Duménil and Lévy 2005: 40, Figure 2.12). Consequently, because of the higher rate of profit of the financial sector, non-financial corporations started making money in the financial sector. General Electric, for instance, made large profits through banking activities (McNally 2009: 56). Similarly, the ratio of portfolio income to cash flow for US non-financial corporations more than doubled between the early 1970s and 2000 (Krippner 2005: 185, Figure 4). Financialization was also marked by the increase in the financialization of individual income through debt, for instance through student debt or mortgages or private pension funds (Lapavitsas 2011: 623). Not only did corporations become financialized, but so did individual income through, for example, a financialization of student debt or American mortgages.

The end of the Bretton Woods financial system and current financialization still need to be explained. Three groups of explanations exist within the Marxian literature. The first (Lapavitsas 2011; Pollin 2007; Wade 2008) considers financialization to be the linear result of a deregulation which resulted in an increase of fictitious capital. This is thought to have prevented the real economy from growing and to have generated a series of crises, including the systemic crisis of 2007–2008. The second explanation claims that financialization corresponds to a crisis of Keynesianism, which may never have been solved; that is, a crisis of over-accumulation (Arrighi 1994, 2007; Bonefeld and Holloway 1995b; Brenner 2006). A third position argues that financialization was able to respond to the Keynesian crisis of over-accumulation even though it has caused a 'world-slump' since the crisis of 2007–2008 (McNally 2009).

The first explanation primarily linking financialization (Lapavitsas 2011; Pollin 2007; Wade 2008) to the deregulation of financial markets does not take account of the crisis of Keynesianism and of the Bretton Woods financial system. The rate of profit at the end of the 1960s had fallen, in particular because of the progressive struggles of the 1960s (Holloway 1995: 22). Keynesianism had been a capitalist response to 'the power of labour . . . dramatically illustrated in the "red October" of 1917', but it was structurally challenged by the struggles of the 1960s (Holloway 1995: 8). Furthermore, this position (Lapavitsas 2011; Pollin 2007; Wade 2008) implies a form of nostalgia for the Fordist era of capitalism, which it might be possible to bring back through a form of re-regulation, as though it were possible to stabilize the dynamic process of capitalism.

The second explanation focuses on more structural issues: financialization brought about by the continuation of the crisis of Keynesianism and of the Fordist regime of accumulation (Arrighi 1994 2007; Bonefeld and Holloway 1995b; Brenner 2006). Arrighi constructs this argument within the framework of world-systems theory (1994, 2007). According to Arrighi, world capitalism has been characterized since the Middle Ages by a series of hegemonies centred round Genoa, the United Provinces, Britain and the United States (2007: 93). A specific hegemony is characterized by a moment of accumulation (American Fordism, for instance) and production, followed by a moment of 'over-accumulation crises to bring about long periods of financial expansions', which correspond to the decline of a global hegemony; that is, of the United States for our contemporary period (Arrighi 2007: 93). The specific issue with Arrighi's interpretation of the current financialization, however, is that China is lending money to the United States, whereas it should be the opposite if China is to be the successor of the United States (Lapavitsas 2011: 616).

Another version of this second explanation is provided by the open Marxist school (Bonefeld and Holloway 1995b). Financialization is understood to be a result of the 'crisis of Keynesianism' (Bonefeld and Holloway 1995a: 3). Keynesianism was a strategy to make sure 'labour's insubordinate power is integrated into the capital relation' through Fordism, that is to say high wages, strong discipline and deskilling (Bonefeld and Holloway 1995a: 4). Because of the revolutionary struggles of the 1960s against capital and the state, however, it became increasingly complicated for capital to exploit living labour (Holloway 1995: 24). Therefore:

> Since the late 1960s, depressed rates of productive accumulation have coincided with a rapid monetary accumulation . . . Credit has not been transformed into command over labour for the purpose of expanded surplus accumulation . . . Speculation does not meet with the same resistance that capital encounters in the factory.
>
> (Bonefeld 1995: 61)

Financialization and the correlative development of debt were the consequence of the incapacity of capital to operate a 'profitable integration of labour into the capital relation' (Bonefeld 1995: 63).

I shall now turn to the third explanation. For all its subtlety, the second explanation was not able to see that the crisis of Keynesianism had been overcome by capitalism through a 'new wave of capitalist expansion . . . centred on East Asia' (McNally 2009: 35). In fact, after the crisis of Keynesianism in the 1970s, a capitalist accumulation started in 1983 in East Asia, which increased the rates of exploitation and profit through, in particular, 'foreign direct investment' and 'lean management' (McNally 2009: 45). Accumulation in East Asia was fostered by financialization through foreign direct investment; that is to say international flows of capital (McNally 2009: 54). It is possible to notice a rebound of the rate of profit in the United States from 1983 till 1997 (Mohun 2006: 348, Figure 1).

The Asian crisis of 1997 'signalled the onset of new problems of over-accumulation that shape the contours of the present crisis' (McNally 2009: 46). Later, a 'massive expansion of credit *did* underpin rates of growth, concentrating profound sources of instability in the financial sector', which brought about the crisis of 2007–2008 (McNally 2009: 46). Therefore, the crisis of 2007–2008 was connected to credit and debt as autonomist Marxists argue (Caffentzis 2013b: 2).

Financialization and neoliberalism

Financialization needs to be understood in relation to neoliberalism. Neoliberalism provided the political conditions that brought about financialization and its effects on the various spheres of the economy, subjectivity or government. Financialization required the intellectual and political operations of neoliberalism. I shall draw on the works of Mirowski to explain the emergence of neoliberalism as a 'neoliberal thought collective' (2009, 2013). Mirowski (2013: 93–102) is partly critical of Foucault's analysis of neoliberalism (2008) with which I shall engage in the next chapter. Mirowski operated a form of ideology critique of neoliberalism. Mirowski explicitly connects neoliberalism, finance and financialization because as a matter of principle 'neoliberals begin with a presumption that capital has a natural right to flow freely across national boundaries' (2009: 438).

The political success of neoliberalism, which makes financialization possible, was brought about by the work of the 'neoliberal thought collective' (Mirowski 2009, 2013). Mirowski explains that the concept 'thought collective' was chosen 'to refer to this multilevel, multiphase, multisector approach to the building of political capacity to incubate, critique, and promulgate ideas' (2013: 43).

Most neoliberals subscribe to the Efficient Market Hypothesis for all, including financial markets (Mirowski 2009: 264). The Efficient Market Hypothesis in relation to financial markets was thought out by a member of the Chicago School, Eugen Fama (1965). A principle for neoliberals is that 'the market . . . can always provide solutions to problems seemingly caused by the market in the first place' (Mirowski 2009: 439). Arguably, this contributed among other factors to the neoliberals' lack of critique of the mechanisms of the financial markets after the crisis of 2007–2008. In particular, neoliberals blamed state interventionism through the voice of Fannie Mae and Freddie Mac (Mirowski 2013: 52). Other neoliberals (Schiller 2013), however, do not subscribe to the Efficient Market Hypothesis and advocate behavioural economics. This allows the neoliberal thought collective to be all the more effective since it is able to play both sides of an argument.

Neoliberalism was first able to take over power in Chile (Taylor 2006), then in Britain, with Margaret Thatcher in 1979 and in the United States with Ronald Reagan in 1980. Later, neoliberalism became the dominant form of governance in the Global South through the International Monetary Fund, the World Banks and a series of adjustment programmes demanding structural reforms, for instance in Africa (Caffentzis 2002). The Washington consensus during the 1990s symbolized this neoliberal governance of globalization (De Angelis 2003).

In fact, neoliberalism was able to promote political ideas based on 'a shared political philosophy and worldview' (Mirowski 2009: 418). Today, these political ideas represent the hegemonic political understanding of reality. Neoliberalism is characterized by a critique of the laissez faire of classical liberalism because it maintains that 'conditions for its existence must be constructed and will not come about "naturally" in the absence of concerted political effort and organisation' (Mirowski, 2013: 434). The neoliberals themselves would not emphasize this point because of rhetorical reasons as the Adam Smith Institute shows. Therefore, neoliberalism is a complex political and cultural phenomenon that was promoted by the 'neoliberal thought collective':

> What holds neoliberals together first and foremost is a set of epistemic commitments, however much it might be ultimately rooted in economics, or politics, or even science. It didn't start out like that; but a half-century of hard work by the neoliberal thought collective has wrought a program that rallies round a specific vision of the role of knowledge in human affairs.
>
> (Mirowski, 2009: 417)

Another important idea of the neoliberal thought collective is that competition should be promoted. In other words, market mechanisms require winners and losers so as to operate successfully: 'It tags every possible disaster as the consequences of risk-bearing, the personal fallout from making "bad choices" in investments. It is a world where competition is the primary virtue, and solidarity a sign of weakness' (Mirowski, 2013: 92). By contrast, the classical liberal conception maintains that the market produces exchange with no losers.

Mirowski argues that the neoliberal thought collective operated as a 'structure of intellectual discourse, perhaps unprecedented in the 1940s, one I would venture to propose to think of as a "Russian doll" approach to the integration of research and praxis in the modern world' (2013: 43). Accordingly, the Mont Pèlerin Society functioned as the centre of the Russian doll of the neoliberal thought collective. The Mont Pèlerin Society was an international organization with figures such as Friedrich von Hayek and Milton Friedman, who effectively constructed and promoted neoliberalism (Mirowski 2013: 49).

The political ideas of neoliberalism were never unified as the Mont Pèlerin society consisted of three schools of thought: 'the Austrian-inflected Hayekian legal theory, the Chicago School of neoclassical economics, and the German Ordoliberals' (Mirowski 2013: 41–42).

Finally, David Harvey argued that neoliberalism operates as 'a *political* project to re-establish the conditions for capital accumulation and to restore the power of economic elites' (2005: 19). Fundamentally according to Harvey, neoliberalism is characterized by an 'accumulation by dispossession', performing a kind of primitive accumulation (2005: 160). For Harvey the class project defined by accumulation by dispossession is characterized by 'privatization' (2005: 160), 'financialization' (2005: 161), 'The management and manipulation of crises' (2005: 162) and 'State redistribution' (2005: 163). Therefore, financialization constitutes an instrument of the economic elite used to restore its class power.

The approaches to neoliberalism that I discussed above are marked by Marxism. Therefore, they are different from Foucault's take on neoliberalism which I will analyse in the next chapter. I will argue in the next chapter that Foucault is critical about Marxism.

Contemporary literature on financialization

I provided, above, a brief history of finance since 1945. The engagement of Deleuze and Guattari with the question of finance was unable to offer a whole analysis of financialization. I shall therefore now turn to the literature on financialization to describe the most important features of the phenomenon.

Financialization and derivatives

Derivatives have been central in the financialization process. This was demonstrated by the importance of specific derivatives backed by American 'subprime' mortgages during the crisis of 2007–2008; that is, credit default swaps and collateralized debt obligations.

Bryan and Rafferty developed an original take on financialization in *Capitalism with Derivatives: A Political Economy of Financial Derivatives, Capital and Class* (2006). Even though Bryan and Rafferty are not orthodox Marxists, their analysis of finance is critical of capitalism and clearly connected to the problematic of Marxism. Bryan and Rafferty argue that derivatives are the most important components of finance and financialization. They date this dominance of derivatives in finance back to the 'mid-1980s' (Bryan and Rafferty 2006: 130). Derivatives have been essential because:

> They reveal finance as a driver of accumulation not just in terms of providing the funds that are used in investment or exchange, but in computing the value of assets, and thereby determining the benchmark of asset performance. This is what inserts derivatives into the explanation of class relations and of social change.
>
> (Bryan and Rafferty 2006: 213–214)

Accordingly, financialization through derivatives has had a huge impact on the evolution of society for 30 years. Against most authors with the exception of some mainstream analysts of finance (for instance, Steinherr 2000), Bryan and Rafferty argue that derivatives have become central to the functioning of finance, as opposed to more traditional securities such as shares or bonds. It is essential to take into account the specific relevance of derivatives in the functioning of contemporary capitalism. Bryan and Rafferty (2006) do not remain at the level of a global perspective of finance because they try to specify the very mechanisms of financialization. The Black–Scholes formula for 'pricing options', for instance, was essential for the development of derivatives (Black and Scholes 1973).

Bryan and Rafferty explain that derivatives operate several tasks. First, derivatives function as money for global capitalism, with all its properties:

> First, money's "invention" was based upon the impracticalities of direct barter in complex processes of exchange. The selected money must have three characteristics of portability, divisibility, homogeneity and indestructibility. Second, money must perform 3 functions: a medium of exchange, a store of value, and a unit of account . . . Third, money can be defined differently according to degrees of liquidity (convertibility into cash).
>
> (Bryan and Rafferty 2006: 143–144)

According to Bryan and Rafferty derivatives constitute a 'commodity money' like gold during the gold standard, as opposed to a pure conventional money such as the dollar since 1971 (2006: 143–144). Bryan and Rafferty argue that derivatives are the commodity money of global capitalism. Second, through derivatives, capital operates a constant commensuration of the different factors of production. Hence, derivatives are facilitators of increased competition between factors of production. This competition operates at all the levels, even though it is particularly ruthless on labour: 'It is a race for profitability . . . Labour that cannot deliver globally competitive levels of productivity must compensate, as it were, for its less than frontier productivity by accepting longer hours and lower wages' (Bryan and Rafferty, 2006: 176).

Financialization is linked to the fact that finance has become connected to the functioning of the everyday economy and production. Derivatives have become the money of contemporary capitalism. Derivatives and finance operate as an instrument of universal pricing of the economy. Anything that can be priced is priced with derivatives. Derivatives have become the instrument of capitalism in order to measure value. Derivatives perform this measuring either for the present of the economy or for the future with specific securities such as futures or forwards. The very fact of providing a universal instrument for measuring value, that is to say a universal money, operates an intensification of exploitation of labour. However, Bryan and Rafferty along with Martin develop the idea in an article that labour has 'become a capital' through financialization (Bryan et al. 2009).

Furthermore, Bryan and Rafferty articulate a historical explanation about derivatives in relation to property and capitalism. Bryan and Rafferty argue that capitalism is characterized by three stages in relation to property of the means of production (2006: 70). The first stage is marked by the fact that the manager of a company is the owner of the means of production. There is no separation between ownership of the means of production and management of a corporation. This corresponds to the beginning of capitalism as was described by Adam Smith and classical liberalism. The second stage is characterized by a separation between the ownership of the means of production and the management of a company (Bryan and Rafferty 2006: 72). This corresponds to the joint stock company. Shareholders own the means of production. However, they do not manage the companies they own, even though they appoint the CEOs.

This second stage started in the 1860s and required the juridical innovation of corporate personhood. According to Bryan and Rafferty, the third stage is related to derivatives because

> Derivatives have taken the logic of capital beyond the bottom line (annual profit rates) and into the details of each phase of production and distribution, because they permit the corporation as legal entity to continually verify the market value of its component "pieces" of capital.
>
> (Bryan and Rafferty 2006: 96)

Through derivatives, capitalism divides corporations into small capitals which are constantly compared, priced and traded beyond the question of the ownership of the shares of a specific joint-stock company.

Derivatives perform the functions of binding the 'future to the present' (Harvie 2008a: 74) and of providing a universal measurement device to capitalism. This increases competition and discipline for labour and different capitals. Financialization therefore allows capitalism to operate a disciplining of labour through derivatives.

Derivatives and social reproduction

Derivatives also allow a novel financialization of the sphere of social reproduction; that is to say outside the workplace. Since the 1970s, it had been possible to trade derivatives on raw materials, agricultural products or currencies; that is, items mainly connected to production and exchange. In the 2000s, however, it also became possible to buy and sell derivatives connected to private life and personal choices; that is to say to the sphere of social reproduction which means everything which is not connected to the workplace, as opposed to the sphere of production: 'capital now dispossesses labour of that haven from market instrumentalities known as private life (Martin et al. 2008: 130).

This was brought about by the financialization of consumption. Arguably, the financialization of consumption was favoured by the relative offsetting of the stagnation of wages with 'cheap credit' since the implementation of neoliberalism (Turbulence Collective 2009: 3). The consumption through credit of the 'neoliberal deal' replaced the consumption through wage of the Keynesian era (Turbulence Collective 2009: 3). Derivatives on individual debt such as students' loans and later mortgages appeared so as to diversify financial innovation (Lewis 2010: 71).

Then, in 2004, derivatives backed on American subprime mortgages were developed by investment banks in Manhattan: 'Stage Two, beginning of the end of 2004, was to replace the student loans and the auto loans and the rest with bigger piles consisting of nothing but US subprime mortgages loans' (Lewis

2010: 71). In fact, the securitization of the mortgages of American households was involved in the financial crisis of 2007 and 2008.

The crisis of 2007–2008 was brought about by a financialization of the sphere of private life and social reproduction through home mortgages and debt. Students' loans or personal loans are also traded through derivatives and could lead to other financial crises. The analyses of financialization (Bryan and Rafferty 2006; Bryan et al. 2009; Martin et al. 2008) showed that financialization through derivatives have permeated the spheres of production and social reproduction with, in particular, private life. Financialization through derivatives has operated the real subsumption of capital. This means that capital does not only exploits labour inside factories and corporations, but as well private life and the sphere of social reproduction through providing loans to individuals in order to consume, that is to say study, buy their homes or get a medical treatment (Bryan et al. 2009: 464) and then transforming these loans into securities.

In sum, financialization has not only been about providing more credit to corporations and encouraging shareholder value (Froud and Williams 2000a, 2000b). The financialization of the economy has also implied a financialization of private life and the sphere of social reproduction. Private life and private choices have become sources of income for finance as the development of credit default swaps and collateralized debt obligations based on subprime mortgages have demonstrated.

Financialization of subjectivity

Similarly, financialization of the economy and social reproduction so as to make money had subjective and ontological consequences. People increasingly think, behave and feel like financial subjects; that is, as though they were traders or financiers managing portfolios composed of shares, bonds and derivatives within the framework of an investing strategy. Contemporary subjectivity is increasingly shaped by the financial logic. In this section, I shall draw on the works of Martin (2002) and Mirowski (2013), both of whom can be depicted as Marxian philosophers. Both in different ways perform an ideology critique of capitalism.

Martin provided a specific analysis of the notion of financialization in *Financialization of Daily Life,* the first book to connect the question of subjectivity and the question of a process of financialization (2002). Martin argues:

> But the present invitation to live by finance . . . is still being extended to players beyond the corporate world . . . Finance . . . presents as the merger of business and life cycles, as a means for the acquisition of self. The financialization of daily life is a proposal for how to get ahead, but also a medium for the expansive movements of body and soul.
>
> (2002: 3)

According to Martin, financialization has substantially increased the influence of capitalism on our ways of living, feeling and thinking on a daily basis, even though capitalism had always had some influence on subjectivities: 'In a market economy, money is both the means and ends of life' (2002: 3). This means that for Martin finance has permeated our experience of living. The financialization of life is a continuation and an embodiment of the capitalist functioning, which already meant dealing with the economy on an everyday basis. Marx identified the destructive effect of capitalism that 'drowned the most heavenly ecstasies of religious fervour, of chivalrous enthusiasm, of philistine sentimentalism, in the icy water of egotistical calculation' (Marx and Engels, 1969: 15–16). Financialization operates a qualitative leap in relation to the connection between subjectivity and capitalism. Whenever we think, feel or act we are in fact to a certain extent determined by finance. Martin, however, adds that: 'This is not to say that financialization occupies all the room of the self or monopolizes the ethical domain, but that its medium and its message make themselves known and heard above the din' (2002: 10).

According to Martin, finance greatly influences our experience of living, as opposed to totally and univocally organizing it. Clearly, for Martin finance is not just about shares, bonds stock markets or abstract figures since it shapes our most inner self. There is a social pressure to impose the idea that the life of the self should be organized and managed as a financial portfolio:

> With the new model of financial self-management, making money does not stop with wages garnered from employment. Money must be spent to live, certainly, but now daily life embraces an aspiration to make money as well. These are opportunities that quickly have obligations to invest wisely, speculate sagely, and deploy resources strategically. The market is not only a source of necessary consumables; it must be beaten. To play at life one must win over the economy.
>
> (Martin 2002: 17)

There is pressure to make money all the time and to maximize profit not only in the workplace, but also in our daily activities. According to Martin, this is well illustrated by 'day trading', which developed in the 1990s in the USA (2002: 46). The promise is that anyone can become rich by gambling on securities from home through the internet. Financialization develops the idea that anyone can become extremely wealthy irrespective of power relations and the class structure through 'hard work' and good financial decisions (Martin 2002: 51). Similarly, education since childhood should promote financialization:

> For the family to operate on a rational basis, rules must be made explicit, and all information regarding how the household is run needs to be transparent and available. But financially literate families are not only rational; they are successful.
>
> (Martin 2002: 59)

Nobel Prize winner and finance mainstream scholar Robert Schiller advocated the idea that to promote financial education could contribute to the creation of a morally better society (2013: 106). Financial literacy could help people economically realize their projects. According to Schiller therefore financializing subjectivity seems to bring about more ethics. Martin argues that finance has permeated education in the United States because parents are encouraged to teach their children how to manage money. In reality, the main principle of financialization is 'risk management':

> Risk management in terms of finance is the willingness to let capital decide one's fate but, given this decision, to place that future in the hands of others in the present. Financialization . . . makes . . . a present obligation to embrace a risk of what can be made of a promised return.
>
> (Martin 2002: 146)

Every action or behaviour should be guided by the goal to decrease risk and increase utility according to an optimum; that is to say the best possible ratio. Financialization entails a constant rational calculation of risks and benefits. Education is supposed to teach children how to calculate efficiently, or to always act as if they were traders on a trading floor. At the same time, more risks should be taken to increase possible returns. Risk management can therefore be an ambiguous notion because zero risk financial portfolios entail very little profits.

The financialization of subjectivity caused a transformation of the subjective relationship to one's body. The body is thought of as a financial portfolio that requires to be managed according to the best investment strategy. The body is divided into parts which correspond to shares, bonds or securities of a financial portfolio. This leads to what Mirowski calls a 'fragmentation of the neoliberal self' (2013: 108). Good assets need to be kept, whereas bad assets need to be sold. Therefore, every part of the body: hair, nose, breasts, muscles can be replaced, transformed or improved according to a financial management strategy.

This financialization of the subjective relationship to the body is documented in relation to plastic surgery (Mirowski 2013: 114). With plastic surgery a specific part of the body is transformed. A 'big' nose is considered as a bad asset that needs to be sold through plastic surgery. The dividend produced by the 'big' nose is not high enough. It is therefore necessary to buy another share or security with a better dividend, which the newly operated nose should provide. This financial arbitrage implies calculating the risk of the operation, which can fail. However, this risk is inferior to the risk of keeping a 'big' nose inside the financial portfolio of one's own body.

The debates around the markets of organs are another symptom of the financialization of the body. Neoliberal theorists have advocated the right to sell or buy organs, in particular Gary Becker (Becker and Elias 2007). Becker and Elias argue that 'incentives' should be provided to promote a market of organs. Accordingly, the price of 'live donations' of organs will determine the price of 'cadaveric donations' (Becker and Elias 2007: 1). According to Becker and Elias, the creation of a legal market of organs would end the current shortage of organs and would challenge the illegal market (2007: 1). Creating a market that puts a price on organs constitutes a financialization of the body, and so also of subjectivity in as much as it is embodied. This financialization of the subjective experience of the body implies a form of dematerialization of subjectivity along with a 'fragmentation' (Mirowski 2013: 107).

In particular, the internet is an environment characterized by the financialization of subjectivity. Subjectivity is turned into a financial portfolio that needs to be adequately managed to provide the highest rate of return. Internet profiles such as Facebook work in this way:

> It forces the participant to construct a "profile" from a limited repertoire of relatively stereotyped materials, challenging the person to somehow attract "friends" by tweaking their offerings to stand out from the vast run of the mill. It incorporates subtle algorithms that force participants to regularly change and augment their profiles, thus continuously destabilizing their "identity", as well as introducing real-time metrics to continuously monitor their accumulated "friends" and numbers of "hits" on their pages.
>
> (Mirowski 2013: 112–113)

I would argue that this destabilising of identities is related to Deleuze's 'dividual' within the framework of societies of control as capitalism is able to produce more fluid forms of control (1992a: 5). The Facebook profile corresponds to a financial portfolio requiring constant monitoring from the user to sell the bad assets and keep the good ones according to the number of 'likes'. Augmenting a Facebook profile is like managing a financial portfolio. From this perspective, Facebook with its millions of profiles corresponds to a financial market that creates a competition between securities. There is an ontological correspondence between Facebook profiles and financial markets. There is competition between Facebook profiles to attract more 'friends' and get more 'likes'. The competition between profiles on Facebook implies that some profiles are bullish if they get many friends. By contrast, a profile's 'price' can decrease if it receives fewer 'likes' than its competitors; that is to say other Facebook profiles. Finally, Facebook profiles trading as financial markets trading – in particular day trading – are online and computerized.

Nevertheless, there is another similarity between a Facebook profile and a portfolio of securities. If the shares of a corporation decrease, this corporation can be bought and the management can change. Similarly, Facebook profiles and internet subjectivity has a profound impact on people's 'actual' lives: 'Facebook profiles then feed back into "real life": employers scan Facebook pages of prospective employees, parents check the pages of their children, lovers check Facebook pages for evidence of philandering' (Mirowski 2013: 113).

More generally, I would argue that other online services operate a financialization of subjectivity. Online dating services require users to provide profiles whose way of functioning is usually quite close to that of Facebook, even though some of them require payment from male users. In particular, users of the French dating site Meetic have to provide profiles. Other users are then contacted, and they can decide or not to start chatting. Professional networking sites like LinkedIn also require profiles.

It should be noted that internet and Facebook are becoming increasingly global. The financialization of subjectivity connected to the internet is becoming increasingly global, including in the Global South. There is evidence of an increasing usage of online social networks in the Global South, which were shown in a different context during the Arab Spring (Howard and Muzammil 2011). The financialization of subjectivity at least through the internet is therefore not limited to the United States or the Global North, but affects important fractions of the Global South as well (Martin 2002: 169).

The financial logic increasingly influences subjectivities. Subjectivity is thought of as a financial portfolio that needs to be managed to maximize profitability. It was argued that this entailed a fragmentation of subjectivity, including the subjective relationship with the body. Similarly, I argued that the internet is an important vector of the financialization of subjectivity.

Financialization and debt

Furthermore, financialization as a process is strongly connected to the question of debt. Debt is related to the financialization of the economy as well as to the financialization of subjectivity. The financial securities that brought about the crisis of 2007–2008, that is credit default swaps and collateralized debt obligations, were based on debt. In other words, the crisis of 2007–2008 can be understood as a crisis of debt (Caffentzis 2013a).

Lazzarato (2012) understands the recent transformations of capitalism in relation to the question of subjectivity and debt. Lazzarato develops an understanding of debt that draws on Nietzsche's concept of genealogy, the Marxian theory of money as well as Deleuze and Guattari's thinking on debt to which I shall return in the next chapter. His understanding of debt in the political economy of neoliberalism is twofold. According to him debt operates at the subjective molecular level as well as at the macro level of global finance: 'What is called financialization represents less a form of investment financing than an enormous mechanism for managing private and public debt and therefore, the creditor-debtor relation, through methods of securitization (Lazzarato 2012: 23).

According to Lazzarato, global finance and the financialization of the global economy that started in the 1970s is fundamentally connected to debt. Finance consists primarily of managing securitized debt. Securitized debt can be either public or private debt. Public debt corresponds to states' sovereign debt, whereas private debt corresponds to credit provided to individuals. Financialization allows the creation of specific securities and financial markets in relation to debt. In particular, sovereign debt derivative markets exist (Marazzi 2011: 120) that were responsible for the European sovereign debt crisis (Lazzarato 2012: 122).

Nonetheless, at the subjective level, that is to say at the level of personal feeling and thinking, debt can be understood as follows:

> What matters is finance's goal of reducing what will be to what is, that is, reducing the future and its possibilities to current power relations. From this

perspective, all financial innovations have one sole purpose: possessing the future in advance by objectivizing it. This objectivation is of a completely different order from that of labor time; objectivizing time, possessing it in advance, means subordinating all possibility of choice and decision which the future holds to the reproduction of capitalist power relations.

(Lazzarato 2012: 46)

According to Lazzarato, financialization operates a reification of the future of subjective life. Therefore, finance is not just about the appropriation of the labour power of a worker in an organization, but about the totality of the worker's subjectivity, which includes his future subjectivity. The financialization through debt not only captures the immediate labour power; it also captures the freedom to reflect on or imagine an alternative future. Financialization does not appropriate the future, because only an omnipotent God could succeed in doing so. Rather, it captures the virtuality of the present, or the existential experience that different possibilities are embodied in our present.

Furthermore, drawing on Deleuze and Guattari, Lazzarato argues that money as such implies a relation of power through credit and debt:

Deleuze and Guattari interpret Marxian theory starting from the relation-ship between creditor and debtor and at the same time from the univocity of the concept of production . . . It is instead the expression of an asymmetry of forces, a power to prescribe and impose modes of future exploitation, domination, and subjection. Money is first of all debt-money, created ex nihilo, which has no material equivalent other than its power to destroy/create social relations and, in particular, modes of subjectivation.

(2012: 34–35)

Money implies a power relation between a money creator, who is a creditor, and a money user, who is a debtor. This relationship of power materializes through the ontological difference between credit-money and payment-money. Finally, Lazzarato's conceptualization of debt argues that the creditor/debtor relationship is not only ontological but also anthropological:

The paradigm of the social lies not in exchange (economic and/or sym-bolic) but in credit. There is no equality (of exchange) underlying social relations, but rather an asymmetry of debt/ credit, which precedes, histori-cally and theoretically, that of production and wage labor.

(Lazzarato 2012: 11)

Students' debt, in particular, in the United States, provides an example of the financialization of social reproduction and of subjectivity. In fact, education is related to the cultural conditions of reproduction of capitalism. In the Fordist context therefore education and higher education were not primarily dedicated to the accumulation of capital. Neoliberalism, however, has transformed higher education as a source of accumulation of capital with the privatization of higher education or the considerable increase of fees. Fees for an undergraduate in Britain could cost up to £9,000 a year (Sedghi and Shepherd 2011). In the United States there is also an important increase of students' debt (Adamson 2009).

The United States' legislation in relation to students' loans and students' debt is particularly harsh. It is extremely complicated to file for personal bankruptcy in relation to students' debt, as opposed to other forms of bankruptcy: 'The 1976 bankruptcy laws passed by congress assured that student debtors have a singular status under the law, further illustrating the exceptional situation created for the financial control over this population' (Adamson 2009: 101). This can be compared to a form of serfdom.

Similarly, students' debt has implied a financialization of the subjectivity of students in relation to education beyond actual money and bankruptcy problems: 'As a figure fully imbricated in debt, the student is formed in and through the instruments of power that produce debt as a form of life' (Adamson 2009: 106). Students are encouraged to think of studying as an investment in relation to the future. Therefore, studies can be considered as a portfolio of securities which requires to be managed adequately. Philosophy, humanities or social sciences degrees, for example, are not valuable financial assets with important returns unlike finance or law degrees.

Students have to spend more time thinking about financing their studies and paying off their student debts: 'It would perhaps not be an exaggeration to suggest that students spend more time on personal finance . . . than on actual study. All the while, students are asked to consider their very education as an investment in their future' (Beverungen et al. 2009: 265).

Studying is not considered a human experience, which is supposed to provide an intellectual engagement with an academic discipline: 'By assigning measure to the life of the mind, student debt relegates it to an indefinite and controlled existence' (Adamson 2009: 107). Studying is no longer considered a *Bildung*; that is, the construction of a humanistic culture allowing someone to become a responsible person and citizen. The classical relationship to higher education was also harshly criticized as being a bourgeois relationship to knowledge (Bourdieu and Passeron 1979). The classical relationship to higher education and culture, however, is challenged by financialization and student debts.

Microfinance is another important form of financialization through debt. Microcredit means providing small loans to poor people, who do not have access to traditional forms of credit. Supposedly, microcredit should be able to alleviate poverty especially in the Global South. Microcredit was launched by the Grameen bank in Bangladesh, in 1976 (Martin 2007: 32). Microcredit was 'adopted by the World Bank' (Morgan and Olsen 2011: 192). The founder of the Grameen bank, Mohammed Yunus, was awarded the Nobel Prize in 2005. Microcredit can be provided by a variety of financial actors such as commercial banks, state banks, cooperative banks, NGOs and self-help groups (Morgan and Olsen 2011: 189).

Arguably, there is a relationship between microcredit and the increase in debt in the Global South because 'debt does not tend to be a short-term commitment that is then paid off. Debt tends to be renewed, and possibly expanded' (Morgan and Olsen 2011: 205). Martin argues that the relationship between the Global North and the Third World is marked by financialization through microcredit, which is based on credit and debt:

> One vehicle has been the advent of the village bank, a microfinance institution backed by government, nongovernmental organization (NGO), or private bank. Rather than placing blame for success or failure on a state or development agency, these banks operate through "peer pressure".
>
> (2002: 165)

According to Martin, the exploitation of the Third World by the Global North is characterized by microcredit, and hence debt. Rather than just plundering the resources of the Third World as within the imperialist paradigm (Lenin 1999; Luxembourg 1971), financialization transfers the responsibility of repaying the interest on their loans on the inhabitants of the Third World. This brings about a financialization of the subjectivities of Third World people, which creates a subjective disciplinarization (De Angelis 2001) of the users of microfinance since they have to behave correctly in order to meet their financial obligations; namely, repay their debts. Finally, disciplinarization through debt is usually targeted at 'women', because they tend to be granted loans, for example in India (Morgan and Olsen 2011: 190). This implies the exercising of power upon women through gendered violence (Johnson 2005).

Financialization and the state

Furthermore, financialization processes influenced state functioning. State action was permeated by the financial logic. Arguably, a Fordist logic of state functioning was replaced to a certain extent by a financialized logic. I shall analyse two domains of state action, namely the welfare state and war. Welfare was a trademark of Fordism and of the Keynesian form of capitalism. The main idea developed, by Beveridge in particular, was that the state should provide everyone with education, healthcare, unemployment benefits, pensions as well as a number of other entitlements (Hobsbawm 1994: 267). Citizens had a right to claim what they were entitled to. In Marxist terms, the welfare state implied that the state had to organize the social and cultural reproduction of capitalism.

Neoliberalism has consistently attacked the welfare state for being too expensive and not sufficiently efficient. In the French context, the benefits of 'contract workers in the cultural industry' were cut as a result of a neoliberal reform in 2003 (Lazzarato 2009: 117). Similarly, as I have already argued, higher education tends to be increasingly privatized and financialized. The creation of social impact bonds in Britain demonstrated the government's intention of financializing social reproduction and its traditional functions (Dowling and Harvie

2014). Social impact bonds operate through social impact bonds markets set up by the British government.

The rationale is that social impact bonds would help promote entrepreneurship within the framework of traditional state functions. This would contribute to more efficiency for these state functions, which supposedly had been carried out insufficiently by civil servants. Bonds are supposed to be issued for a specific social problem like the reduction of poverty in a specific zone or the rehabilitation of former convicts. Social impact bonds would represent a financialization of the crisis of social reproduction (Caffentzis 1999). If the objectives are met according to measurable targets, when bonds mature then bonds are paid. These social impacts bonds can be traded and exchanged on a market like any other financial securities. In other words, social impact bonds are a literal financialization of state action. Even though they are not yet very developed, they could become more used in the future. The fiscal crisis of the state is connected to the implementation of this measure, because it is a means to reduce expenditure in relation to the welfare state.

Furthermore, war and the army have become increasingly financialized, in particular in the United States (Martin 2007). Martin argues that American foreign policy no longer operates through Fordist imperialism, which plans the exploitation of Third World's resources to supply its domestic industry (Lenin 1999; Luxembourg 1971). In contrast, current American foreign policy operates through a financialized logic: 'While not reducible to the interests of finance capital, war today takes on a financial logic in the way it is organized and prosecuted' (Martin 2007: 2). Military operations operate through 'securitization' (Martin 2007: 18); that is, the breaking up and spreading of risk in financial assets is a technique of risk management.

According to Martin, the notion of pre-emptive war is connected to the financial logic of risk management:

> Enemies are to be defeated before they can make their antagonism manifest. Contingencies of the future are to be lived out in the present, blurring the distinction between the not-yet and the now. By converting potential threats into actual conflicts, the war on terror transfers uncertainty into present risk
>
> (2007: 3)

For instance, waging a pre-emptive war in Iraq would have been a means of reducing global uncertainty in the Middle East from the point of view of American strategic logic. Furthermore, according to Martin, American foreign policy is capable of dealing with volatility:

> Special Forces are meant to eliminate targets before a formal battle is joined. They are trained to undertake greater personal risk in exchange for the prospect of substantial politico-military reward. In this regard they are the military's arbitrageurs. The volatility of war is isolated and contained by

concentrated and precise intervention. The small-scale operation of the quick and clean surgical strike on highly focused targets is leveraged to the larger strategic ambitions of the larger war theatre.

(2007: 10)

Special Forces can be viewed as corresponding to traders operating highly specific and leveraged operations on financial markets. The profits made by a trader on a single trade can be very important as is for instance an intervention by the Special Forces to eliminate a terrorist leader. From this perspective, the concept of 'war on terror' corresponds to financialization of war and foreign policy, as opposed to the Fordism of the Cold War and its industrial competition measured in terms of atomic missiles and tanks between the United States and the Soviet Union.

A specific market was developed in relation to the military, namely the policy analysis market: 'This betting market, known as the "Policy Analysis Market" (PAM) was part of a US Defense Department Advanced Research Projects Agency (DARPA) sponsored programme entitled "FutureMAP" (an acronym for "Futures Markets Applied to Prediction")' (Lightfoot and Lilley 2007: 83–84). The policy analysis market project was designed by the Pentagon. The project was abandoned, however, after two senators announced on 28 July 2003 that the Pentagon wanted to create a market that could predict terrorist attacks and that terrorists could bet on it (Lilley and Lightfoot 2007: 83). Even though the project was finally rejected, the very project of a policy analysis market to predict future terrorist attacks demonstrates the influence of financial logic on the American military. The Pentagon saw markets as super-efficient information-processing machines that could be operated for intelligence and foreign-policy ends through a policy analysis market.

I have provided an analysis of the phenomenon of financialization that draws on a Marxian literature. Financialization is a phenomenon that has permeated the spheres of production, social reproduction, subjectivity and the state.

Social studies of finance

Social studies of finance and the scholarship on finance that draws on actor network theory provide revealing descriptions of financial processes in terms of social, technological and material processes. Social studies of finance can cause some challenging of mainstream finance through an emphasis on the materiality, the social construction or the performativity of financial markets (Callon 2007; MacKenzie 2006; MacKenzie and Millo 2003). Social studies of finance and actor network theory approaches to finance do not, however, provide the historical and international understanding of financialization provided by the Marxian literature on financialization because they remain stuck at micro levels. Also, social studies of finance and actor network theory approaches to finance seem unable to articulate any politics or ethics that might resist financialization.

Actor network theory deals with the question of the role of the agents that produce finance through material processes. Actor network theory develops an alternative social science for which the social reality is constructed by material, technical and natural objects as much as by humans through a series of translations between actors. The difference between the social world and the natural worlds are deconstructed (Latour 2005: 10–11). In particular, through the material construction of financial markets, actor network theory confronts the issue of the subjectivity of professionals working in financial organizations and how subjectivity is shaped by boundary objects such as shares for instance (Blomberg et al. 2012).

Social studies of finance envisage finance as a social phenomenon. According to social studies of finance, finance is a socially constructed phenomenon that can be investigated unlike natural phenomena using a sociological methodology. Social studies of finance can therefore be understood as a critique of the mainstream view that considers finance as efficient markets (Fama 1965). Social studies of finance are multidisciplinary and, hence, combine different approaches mainly from sociology and social studies of science and technology (MacKenzie 2009: 8).

Social studies also draw from actor network theory and ethnography (MacKenzie, 2009: 9); they should, however, not be confused with actor network theory, because 'individual human beings are embedded in *agencements*' (MacKenzie 2009: 9) rather than considered on a par with other types of actors. In other words, social studies of finance still describe individuals even though they are embodied, contextualized and embedded (Preda 2009: 7).

Politics of the financialization literature

I have engaged with the question of financialization. I have reviewed an important Marxian literature upon financialization, because for historical reasons the works of Deleuze and Guattari do not provide extensive analyses on the subject. Having drawn on the analyses of financialization provided by Marxian literature, I would like to examine political responses to financialization in terms of political resistance. In order to operate this task, I shall focus on two central themes: class politics and revolutionary subject.

Class politics

Financialization was analysed as an economic as well as a subjective process. Harvey identifies financialization as a distinctive feature of neoliberalism (2005: 33). Neoliberalism, however, and hence also financialization are understood in terms of class politics; that is to say as an upper-class offensive (Harvey 2005: 62). Resisting financialization would therefore for Harvey imply an alternative class project that would allow the victims of neoliberalism to unify as a class. Since neoliberalism, of which financialization is an essential trait, is a conscious and clear class strategy of the upper class (Harvey 2005: 201), a counter class strategy needs to be operated. The upper class however, as opposed to the working class, initiated the fight by attacking Keynesianism and 'class compromise between capital and labour' (Harvey 2005: 10) because of the fall of the rate of profit at the end of the 1960s. Accordingly, the 'restoration power' operated by the upper class was demonstrated by the increase in inequalities as a result of, for example, the reduction of higher tax brackets in the US (Harvey 2005: 26).

Identifying the class enemy is not easy since neoliberalism 'changed the locus of upper- class economic power significantly' (Harvey 2005: 31). Harvey therefore characterizes the new upper class of neoliberalism, and hence of financialization as:

> Disparate groups of individuals embedded in the corporate, financial, trading, and developer worlds do not necessarily conspire as a class, and while there may be frequent tensions between them, they nevertheless possess a certain accordance of interests that generally recognizes the advantages (and now some of the dangers) to be derived from neoliberalization.
>
> (2005: 36)

Class resistance against financialization could be organized through elections and social-democratic politics: 'Given the volatility, there is no reason to rule out the resurgence of popular social democratic . . . politics within the US in future years' (Harvey 2005: 199). The idea would be to operate class struggle through representative democracy and then to perform a regulation of finance through the state.

Similarly, Martin, Rafferty and Bryan insist on 'class politics' to resist financialization (2008: 127). Their description of financialization is supposed to favour a class politics allowing 'transformative politics and profound historical reconfigurations' (Martin et al. 2008: 128). Bryan and Rafferty, however, admitted in 2009 that 'an emergent politics of financialization awaits' and that it still needed to be operated along the lines of a class politics (2009: 360). Bryan and Rafferty argue that financialization intensify the exploitation of labour. This means that a politics that resists financialization should be grounded on living labour. McNally also considers that a crisis produced by financialization is an opportunity to operate class politics from a clearly Marxist perspective to provide the 'revolutionary capacities of the world's workers to remake the world' (2009: 79).

Furthermore, Lazzarato understands the debt problem created by financialization in terms of 'class struggle' (2012: 7). For Lazzarato, debt consists of 'the most general and most deterritorialized power relation through which neoliberal power governs the class struggle' (2012: 51). Financialization becomes the operation of the capitalists since financiers are equated to the capitalists: 'Finance is no longer a simple convention, nor a mere function of the real economy. It represents social capital and the "collective capitalist," the "common" capital of the capitalist class, as Marx and Lenin well knew' (Lazzarato 2012: 74). Resisting debt and finance corresponds to performing class struggle. According to Lazzarato, the aim of a class politics should be 'the cancellation of debt, for debt, one will recall, is not an economic problem but an apparatus of power designed not only to impoverish us, but to bring about catastrophe' (2012: 164). Lazzarato makes the point that resisting financialization implies a class politics. It seems therefore that the class of the oppressed who should combat the 'collective capitalist' of finance are the debtors. Caffentzis also argues that class struggle should be performed on the question of debt (2013b: 2).

The politics advocated by Mirowski is not as explicit, however. Mirowski (2009, 2013) operates an ideology critique of neoliberalism and hence of financialization (2013: 62). Mirowski demonstrates that the 'neoliberal thought collective' operates an 'agonotology' (2013: 227) whose aim is to take over power and not to provide a truthful analysis of society. I hypothesize that Mirowski's ideology critique is not neutral and that he is engaged in a political struggle for cultural hegemony to implement a class politics. Mirowski aims to resist the politics of the neoliberal thought collective which is class based. Mirowski's ideology critique therefore operates a form of class politics.

Finally, Bonefeld and Holloway also insist on class politics to resist the power of finance, namely financialization (1995a, 1995b, 1995c). Bonefeld and Holloway can be described as open Marxists. According to Bonefeld and Holloway, money and hence finance consist of a class relation (1995a). Financialization therefore corresponds to a form of class confrontation to which class politics is a response. Their main thesis is that finance allows a displacement of capital's conflict with labour: 'The significance of monetary speculation lies in the avoidance of a direct relationship with the working class. Speculation does not meet with the same resistance that capital encounters in the factory' (Bonefeld 1995: 61). Financialization can be seen as a consequence of the crisis of Keynesianism. A class politics of labour against capital would then provide a resistance against finance and capital.

Caffentzis therefore argues that debt and credit correspond to class relations between workers and capital, as opposed to the traditional Marxist view, which insists debt and credit are related to conflicts among capitalists; for example, between finance capital and industrial capital through interest rates (2013b: 6). For Caffentzis, who can be described as an autonomist Marxist, class struggle and class politics are not limited to the conflict between employers and wage earners. Consequently, workers should organize political struggles to refuse to pay their debts for instance. Notably, the Zapatista movement in Chiapas was able to confront the financial markets during its 19 December 1994 uprising when capital fled financial assets denominated in Mexican pesos in Wall Street and Mexico City's stock exchange (Holloway 2000: 173).

Within a Marxian framework, Duménil and Lévy also insist on class politics to resist financialization: 'the unquenchable quest for high income on the part of the upper classes must be halted. Much will depend on the pressure exerted by the popular classes and the peoples of the world' (2011: 2). Both agree that neoliberalism, of which financialization is the expression, is a clear class strategy of the upper class to which the only response rests in a class politics.

In sum, the financialization literature I reviewed subscribes to class politics and class antagonism as a form of resistance against financialization, beyond its differences within the Marxist or the Marxian tradition, in particular between open Marxists, autonomist Marxists and other forms of Marxism. It can be noted that although these authors advocate class politics, few of them discuss concrete struggles, except Holloway (2000).

Revolutionary subject

I shall now examine the question of a revolutionary subject from the perspective of the financialization literature. The financialization literature that I reviewed belongs to the Marxian tradition and provides an analysis of financialization within the framework of Marxism. Furthermore, this financialization literature despite its differences – open Marxism, autonomist Marxism, orthodox Marxism, heterodox Marxism – agrees that a politics against the power of finance would consist of a class politics. The notion of a revolutionary subject, however, implies that there is an identified agent that is able to bring about a revolutionary transformation of history; that is, the transcending of capitalism.

Marx argued in *The Communist Manifesto* that the proletariat though its victorious struggle against the bourgeoisie was the revolutionary agent of history and that it would bring about communism (Marx and Engels 1969). Later, Lenin in *What Is to Be Done?* maintained that the proletariat would not spontaneously operate a revolutionary struggle against the bourgeoisie (1969). The proletariat therefore needed to be led by a vanguard of professional revolutionaries organized within a disciplined political party, namely the Communist Party (Lenin 1969). From the Leninist perspective, the political party became the revolutionary subject that the proletariat and the masses needed.

The financialization literature primarily provides an analysis of financialization. Its politics is therefore sometimes harder to understand. Harvey considers that a struggle against financialization could be brought to a successful end through a social democratic class politics (2005: 199). His position is not primarily revolutionary since a social democratic politics against financialization would imply a series of regulatory measures in particular to restrict international flows of finance. Nevertheless, in theory at least, a social-democratic politics is not antithetical to revolution if it is viewed in gradualist terms as members of the Second International used to argue (Bernstein 1961). As Harvey understands financialization within the framework of a conflict between labour and capital, the historical agent that could implement a decisive historical change is labour within the framework of a class politics (2005: 10).

Similarly, Bryan and Rafferty understand financialization as a complex process operating, *inter alia*, through derivatives, which intensifies capital's exploitation of labour (2006). This exploitation of labour is to be found not only in the sphere of production, but also in the sphere of reproduction and private life, in particular through debt (Martin et al. 2008). This implies that the revolutionary subject that would able to confront financialization is related to labour, because it is the substance that financialization tries to capture. McNally also considers that labour is the revolutionary subject that could resist financialization (2009).

The position of Lazzarato is different, even though he subscribes to the notion of class politics. Lazzarato is quite critical of the Marxist concept of labour because of the post-Fordist transformations of capitalism since the 1970s:

> The debtor–creditor relationship – the subject of this book – intensifies mechanisms of exploitation and domination at every level of society, for within it no distinction exists between workers and the unemployed, consumers and producers, working and non-working populations, retirees and welfare recipients. Everyone is a "debtor," accountable to and guilty before capital.
>
> (2012: 7)

For Lazzarato, the main antagonism in our contemporary financialized capitalism is the struggle between debtors and capital. This entails that debtors are able to operate as historical agents that would operate a revolutionary transformation of capitalism. In other words, according to Lazzarato, debtors have replaced the proletariat or the working class as revolutionary subject within the framework of financialization.

Mirowski provides an ideology critique of the neoliberal project of which financialization is a part (2009, 2013). Even though Mirowski operates within a Marxian framework, he does not propose an explicit politics. It seems that providing an ideology critique of financialization implies a struggle for cultural hegemony, which is the condition of the possibility of finding a revolutionary subject against neoliberalism and financialization. Intellectual and cultural work would be the priority to provide cognitive arms to fight financialization.

The open Marxist literature on financialization advocates a class politics to fight against capital (Bonefeld and Holloway 1995b). Accordingly, the main social antagonism within a capitalist society is to be found in the conflict between capital and labour, as capital constantly seeks to exploit living labour. Financialization and debt are ways for capital to displace class struggle. A revolutionary transcending of the power of capital is therefore connected to labour. Labour is the revolutionary subject that could not only resist financialization, but could also resist the power of capital through its power of insubordination.

For the open Marxist literature, financialization through credit and debt implied the 'decomposing of class relations' (Bonefeld and Holloway 1995c: 216). Debt operated a 'disciplining power' over labour (Bonefeld and Holloway 1995c: 217). However, financialization and debt through credit expansion cannot be used eternally by capital: 'Capital has to face labour in the contested terrain of production. It cannot run away forever because the rising ratio of debt to surplus value will make it increasingly difficult to make money out of debt' (Bonefeld and Holloway 1995c: 223). A final confrontation between capital and labour can therefore not be suppressed for ever. This confrontation might bring about a victory of the revolutionary subject; that is to say living labour.

Finally, Duménil and Lévy provide a different understanding of what might be a historical agent able to resist neoliberalism and financialization (2011). For Duménil and Lévy, labour alone would not be able to resist financialization and neoliberalism. Duménil and Lévy distinguish between three groups of classes in modern capitalism: the 'capitalist classes', the 'managerialist classes' and the 'popular classes' (2011: 14). Neoliberalism of which financialization might be an expression would be characterized by an alliance between the capitalist classes and the managerialist classes (Duménil and Lévy 2011: 19).

By contrast, the Keynesian compromise consisted of an alliance between the managerialist classes and the popular classes (Duménil and Lévy 2011: 18). Only an alliance between the managerial classes and the working class would be able to challenge financialization within a social democratic framework (Duménil and Lévy, 2011: 19). According to Duménil and Lévy, the most important social group is therefore the managerialist classes, which can either make an alliance with the capitalists or with the wage earners. For Duménil and Lévy, the subject of history are the managerialist classes. The alliance between the managerialist classes and the popular classes, however, would create a 'centre-left' politics, as opposed to a revolutionary alternative to financialization and capitalism.

Most of the financialization literature I have reviewed considers labour to be the revolutionary subject, except Lazzarato who argues that debtors are the new revolutionary subject within the framework of financialization. Other authors I shall refer to in the last chapter also consider that debtors have a revolutionary potential (Caffentzis 2013a; Graeber 2011a). Duménil and Lévy do not consider that a revolutionary subject exists in the current situation. Some authors consider that the state is a major instrument that can resist financialization through regulations (for instance Duménil and Lévy 2011; Harvey 2005; Lapavitsas 2011), unlike Lazzarato, the autonomist literature and the open Marxist literature, who generally speaking do not identify the state as an instrument that would allow a revolutionary subject to resist financialization. From the perspective of autonomist Marxism, the state as well as finance remain enemies of labour or debtors.

Conclusion

I have tackled the notion of financialization in this chapter. I argued that financialization corresponded to the centrality of finance in the current functioning of capitalism. This phenomenon took place in the 1970s when the Bretton Woods financial system collapsed. Financialization did not only concern the sphere of economic production; it also concerned the spheres of social reproduction, state and subjectivity.

Nonetheless, the works of Deleuze and Guattari do not provide an analysis of financialization for historical and epistemological reasons since both authors died in the first half of the 1990s. I therefore reviewed a contemporary Marxian literature on financialization (Bonefeld and Holloway 1995b; Bryan and Rafferty 2006; Bryan et al. 2009; Duménil and Lévy 2011; Harvey 2005; Lazzarato 2009, 2012; McNally 2009; Martin et al. 2008; Martin 2002, 2007; Mirowski 2009, 2013).

Finally, I analysed the politics of this financialization literature. In particular, class politics was advocated to resist financialization (Bonefeld and Holloway 1995b; Bryan and Rafferty 2006; Bryan et al. 2009; Duménil and Lévy 2011; McNally 2009; Martin et al. 2008; Martin 2002, 2007). Labour is considered to be the revolutionary subject by most of the literature (Bonefeld and Holloway 1995b; Bryan and Rafferty 2006; Bryan et al. 2009; McNally 2009); for Lazzarato, however, the debtors are the revolutionary subject (2012).

In the next chapter, I shall explain how Deleuze and Guattari as well as Foucault anticipated some of the aspects of financialization. Next, I shall show how their politics is different from the Marxian literature on financialization.

6 Anticipating financialization

Introduction

For epistemological and historical reasons, Deleuze and Guattari could not have completely described financialization. Financialization is a process that started in the 1970s and was not properly described and analysed before the last decade by the Marxian authors mentioned in the previous chapter (Bonefeld and Holloway 1995b; Bryan and Rafferty 2006; Bryan et al. 2009; Duménil and Lévy 2011; Harvey 2005; Lazzarato 2009, 2012; McNally 2009; Martin et al. 2008; Martin 2002, 2007; Mirowski 2009, 2013). Deleuze and Guattari could not have come to terms in the 1970s and 1980s with a historical phenomenon that could only have been understood in the 2000s. It is epistemologically impossible to explain historical phenomena before they actually take place.

Nevertheless, the writings of Deleuze and Guattari provided a critical understanding of some of the aspects of the transformations of capitalism in the 1970s and the 1980s. Therefore, I shall argue that their thinking operated an anticipation of financialization, even though the phenomenon could not have been described before the 2000s. In order to do this, I shall focus mainly on *Anti-Oedipus* (1977), *A Thousand Plateaus* (1987) and the *Postscript on the Societies of Control* (1992a). In other words, Deleuze and Guattari provided analyses that anticipated the processes of financialization, which I have described in the previous chapter.

Arguably, Deleuze and Guattari on the one hand and Foucault on the other were the theorists who were most successful in understanding the social movements and the struggles of the 1960s and 1970s. In particular, Deleuze and Guattari as well as Foucault operated a far-reaching reflection on the political and social significance of May '68 (Dosse 2010: 521). It makes sense therefore to also analyse their understanding of the transformations of capital of which financialization is an essential feature.

Five other reasons can be provided within this general context to justify the relevance of the oeuvres of Deleuze and Guattari and of Foucault in relation to financialization. Foucault strived to understand neoliberalism in the courses he taught at the Collège de France in 1977–1978, in *Security, Territory, Population* (2007) and in 1978–1979, in *The Birth of Biopolitics* (2008). First, Foucault,

Deleuze and Guattari can all be classified as poststructuralist thinkers (James 2005). This implies that Foucault and Deleuze and Guattari share a number of theoretical positions such as the critique of the truth correspondence theory and the critique of the notion of subject. Similarly, Foucault and Deleuze and Guattari provided critiques of structuralism and of traditional Marxist politics.

Second, Foucault and Deleuze and Guattari knew each other. In fact, Deleuze wrote a book about the oeuvre of Foucault after the author's death (1988). Deleuze's Foucault, however, is arguably a 'metaphysical fiction' (Gros 1995). Foucault wrote a text on *Difference and Repetition* and *The Logic of Sense* (Foucault 1998b) as well as the English preface to the *Anti-Oedipus* (1977b: xi–xiv).

Third, some authors of the financialization literature I have considered provide a careful discussion of Foucault's concepts and understanding of neoliberalism (Lazzarato 2009, 2012; Martin 2007; Mirowski 2013). It makes sense therefore to operate an analysis of Foucault's take on neoliberalism and financialization so as to contextualize and clarify their conceptual positions.

Fourth, an influential autonomist Marxist literature performed a combined reading of the oeuvre of Foucault on the one hand and of Deleuze and Guattari on the other (Hardt and Negri 2000, 2004, 2009). Hardt and Negri, however, developed the construction of a novel revolutionary subject, which for them is 'the multitude' and will oppose 'Empire' (2000 2004, 2009). This antagonistic relationship of 'the multitude' and of 'Empire' based on relations of production corresponds to a class analysis and a class politics (Mandarini 2005: 192). By contrast, I argue below that Foucault as well as Deleuze and Guattari criticized the notions of revolutionary subject and of class politics.

Fifth, Deleuze provided an understanding of the transformations of capitalism and anticipated financialization by drawing on the oeuvre of Foucault in the *Postscript on the Societies of Control* (1992a). It is therefore relevant to analyse Foucault's analysis of neoliberalism to contextualize and augment the understanding of Deleuze and Guattari's own analysis of the transformations of capitalism.

Foucault on the one hand and Deleuze and Guattari on the other anticipated the analyses of financialization by the authors I refer to in the final chapter, even though their understanding of financialization could only be partial. All these authors of the financialization literature were either Marxist or Marxian (Bonefeld and Holloway 1995b; Bryan and Rafferty 2006; Bryan et al. 2009; Duménil and Lévy 2011; Harvey 2005; Lazzarato 2009, 2012; McNally 2009; Martin 2002, 2007; Martin et al. 2008; Mirowski 2009, 2013). The works of Foucault and of Deleuze and Guattari, however, did not share the Marxian politics of the literature on financialization, in particular on two crucial points: the notion of revolutionary subject and the notion of class politics. I shall discuss these points irrespective of the broader question of the relationship between Marxism and Deleuze and Guattari on the one hand and Foucault on the other hand, which would require a much more extensive study.

Next, I shall perform another task. I shall examine another literature that draws on the oeuvre of Deleuze and Guattari to operate an analysis of financialization. I shall criticize some of this literature because it provides a capitalist

reading of Deleuze and Guattari (Armstrong et al. 2012; Hillier and Van Wezemael 2008; Lozano 2013a, 2013b; Neu et al. 2009; Vlcek 2010). I shall, however,
show sympathy towards authors who try to combine a Deleuzian approach to
financialization and a critical perspective (Bay 2012; Bay and Schinckus 2012;
Ertürk et al. 2010; Ertürk et al. 2013; Forslund and Bay 2009; Holland 2013;
Jameson 1997; Lightfoot and Lilley 2007; Shaviro 2010).

In sum, I shall operate three tasks in this chapter. First, I shall attempt to show
how Foucault and Deleuze and Guattari partly anticipated financialization.
Second, I shall explain how Foucault and Deleuze and Guattari criticized the
notions of class politics and of revolutionary subject, which are central to the
Marxian financialization literature. Third, I shall analyse the literature that draws
on Deleuze and Guattari to study financialization. I shall criticize some of the
literature, but occasionally refrain from criticism on political grounds, from my
own revolutionary perspective.

Foucault and the analysis of neoliberalism

In this section I will provide an analysis of Foucault's anticipation of financialization, that is to say mainly his analysis of neoliberalism, through a qualitative
engagement with in particular *Security, Territory, Population* (2007) and *The Birth of
Biopolitics* (2008). This implies an active reading through a selection of concepts
as opposed to others, and a selection of possible senses as opposed to others.
Some authors of the financialization literature draw on Foucault (Lazzarato 2009,
2012; Martin 2007; Mirowski 2009, 2013). The oeuvre of Foucault is characterized by different periods. In the 1960s, the first period of Foucault is marked
by structuralism and the methodology of archaeology, in particular with *The
Order of Things* (1989) and *Archaeology of Knowledge* (2002). Then, in the 1970s,
the second period of Foucault is characterized by an analysis of the question of
power and the methodology of genealogy taken for Nietzsche (Oksala 2010:
86). In particular, Foucault (1977a) provides in *Discipline and Punish* a specific
analysis of the question of prison and penalty.

Foucault (1977a) argued in *Discipline and Punish* that a new form of power
appeared at the end of the eighteenth century, namely disciplinary power. It was
defined as specific apparatuses of power/knowledge operating within specific
closed institutions such as prisons. The operating of discipline implied a microphysics of power. Power was no longer exercised by subjects on objects, but
rather through 'capillarity' (Feder 2010: 60). Discipline achieved a normalization
of convicts within the prison, or of bodies within institutions. Foucault draws
on Bentham's notion of panopticon to argue that discipline corresponded to a
'panoptic' form of power (Foucault 1977a: 195). Furthermore, Foucault argued
that the power of sovereignty has been replaced by the power of discipline
defined by the spectacle of the violence exercised on the body of the condemned
as demonstrated by the case of the regicide Damiens (1977a: 2).

Foucault pursued his reflexion on power in *The Will to Knowledge: History
of Sexuality, Volume 1* (1978) via the issue of sexuality. In *The Will to Knowledge*

Foucault developed another theorization of power with the concept of bio-power, which emerged along with the power of discipline:

> There was also the emergence, in the field of political practices and eco-nomic observation, of the problems of birth rate, longevity, public health, housing, and migration. Hence there was an explosion of numerous and diverse techniques for achieving the subjugation of bodies and the control of populations, marking the beginning of an era of "biopower".
>
> (Foucault 1978: 140)

Biopower consisted in the 'methods of power capable of optimizing . . . life' (Foucault, 1978: 141). Statistical techniques helped measure life to control and increase it through, for example, the introduction of the notion of demographics (Foucault 1978: 142). Statistical techniques are also central to modern finance. In *Security, Territory Population*, Foucault developed the notion of 'biopower', which he connected to the concept of 'apparatuses of security':

> Putting it in a still absolutely general way, the apparatus of security inserts the phenomenon in question . . . within a series of probable events. Second, the reactions of power to this phenomenon are inserted in a calculation of cost. Finally, third, instead of a binary division between the permitted and the prohibited, one establishes an average considered as optimal on the one hand, and, on the other, a bandwidth of the acceptable that must not be exceeded.
>
> (2007: 20–21)

Biopower is implemented by apparatuses of security that try to regulate and increase life. The apparatus of security implies a calculative rationality and a measuring as for modern finance. Unlike disciplinary power, security does not try to normalize individual bodies, but rather to control large numbers of bod-ies. There is a strong connection between the power of security and economics:

> For some time now, for a good dozen years at least, it has been clear that the essential question in the development of the problematic of the penal domain, in the way in which it is reflected as well as in the way it is prac-ticed, is one of security. Basically, the fundamental question is economics and the economic relation between the cost of repression and the cost of delinquency.
>
> (Foucault, 2007: 23)

The emergence of the apparatus of security was connected to the emergence of political economy. Foucault argued that security as a form of power was related to the emergence of physiocratism, as opposed to mercantilism (Foucault 2007: 56). Physiocratism was the first economic school of thought to advocate free trade. The notion that free trade should be implemented for grain to avoid famines was connected to the idea of increasing life. Security is therefore related to the laissez-faire of classical liberalism (Foucault 2007: 68).

Foucault elaborated, in *The Birth of Biopolitics*, the notion of governmentality, which he had already developed in *Security Territory Population* (2007). Governmentality is the 'art of government . . . insofar as it appears as the exercise of political sovereignty (Foucault 2008: 1–2). Fundamentally, Foucault argued that modern governmentality appeared in the eighteenth century along with political economy, physiocratism and liberalism. The former governmentality of state absolutism was characterized by the 'raison d'état'; that is, a governmentality organized around a strong state. The raison d'état implied mercantilism (Foucault 2008: 5).

By contrast, modern governmentality is connected to liberalism and political economy:

> The market now means that to be good government, government has to function according to truth. In this history and formation of a new art of government, political economy does not therefore owe its privileged role to the fact that it will dictate a good type of conduct to government.
>
> (Foucault, 2008: 32)

Political economy became the founding discipline of governmental reason. Political economy became the discipline that informed the exercising of state power. This implied that the market became the 'site of truth' (Foucault 2008: 30). The market became the cornerstone of the actions of the state, as opposed to mercantilist accumulation of money. Markets should therefore be liberalized to enable them to perform their function of veridiction of modern governmentality as the physiocrats argued. This meant that the state should not attempt to control the market because: 'with this conception of the physiocrats and Adam Smith we leave behind a conception of the economic game as a zero sum game' (Foucault 2008: 54). In other words, free trade was held to be beneficial to all.

According to Foucault, neoliberalism should be understood within the framework of this modern governmental reason and its operating of the market as an instrument of veridiction; that is, of the production of truth. Neoliberalism, however, does not only consist of a repetition or a reactivation of classical liberalism and laissez faire. Neoliberalism consists of a substantial transformation of classical liberalism. Consequently, there are a number of differences between classical liberalism and neoliberalism. First, neoliberalism insists on competition as opposed to exchange: 'Now for the neo-liberals, the most important thing about the market is not exchange that kind of original and fictional situation imagined by eighteenth century liberal economists. The essential thing of the market is elsewhere; it is competition' (Foucault 2008: 118).

Neoliberal competition implies that there should be losers and winners so that the market can operate. By contrast, classical liberalism laissez faire implies that exchange is beneficial to all participants. The market becomes a form of Darwinian machine that selects the best entrepreneurs. Neoliberal competition is therefore characterized by a form of tragedy: entrepreneurs need to survive the destructive test of the market to be successful.

Second, competition is not a natural phenomenon that appears spontaneously as is claimed by classical liberalism. By contrast, competition should be constructed through a specific governmental reason: 'Pure competition must and can only be an objective, an objective thus presupposing an indefinitely active policy. Competition is therefore an historical objective of governmental art and not a natural given that must be respected' (Foucault 2008: 120). In other words, neoliberalism is not a form of anarchism that refuses the state as an institution. Neoliberalism provides a novel thinking of state action. The neoliberal state should continually ensure that competition operates, for instance, through the creation of new markets or the privatization of state-owned corporations. This analysis is different from the Marxist takes on neoliberalism which I discussed in the previous chapter (Harvey 2005; Mirowski 2009, 2013). For Foucault, the neoliberal state is disconnected from class politics.

Third, competition can never be wrong as long as it operates adequately. According to Foucault, neoliberalism does not therefore consider monopoly as an inherent flaw in market competition (2008: 130). According to neoliberalism, monopoly happens only if competition does not adequately operate because of state interventionism. By contrast, according to Foucault, classical liberalism considers that monopoly can be brought about by inherent flaws in the mechanisms of the market and that: 'For freedom of the internal market to exist, the effects of monopolies must be prevented, and so anti-monopoly legislation is needed' (2008: 64).

As far as Foucault is concerned, the project of neoliberalism therefore consists of the following:

> This means that what is sought is not a society subject to the commodity effect, but a society subject to the dynamic of competition. Not a supermarket society, but an enterprise society. The homo oeconomicus sought after is not the man of exchange or man the consumer; he is the man of enterprise and production.
>
> (2008: 147)

The project of neoliberal governmentality is to construct a society shaped by the logic of competition as though the ultimate social unit were the enterprise. The enterprise should take risks and innovate on the market to be competitive. The neoliberal 'social ethic' is connected to Schumpeter's understanding of enterprises (Foucault 2008: 147). In other words, it is related to permanent 'creative destruction'.

Methodologically and politically, Foucault analysed matters that were connected to contemporary political issues. Providing an understanding of the market and of the novel neoliberalism of the 1970s therefore entailed providing a history of the market and of the origins of neoliberal governmentality, which was connected to classical liberalism (Foucault 2008: 186). In *The Birth of*

Biopolitics, Foucault provided specific analyses of German neoliberalism, French neoliberalism and of American neoliberalism. German neoliberalism was characterized by ordoliberalism, whereas American neoliberalism was connected to the School of Chicago. However, Hayek and the Austrian school were considered to have bridged the gap between the different forms of neoliberalism (Foucault 2008: 79). Foucault operated a conceptual analysis of the different forms of neoliberalism.

Ordoliberalism was connected to the idea that the German and Nazi states should be radically different. The German state should be grounded on a democratic ideology. The very existence of the German state was connected to the market: 'This objective . . . was to found the legitimacy of a state on the basis of a space of freedom for the economic partners' (Foucault 2008: 106). The market as a space of freedom for economic actors entailed a limitation of state power and a guarantee of democracy. Ordoliberalism therefore developed the idea that too much state interventionism would lead to Nazism (Foucault 2008: 110). The ordoliberal scholar Röpke in particular produced a text in 1943 arguing that the Beveridge plan could lead to Nazism (Foucault, 2008: 110).

Ordoliberalism is characterized by more importance granted to the state than is the case with American neoliberalism (Foucault 2008: 140). For the ordoliberals, the governmental reason should make sure that the framework allows competition to operate through specific forms of actions, which involves acting 'on facts that are not directly economic facts, but which are conditioning facts for a possible market economy' (Foucault 2008: 140). In particular, according to Foucault, the framework that should be provided by the neoliberal state corresponds to the legal framework and to the management of populations and technology.

Similarly, Foucault provides an analysis of French neoliberalism. French neoliberalism is connected to German neoliberalism. First, according to Foucault, German ordoliberals influenced French liberal intellectuals at the Walter Lippman colloquium in 1939 (2008: 132). Second, still according to Foucault, French neoliberalism corresponded to a state doctrine like German ordoliberalism. Neoliberal policies in France were implemented from above by President Giscard d'Estaing as a response to the French statist tradition and the increase of oil prices in 1973 (Foucault 2008: 196). The analysis of the intellectual history operated by Foucault is continued and transformed along the Marxist line of ideology critique by Mirowski (2009, 2013) as I have argued in the previous chapter.

According to Foucault, however, American neoliberalism was much more radical than ordoliberalism, which is why American neoliberalism was the most relevant to analyse the situation that prevailed at the end of the 1970s. According to Foucault, American neoliberalism was connected to 'criticism of the New Deal and what we can broadly call the Keynesian policy developed by Roosevelt from 1933–34' (2008: 216). American neoliberalism was related to the Chicago school and economists like Milton Friedman.

Unlike German and French neoliberalism, American neoliberalism corresponded much more to culture and society since: 'Liberalism in America is a whole way of being and thinking. It is a type of relation between the governors and the governed much more than a technique of governors with regard to the governed' (Foucault 2008: 218). The liberal governmental reason was part of American identity since the American Revolution with, for instance, the romanticized figures of the founding fathers (Foucault, 2008: 217). By contrast, in France and Germany, neoliberalism was 'just an economic and political choice formed and formulated by those who govern and within the governmental milieu' (Foucault 2008: 218).

American neoliberalism provided an innovative conceptualization of labour through the notion of 'human capital' (Foucault 2008: 219). The concept of human capital implies a critique of the Marxist analysis of the opposition between capital and labour. Similarly, labour is no longer a factor of production as in Keynesian economics (Foucault 2008: 220). The analyses of Foucault on human capital drew on the works of, in particular, neoliberal economist Gary Becker, who argued that workers became entrepreneurs of their selves as they needed to think of themselves as enterprises. Class struggles were negated, the only relevant social phenomenon being exclusively competition between enterprises.

This allowed American neoliberalism to conceptualize 'the economization of the entire social field' (Foucault 2008: 242). The social was thought of by neo-liberalism in terms of competition between enterprises: that analysis in terms of the market economy 'or, in other words, of supply and demand, can function as a schema which is applicable to non-economic domains' (Foucault 2008: 243). Therefore, neoliberal scholars provided economic descriptions of non-monetary economic phenomena. In particular, Gary Becker operated a neoliberal analysis of criminality arguing that criminals behaved as homo oeconomicus (2008: 248). I discussed in the previous chapter how Gary Becker proposed a financial-ization of organ donations (Becker and Elías 2007). Neoliberal governmentality meant that it was not possible to provide a total knowledge about the economy and society. Accordingly, the market is the only reliable provider of information about the economy and society: 'Thus the economic world is naturally opaque and naturally non-totalizable' (Foucault 2008: 282).

Foucault provides an analysis of the emerging phenomenon of neoliberalism, mainly in *The Birth of Biopolitics* (2008), even though it is strongly connected to the argumentation of *Security, Territory, Population* (2007). It should be noted that his methodology largely consists of textual analysis of important theoreticians of neoliberalism, in particular Gary Becker, or of the debates that took place during the Walter Lippman colloquium. Foucault's methodology in relation to neoliberalism was mainly based on his reading of a number of important authors: a methodology very much in contrast to the substantial archival work he performed in *Discipline and Punish* (1977a) or in *Madness and Civilization* (2006). Foucault's understanding of neoliberalism is therefore not exhaustive and corresponds rather more to a series of anticipations and intuitions. It should be stressed that Foucault's courses at the Collège de France were not meant to be published.

Remarkably, however, Foucault was able to anticipate some of the later developments of neoliberalism and financialization. American neoliberalism with its construction of the notion of human capital and the idea that society can be economized constitutes the closest anticipation of our contemporary financialized world of the sphere of subjectivity (Martin 2002) and of social reproduction (Bryan and Rafferty 2006; Bryan et al. 2009). More generally, Foucault understands neoliberalism as a transformation of the modern governmental reason, i.e. of classical liberalism. Neoliberalism constitutes a specific form of security apparatus aimed at regulating populations through the market. For historical and epistemological reasons Foucault was not able to provide an analysis of the mechanisms of financialization through derivatives.

Mirowski's analysis (2009, 2013) of neoliberalism on which I have drawn in the previous chapter provides a continuation of some of Foucault's insights into the neoliberalization of the self. Foucault does not, however, understand neoliberalism in terms of class analysis and capitalist exploitation, for example through debt, as opposed to the Marxian literature on financialization, which I considered in the previous chapter (Bryan and Rafferty 2006; Harvey 2005; Mirowski 2009, 2013). In particular, Mirowski blames Foucault for not identifying the conscious strategy of the Neoliberal Thought Collective (2013: 100). Nevertheless, some of Foucault's points anticipated the analysis of the Marxian literature, in particular in relation to the financialization of subjectivity (Martin 2002).

Deleuze and Guattari: anticipating financialization

I argued above that Foucault anticipated some of the transformations of capitalism described by the literature on financialization in the 2000s. In particular, his analysis of neoliberalism as a form of governmental reason applying biopower through the economizing of society and the reducing of labour to human capital has proven remarkably far-sighted.

Similarly, Deleuze and Guattari anticipated some of the transformations of capitalism in the 1970s and 1980s, though no more than Foucault were they able to theorize financialization, because of epistemological and historic reasons. Social processes produce new phenomena that cannot be understood before they fully develop. Below, I shall introduce the critique of capitalism by Deleuze and Guattari to be found mainly in *Anti-Oedipus* (1977), *A Thousand Plateaus* (1987) and *Postscripts on the Societies of Control* (1992a). My analysis of the Deleuzian oeuvre operates through a qualitative engagement with these texts. This implies an active reading through a selection of concepts as opposed to others, and a selection of possible senses as opposed to others.

Deleuze, Guattari and finance

At this point, it is necessary to assess the engagement of Deleuze and Guattari with the very notion of finance. The notion of financialization does not exist in the works of Deleuze and Guattari, even though they analyse specific financial issues such as banks and money. The question of money is tackled by Deleuze and Guattari in *Anti-Oedipus* (1977: 218) and *A Thousand Plateaus* (1987: 214). Similarly, the question of banking is dealt with in *Anti-Oedipus* (1977: 104, 229) and in *A Thousand Plateaus* (1987: 226). Deleuze and Guattari closely associate the issues of banking and money as the role of banking in the capitalist machine is related to the creation of money.

The analysis carried out by Deleuze and Guattari on financial issues is strongly linked to the Marxist approach and makes use of a Marxist vocabulary with concepts such as 'merchant capital' (1977: 225). Similarly, Marx's analyses of money and banking in *Capital, Volume I* and most of all in *Capital, Volume III* are referred to (Deleuze and Guattari 1977: 230). Deleuze and Guattari, however, are relatively critical of the Marxist understanding of the question of money and praise Keynes in passing:

> One of Keynes's contributions was the reintroduction of desire into the problem of money; it is this that must be subjected to the requirements of Marxist analysis. That is why it is unfortunate that Marxist economists too often dwell on considerations concerning the mode of production, and on the theory of money as the general equivalent as found in the first section of *Capital*, without attaching enough importance to banking practice, to financial operations, and to the specific circulation of credit money – which would be the meaning of a return to Marx, to the Marxist theory of money.
>
> (1977: 230)

The Marxist understanding of money and banking is criticized for not drawing enough attention to the issue of desire and the specific role of 'credit money'. Deleuze and Guattari therefore refer to the Marxist work on credit and money (1977: 230) by the French economist Suzanne De Brunhoff (1967, 1977). According to De Brunhoff, there is a fundamental 'dissimulation' of the functioning of money, which operates either as credit-money or as income-money (Deleuze and Guattari 1977: 229). Finally, Deleuze and Guattari refer to French economist Bernard Schmitt, who understands money in terms of flows, and in particular flows of credit-money in terms of 'infinite debt' (1977: 237). The analysis of Deleuze and Guattari on financial analyses can therefore be described as Marxian.

Furthermore, drawing on De Brunhoff banking is described as operating according to a 'dualism of money' (Deleuze and Guattari 1977: 229). Banks are creditors of an 'infinite debt', because they can produce as much credit-money as they wish, whereas the actual money that circulates is only used to buy and consume (Deleuze and Guattari, 1977: 229). There is therefore an ontological difference and an asymmetric relation of power between the credit-money produced by banks and finance, that is the 'signs of the power of capital' (Deleuze and Guattari 1977: 228), and the powerless payment-money used by wage-earners and people in actual life. The question of banking and the production of two heterogeneous flows of exchange-money and credit-money are connected to a problematic of power. Banks are centres of power that can produce credit-money, which the powerless users of exchange-money have no other choice but to accept.

Precisely the creation of credit-money by banks corresponds to an 'infinite debt' within the capitalist machine (Deleuze and Guattari 1977: 237). This is to be understood in relation to a history of debt. Deleuze and Guattari describe the evolution of history in terms of three social machines: the primitive machine, the imperial machine and the capitalist machine. Debt is 'finite' within the framework of the primitive machine, whereas it is already infinite within the framework of the imperial machine because of the emergence of State power (Deleuze and Guattari 1977: 192).

Deleuze and Guattari also specifically analyse the question of the role of merchant capital, as opposed to industrial capital in the historical process of emergence of capitalism (1977: 225, 1987: 452). The reflections on the role of merchant capital are connected to the Marxist problematic of the transition from feudalism to capitalism. Deleuze and Guattari argue that merchant capital already exists in pre-capitalist societies with no possibility of developing because it is controlled by the state (1977: 197). In order to make this point, they draw on the analyses of historian Etienne Balazs (1968), who points out that capitalism did not start in the Chinese empire despite favourable economic conditions (Deleuze and Guattari 1977: 197). Merchant capitalism therefore becomes important with the capitalist machine, even though it remains dependent upon industrial capital: 'capitalism . . . cannot be defined by commercial capital or by financial capital – these being merely flows among other flows and elements among other elements – but rather by industrial capital' (Deleuze and Guattari 1977: 226).

In *Postscript on the Societies of Control* (1992a), Deleuze refers to the end of disciplinary societies and the emergence of societies of control. In passing, Deleuze makes an important point on finance when he compares capitalism to 'a single corporation' with shareholders (Deleuze 1992a: 6). It is important to remember that Deleuze wrote *Postscript on the Societies of Control* in 1990, that is clearly in a period of neoliberal and financialized capitalism, 11 years after the first victory of Margaret Thatcher in the British general election. Even though Deleuze does not employ the term financialization, there are clear analogies between his argument and this concept as societies of control would be 'debt' societies (Deleuze 1992a: 6).

Finally, Guattari provided some analyses of finance in his own work in the 1980s. Guattari develops the notion of Integrated World Capitalism with Eric Alliez (Guattari and Alliez 1996; Guattari 2000) and Antonio Negri in the 1980s (Guattari and Negri 1990). Integrated World Capitalism is founded on the understanding of capitalism as a semiotic system:

> I would propose grouping together four main semiotic regimes, the mechanisms on which IWC is founded: (1) *Economic semiotics* (monetary, financial, accounting and decision-making mechanisms); (2) *Juridical semiotics* (title

deeds, legislation and regulations of all kinds); (3) *Techno-scientific semiotics* (plans, diagrams, programmes, studies, research, etc.); (4) *Semiotics of subjectification,* of which some coincide with those already mentioned, but to which we should add many others, such as those relating to architecture, town planning, public facilities, etc.

(Guattari 2000: 48)

Integrated World Capitalism corresponds to the centralization of finance, cybernetics, mass media, precarization of labour and a terroristic exploitation of the Global South (Guattari and Negri 1990: 75). Nevertheless, the concept of Integrated World Capitalism is not specific to financialization or the processes of finance; rather, it provides a reformulation of the problematic of uneven development.

Anticipating financialization

Beyond the specific questions of banking and money, the very understanding of capitalism by Deleuze and Guattari provided an anticipation of the literature on financialization. It is therefore necessary to examine Deleuze and Guattari's understanding of capitalism. The analysis of capitalism developed by Deleuze and Guattari is articulated around key concepts such as desiring production and socius, or axiomatization, but also deterritorialization and reterritorialization. In *Anti-Oedipus*, Deleuze and Guattari argued that: 'The truth of the matter is that *social production is purely and simply desiring-production itself under determinate conditions . . . There is only desire and the social, and nothing else*' (1977: 28–29).

Capitalism corresponds to a certain configuration of the production of desire within history, as with any historical system. Deleuze and Guattari describe the capitalist system, as a 'capitalist machine' characterized by a socius whose role is to 'codify the flows of desire, to inscribe them, to record them, to see to it that no flow exists that is not property dammed up, channeled, regulated' (1977: 33). However, the capitalist socius is different from other social organizations (primitive, and imperial societies), as it needs to combine two heterogeneous phenomena: the flows of money and the flows of labour (Deleuze and Guattari 1977: 33). Therefore:

> By substituting money for the very notion of a code, it has created an axiomatic of abstract quantities that keeps moving further and further in the direction of the deterritorialization of the socius. Capitalism tends toward a threshold of decoding that will destroy the socius in order to make it a body without organs and unleash the flows of desire on this body as a deterritorialized field.

(Deleuze and Guattari 1977: 33)

The capitalist processes through the power of abstraction and universal equivalence deterritorializes the socius, that is to say social reproduction. According to Deleuze and Guattari, the capitalist socius represses and liberates desire at the same time (1977: 33). Schizophrenia as a process of liberation of desiring production is therefore linked to capitalism, even if it constantly tries to repress it because 'schizophrenia is desiring-production as the limit of social production' (Deleuze and Guattari 1977: 35). This is crucial, because, then, there is no production, circulation and consumption from a strict point of view, but rather production of desire and connections of desiring-machines. Capitalism is both liberating and repressive, deterritorializing and reterritorializing, because 'it continually sets and then repels its own limits' (Deleuze and Guattari 1987: 372).

The role of the state is to regulate for the bourgeoisie the immanent deterritorialization induced by capitalism (Deleuze and Guattari 1977: 253). Capitalism therefore needs the space striation of the states to operate 'worldwide' and stabilize capitalism when it is required, in particular with crises through central banks (Deleuze and Guattari 1987: 434). States can appropriate the dynamism of war machines, in order to apply a capitalist capture of 'land' through 'rent' as proprietor of the land, of 'work' through 'profit' as 'entrepreneur', of 'money' through 'taxation' as 'banker' (Deleuze and Guattari 1987: 443–444).

Unlike in *Anti-Oedipus* (1977), in *A Thousand Plateaus* (1987), Deleuze and Guattari do not address the question of capitalism throughout. Deleuze and Guattari do, however, provide a substantial reasoning about capitalism in *1227: Treatise on Nomadology – The War Machine* and *7000 B.C: Apparatus of Capture*, as well as *1440: The Smooth and the Striated*, which resonate with the analyses of *Anti-Oedipus*. *Anti-Oedipus* and *A Thousand Plateaus* do not belong to the same philosophical genre because *Anti-Oedipus* is more polemical and provides a unified narrative, as opposed to the autonomous plateaus of *A Thousand Plateaus*. However, the main problematic of providing a processualist ontology remains as also the analysis of capitalism.

Some of the concepts developed in these two works are modified. For instance, body without organs in *Anti-Oedipus* corresponds to 'antiproduction' (Deleuze and Guattari, 1977: 9), whereas in *A Thousand Plateaus* it relates to the plane of consistency, as opposed to the plane of organization (Deleuze and Guattari 1987: 507). The body without organs in *A Thousand Plateaus* represents a series of becomings or smooth spaces, which are opposed to any anti-production. Additionally, *Anti-Oedipus*'s key concept of desiring-production is replaced by assemblages which are 'simultaneously and inseparably a machinic assemblage and an assemblage of enunciation' (Deleuze and Guattari 1987: 504). An assemblage is based on a territory and a movement of deterritorialization (Deleuze and Guattari 1987: 504). Consequently, the concept of assemblage pays more attention than does that of desiring-machines to the question of signs.

In *Anti-Oedipus* Deleuze and Guattari describe capitalism as a socius operating the extraction of a 'surplus value of flux' through the confrontation on the market of heterogeneous flows, for instance flows of capital and flows of human labour, or flows of credit-money and flows of wages (1977: 372). By contrast, the imperial socius operates a surplus value of code through direct extortion of crops or the imposition of forced labour. Deleuze and Guattari emphasize the deterritorialization features of capitalism and its capacity to drive the state to its limits, even though its stabilizing and repressive role remains indispensable: 'the modern States of the third age do indeed restore the most absolute of empires, Capitalism has reawakened the *Urstaat*, and given it new strength' (1987: 460).

Surplus value of flux is replaced by machinic surplus value in *A Thousand Plateaus* (Thoburn 2003: 97). For Deleuze and Guattari it is no longer possible to determine from where the surplus value comes, as:

> In these new conditions, it remains true that all labor involves surplus labor; but surplus labor no longer requires labor. Surplus labor, capitalist organization in its entirety, operates less and less by the striation of space-time corresponding to the physicosocial concept of work. Rather, it is as though human alienation through surplus labor were replaced by a generalized "machinic enslavement," such that one may furnish surplus-value without doing any work (children, the retired, the unemployed, television viewers, etc.)
>
> (1987: 492)

Deleuze and Guattari associated machinic enslavement with 'complex qualitative process bringing into play modes of transportation, urban models, the media, the entertainment industries, ways of perceiving and feeling – every semiotic system' (1987: 492). This, then, has arguably replaced the quantitative processes of extortion of the surplus value in Fordist capitalism through, for instance, the measuring and increasing of the productivity of industrial labour by scientific management. In other words, the critique of capitalism by Deleuze and Guattari subscribed to the notion of real subsumption of capitalism. Deleuze and Guattari therefore referred to the autonomist tradition, in particular Negri and Yann Moulier-Boutang, which developed the notion of real subsumption (1987: 469).

The end of Fordist capitalism is characterized by the emergence of machinic enslavement. Machinic enslavement implies a transformation of the relationship between subjectivity and capitalism. Machinic enslavement signifies a real subsumption of labour under capital, as the worker is not a subject acting on a machine, or a consumer consuming a use-value. On the contrary, workers are like cogs in a machine comprising material and immaterial elements such as language. The individual consciousness of subjectivity is challenged by machinic enslavement. However, according to Deleuze and Guattari, machinic enslavement is combined with subjection. Therefore, machinic enslavement does not replace subjection.

Deleuze and Guattari provide the example of television (1987: 458). In fact, the individuals who watch a television programme are subjected by the group of people who own the media and who control the information that they make available, inasmuch as they believe what they watch. This corresponds to subjection. Additionally, these individuals respond as robots to the stimuli of television. This corresponds to machinic enslavement. The circulation and the accumulation of abstract exchange value is therefore operated by subjection and machinic enslavement.

Furthermore, machinic enslavement implies a colonization of private life – that is to say life outside of the workplace – by capital. Private life is integrated into the circuit of valorization of capitalism. Therefore, the presence of capitalism in the lives of people is intensified. People are not only confronted to capitalism in their workplace when a surplus value is extracted from them. Similarly, people are confronted to capitalism when they try to relax or when they are home. This originates from the fact that machinic enslavement and subjection reinforce each other and contribute to the real subsumption of society by capital (Deleuze and Guattari 1987: 459).

In *Anti-Oedipus* Deleuze and Guattari provide a very insightful description of capitalism from which it is possible to draw an analysis of capitalism and subjectivity. In *Anti-Oedipus*, Deleuze and Guattari analyse the intrinsic connection between psychoanalysis and capitalism. According to Deleuze and Guattari, psychoanalysis is connected to the production of subjectivity in capitalist societies. Deleuze and Guattari therefore provide a radical critique of capitalism and of psychoanalysis in *Anti-Oedipus*. According to Deleuze and Guattari, there is a necessary relationship between psychoanalysis and capitalism:

> It is only in the capitalist formation that the Oedipal limit finds itself not only occupied, but inhabited and lived, in the sense in which the social images produced by the decoded flows actually fall back on restricted familial images invested by desire . . . It is not via a flow of shit or a wave of incest that Oedipus arrives, but via the decoded flows of capital-money.
> (1977: 267)

In fact, for Deleuze and Guattari, capitalism needs psychoanalysis in order to produce subjects without psychoses that can be rational and act accordingly on the market. Psychoanalysis uses the Oedipian triangle and the family to provide some stability to the individual, despite the schizophrenic dynamism of capitalism, which endangers the very notions of subject or morals. Psychoanalysis prevents economic agents from becoming schizophrenic in the capitalist context. It is arguable that this corresponds to the Fordist phase of capitalism in which the private sphere and the public and work spheres were clearly separated. For instance, this is true for large Western Fordist factories in the 1950s and 1960s. Similarly, psychoanalysis, in particular Freudian, strongly highlights the unconscious ultimately connected to our family, Oedipus and infancy and the economic and political domains.

By contrast, the highly financialized capitalism in which we live has no need for the relatively stable individuals with no psychoses and only neuroses that psychoanalysis contributed to produce. Psychoanalysis gave individuals a coherent temporality through which they could interpret their lives. For instance, an individual could think I have this type of neurosis because this specific event traumatized me when I was four. In other words, psychoanalysis offered Fordist capitalism individuals with a private history and temporality so they could become workers or students.

I would argue that there is a correspondence between the subjectivity of an individual marked by psychoanalysis and the Oedipus, on the one hand, and the individual working in the context of Fordist capitalism, on the other. Fordist capitalism is related to the extraction of surplus value and the exploitation of labour. Fordist capitalism needs stable subjectivities because they are seen to ground exchanges between individuals on the market. Fluxes of capital and labour need the stable subjectivity provided by the individual.

Second, capitalism entails the favouring of certain affects, as opposed to others. Therefore, according to Deleuze and Guattari, capitalism operates an influence on subjectivity:

> Cynicism is the physical immanence of the social field, and piety is the maintenance of a spiritualized Urstaat; cynicism is capital as the means of extorting surplus labor, but piety is this same capital as God-capital, whence all the forces of labor seem to emanate. This age of cynicism is that of the accumulation of capital – an age that implies a period of time, precisely for the conjunction of all the decoded and deterritorialized flows.
>
> (1977: 225)

Cynicism corresponds to the immediate satisfaction of the capitalist subjectivity that makes a profit. Cynicism implies a refusal of any traditional morals or religion. The only thing that counts is personal interest. A cynical subjectivity tends to neglect priests and piety. This corresponds to the deterritorializing operation of capitalism. Nevertheless, the 'piety' of the 'Urstaat', that is to say the religious respect for the power of the state, is related to capitalism's need of a reterritorializing state. The latter is particularly developed in the specific Fordist form of capitalist subjectivity.

In *Postscript on the Societies of Control*, Deleuze draws on Foucault's conceptualization of power. In particular, he identifies Fordist capitalism with disciplinary power and the new capitalism of the 1980s with 'control'. The new form of capitalism is no longer characterized by the Fordist disciplinary model of the confined factory. By contrast, the logic of this new capitalism is much more flexible and changing: 'In the disciplinary societies one was always starting again (from school to the barracks, from the barracks to the factory), while in the societies of control one is never finished with anything' (Deleuze 1992a: 5). This new form of capitalism can be associated with financialization.

Deleuze noted the importance of debt for control societies: 'Control is short-term and for rapid rates of turnover, but also continuous and without limits, while discipline was of long duration, infinite and discontinuous. A man is no longer a man enclosed, but a man in debt' (1992a: 6). Debt constitutes a much more flexible instrument for exercising power than disciplinary techniques. The centrality of debt implies a transformation of subjectivity related to the end of the Fordist stable form of subjectivity. The unstable and changing form of subjectivity, which is related to the societies of control is called 'dividual' (Deleuze 1992a: 5). The dividual corresponds to a dissolution of the individual subject which psychoanalysis contributed to construct according to Deleuze and Guattari's critique of psychoanalysis in *Anti-Oedipus*.

Deleuze and Guattari did not provide a full understanding of neoliberalism and financialization, which was virtually impossible in the 1970s and 1980s. They did, however, develop a number of illuminating analyses anticipating financialization. First, Deleuze and Guattari fundamentally understood capitalism as a transformative system operating through deterritorialization and reterritorialization. Capitalism is therefore a constantly changing machine with no natural laws. In other words, capitalism needs to be understood historically.

Second, Deleuze and Guattari understood that there was a real subsumption of society by capital, in particular with the concept of 'machinic enslavement' (1987: 428) or 'society of control' (Deleuze 1992a). Therefore, society as a whole contributed to capitalist exploitation and not only the sphere of work through derivatives (Bryan and Rafferty 2006; Martin 2002). This anticipates the financialization of social reproduction through credit and debt, which brought about the crisis of 2007–2008 as was discussed in the previous chapter (McNally 2009). The contemporary financialization took advantage of the real subsumption to increase its business with credit for studies, home mortgages or consumption.

Third, the concepts of 'cynicism' (Deleuze and Guattari 1977: 225) and of 'dividual' (Deleuze 1992a: 183) were anticipations of the fragmentation of the self and of the sheer cynicism of financialization (Martin 2002; Mirowski 2013).

Deleuzo-Guattarian disagreements

I have argued above that Foucault's analyses of neoliberal governmentality and Deleuze and Guattari's understanding of the transformations of capitalism anticipated the Marxian literature on financialization of the 2000s, which I analysed in the previous chapter (Bonefeld and Holloway 1995b; Bryan and Rafferty 2006; Bryan et al. 2009; Duménil and Lévy 2011; Harvey 2005; Lazzarato 2009, 2012; McNally 2009; Martin et al. 2008; Martin 2002, 2007; Mirowski 2009, 2013). This means two things. First, it implies that Foucault, on the one hand, and Deleuze and Guattari, on the other, were remarkable thinkers because they were able to achieve prior understanding of the major transformations of capitalism, which were only beginning to take place. Second, this entails that the analyses by Foucault or Deleuze and Guattari are not sufficient to conceptualize financialization. A Foucauldian or a Deleuzian analysis of financialization needs to integrate the literature on financialization of the previous chapter.

Nonetheless, there are contradictions between Foucault, Deleuze and Guattari and the literature on financialization, despite the relevance of their understanding of financialization. These contradictions are related to the Marxian political agenda of the literature on financialization I engaged with in the last chapter. Beyond the different approaches to Marxism, the literature on financialization shares two political presuppositions: the notion of class politics and the notion of revolutionary subject. Foucault and Deleuze and Guattari reject these two concepts, irrespective of their broader relationship with Marxism.

I shall provide a qualitative and textual engagement with the works of Foucault and more substantially of Deleuze and Guattari to show why they do not agree with the notions of class politics and of revolutionary subject. I shall then assess their critique of these two Marxist notions.

Critique of the notion of class

The question of the relationship of Foucault with Marxism is a complex one as some authors combine a Marxist and a Foucauldian approach (for instance, Hardt and Negri 2000, 2004, 2009), whereas other authors criticize Foucault from a Marxist perspective (Garo 2011a). I shall, however, not deal with this literature and shall concentrate on an analysis of Foucault's relationship with Marxism and class analysis. During his structuralist period in the 1960s, Foucault performed his critical archaeological methodology on Marxism:

> Marxism exists in nineteenth century thought like a fish in water: that is, it is unable to breathe anywhere else. Though it is in opposition to the "bourgeois" theories of economics, and though this opposition leads it to use the project of a radical reversal of History as a weapon against them, that conflict and that project nevertheless have as their condition of possibility, not the reworking of all History, but an event that any archaeology can situate with precision.
>
> (1989: 285)

Foucault understands Marxism as an economic theory of labour limited to the nineteenth-century 'episteme' (1989). Additionally, in the *Order of Things*, Foucault is critical of the notions of ideology and class: 'Their foolishness is to believe that all thought "expresses" the ideology of a class' (1989: 353). During his genealogical period in the 1970s, Foucault does not seem to have used any class analysis, in particular in *Discipline and Punish* (1977a). What Foucault applies are such notions as apparatus of security and governmental reason to populations to provide an understanding of classical liberalism and neoliberalism in *Security, Territory, Population* (2007) and *The Birth of Biopolitics* (2008).

Foucault does not understand classical liberalism and neoliberalism as class projects. By contrast, he considers them as forms of governmental rationality applying a biopower on populations, and not a class relation of power. From the perspective of Foucault, the question of class struggle seems to obscure the understanding of what takes place with neoliberalism, that is to say a form biopower.

The relationship of Deleuze and Guattari to class seems more complex than Foucault's. Deleuze and Guattari explicitly refer to a Marxist notion of class in *Anti-Oedipus* (1977). Deleuze and Guattari, however, oppose class interests to libidinal processes (1977: 104). Working-class aspirations do not always correspond to its better interests, witnesses the fascist phenomenon. Capitalism is therefore fundamentally about deterritorializing and reterritorializing flows, not about contradictions between class interests:

> The wage earner's desire, the capitalist's desire, everything moves to the rhythm of one and the same desire, founded *on the differential relation of flows having no assignable exterior limit, and where capitalism reproduces its immanent limits on an ever widening and more comprehensive* scale.
> (Deleuze and Guattari 1977: 239)

Deleuze and Guattari analyse capitalism as a 'general theory of flows' (1977: 239). In fact, the bourgeosie 'is the *only* class as such, inasmuch as it leads the struggle against codes, and merges with the generalized decoding of flows. In this capacity it is sufficient to fill the capitalist field of immanence' (Deleuze and Guattari 1977: 254). The bourgeoisie as a class is able to deterritorialize society, whereas the working class and its class interests tend to be absorbed and integrated by capitalism through the creation of an 'axiom for wage earners, for the working class and the unions' (Deleuze and Guattari 1977: 238).

According to Deleuze and Guattari, a revolutionary politics based on class interest would entail a bureaucratic and socialist state (1977: 192). Therefore, an actual revolutionary politics should be based on flows of desire that could break social investments (Deleuze and Guattari 1977: 379). The true opposition is not between the bourgeoisie and the working class, but rather between the class and those who are outside the class. Between the servants of the machine, and those who sabotage it or its cogs and wheels. Between the social machine's regime and that of the desiring-machines. Between the relative interior limits and the absolute exterior limit. If you will: between the capitalists and the schizos (Deleuze and Guattari 1977: 379).

This entails that Deleuze and Guattari do not understand capitalism primarily in terms of contradictions between classes, but rather as a theory of flows or looking for the lines of flight of a specific assemblage or territory, that is to say becomings: 'a social field is defined less by its conflicts and contradictions than by the lines of flight running through it' (1987: 90).

Revolutionary subject

Foucault and Deleuze together published an interview dealing with their understanding of politics (Deleuze and Foucault 1977). They published this interview in the context of their political engagement with the Prison Information Group in 1972. The Prison Information Group was a group of prisoners that was articulating its struggles with the specific knowledge of intellectuals. Deleuze argued:

> At one time, practice was considered an application of theory, a consequence; at other times, it had an opposite sense and it was thought to inspire theory, to be indispensable for the creation of future theoretical forms. In

any event, their relationship was understood in terms of a process of totalisation . . . The relationships between theory and practice are far more partial and fragmentary, on one side, a theory is always local and related to a limited field, and it is applied in another sphere.

(Deleuze and Foucault 1977: 205–206)

This constitutes a critique of the philosophies of history and their vision of history as a totality, which allows them to posit a revolutionary subject of world history. The idea defended by Deleuze and Foucault is that there should be practical engagements between theory and political struggles so as to operate 'relays' (1977: 206). This implies a critique of Sartre's vision of the intellectual leading the masses and identifying the revolutionary subject of history.

Additionally, in 'Intellectuals and Power', Foucault advocates the political struggles of new groups:

Women, prisoners, conscripted soldiers, hospital patients, and homosexuals have now begun a specific struggle against the particularised power, the constraints and controls, that are exerted over them. Such struggles are actually involved in the revolutionary movement to the degree that they are radical, uncompromising and nonreformist, and refuse any attempt at arriving at a new disposition of the same power with, at best, a change of masters.

(Deleuze and Foucault 1977: 216)

Specific groups like prisoners should struggle against the power that is imposed upon them and perform strategic cooperation with other groups, including the proletariat. The proletariat is therefore no longer considered the revolutionary subject. The very notion of subject and its presupposed totalized vision of history is criticized for corresponding to the operating of repression (Deleuze and Foucault 1977: 211). The proletariat or the working class becomes a struggling group among others.

The concept of subject is criticized throughout the oeuvre of Deleuze and Guattari, which implies a rejection of the notion of revolutionary subject. The notion of schizophrenia in *Anti-Oedipus* entails a critique of the rational reterritorialization of subjectivity to which psychoanalysis contributes: 'Desire does not lack anything; it does not lack its object. It is, rather, the *subject* that is missing in desire, or desire that lacks a fixed subject; there is no fixed subject unless there is repression' (Deleuze and Guattari, 1977: 26). According to Deleuze and Guattari, the concept of subject is related to representation, that is to say a form of repression and capture of desiring production (1977: 54).

In *A Thousand Plateaus*, Deleuze and Guattari continue their critique of the concept of subject:

A book has neither object nor subject; it is made of variously formed matters, and very different dates and speeds. To attribute the book to a subject is to overlook this working of matters, and the exteriority of their relations . . . All this, lines and measurable speeds, constitutes an *assemblage* . . . It is a multiplicity.

(1987: 3–4)

In fact, Deleuze and Guattari oppose the notion of material and processual movement of the multiplicity and of assemblages to the idea of a unique and stable subject. For Deleuze and Guattari, there are multiplicities and becomings, that is to say rhizomatic logics (1987: 5). Reality is made up of different flows of matter. In contrast, the subject is constituted by an 'organism' and is therefore constructed by an exercising of power.

Deleuze and Guattari therefore articulate a strong critique of Leninism (1977: 256) and the notion of vanguard party that should lead the masses of proletarians and transform them into a revolutionary subject. From the perspective of Leninism, the revolutionary subject is the working class. The working class, however, could not perform historical agency without the self-conscious group of professional revolutionaries forming the Leninist vanguard party.

Deleuze and Guattari reject the idea that the working class could be the revolutionary subject in the Marxist sense because revolution is conceptualized as a schizophrenic rupture in *Anti-Oedipus*. Similarly, Deleuze and Guattari insist on the revolutionary potential of different minority processes in *A Thousand Plateaus* (1987: 106). The connection of heterogeneous lines of flights does not consist of a unitary and totalized revolutionary subject such as the working class. Deleuze and Guattari eventually conceptualize the concept of revolutionary becoming in *What Is Philosophy?* (1994: 112) which refers to revolution as a virtuality without mentioning any revolutionary subject.

If it is true that Foucault as well and Deleuze and Guattari really did anticipate financialization, they do not agree with the notions of class politics and revolutionary subject, which constitute the foundation of the politics of the financialization literature that I analysed in the previous chapter (Bonefeld and Holloway 1995b; Bryan and Rafferty 2006; Bryan et al. 2009; Duménil and Lévy 2011; Harvey 2005; Lazzarato 2009, 2012; McNally 2009; Martin et al. 2008; Martin 2002, 2007; Mirowski 2009, 2013). Deleuze and Foucault (1977) criticize the notion that the proletariat, or some Leninist party could be a revolutionary subject leading a class politics towards revolution. What they do advocate are specific struggles with strategic articulations as demonstrated by the Prison Information Group.

The notion of class politics was criticized both by Deleuze and Guattari because it could lead to a molarization of revolutionary desire by bureaucracies and bring about the creation of a 'socialist State' (1977: 236). A politics against financialization should be based on desire so as to avoid the temptations of the Leninist or social-democratic bureaucracies, which are related to politics based on class interest (Deleuze and Guattari 1987: 470). In other words, a Deleuzian politics of resistance against financialization should advocate an 'anti-state force' (Zibechi 2010).

Advocating the notion of revolutionary subject and class politics would entail the disciplining of a political party, a trade union or a working-class organization, either Leninist or social democratic. These forms of political organizations correspond to Fordist capitalism. In fact, the Leninist political party is a 'space of enclosure' characterized by a disciplinary power exercised upon militants (Deleuze 1992a: 3). Financialization has fragmented subjectivities, however. In other words, it seems unrealistic to transform financialized subjectivities into disciplined militants. I therefore endorse the poststructuralist critique of the Marxist notions of class politics and revolutionary subject operated by Foucault and Deleuze and Guattari, even though the Marxian financialization literature is indispensable to understand contemporary capitalism. In the final chapter of this book, I shall proceed to a synthesis of the Deleuzo-Guattarian poststructuralist and revolutionary politics and of the Marxian financialization literature.

However, to analyse finance I now need to engage with the literature that draws upon Deleuze and Guattari. I shall operate a critique of some of the literature because, even though it is interesting and illuminating, it is ultimately capitalist or reformist. I shall however show sympathy to another part of the literature, which is critical about finance and capitalism.

Deleuzo-Guattarian literature in finance studies

In this section I shall provide a literature review of the Deleuzo-Guattarian approaches to finance. My project is not to use Deleuzo-Guattarian concepts to engage with financialization because, as I have argued, the Marxian literature on this issue is more relevant than the works of Deleuze and Guattari, who died in the early 1990s, that is before the full development of financialization. Second, my work is on financialization, whereas most of the literature is about finance.

There are two main takes in the field of Deleuzo-Guattarian approaches to finance. Actually, a number of works in finance studies operate a pro-market take on finance based on Deleuzo-Guattarian concepts. This scholarship considers that the oeuvre of Deleuze and Guattari is not radically critical of capitalism. In other words, as far as this Deleuzo-Guattarian and pro-market take on finance is concerned, it is possible to be at the same time pro-capitalist and Deleuzo-Guattarian. Then there are a number of works that are critical of finance and that try to use Deleuzo-Guattarian concepts to criticize finance, in particular scholarship related to critical finance studies. My project is different from their work, but I do sympathize with their approach.

Pro-market Deleuzo-Guattarian literature in finance studies

I shall deal below with the overtly pro-capitalist Deleuzo-Guattarian analysis of finance. Benjamin Lozano develops an ambitious project using the oeuvre of Deleuze and Guattari in relation to finance, in which he conducts an implicit liberal reading of Deleuze and Guattari. Lozano wants to proceed to a Deleuzo-Guattarian reading of finance. He explains his position on his blog Speculative

Materialism and in a number of texts. The project of Lozano needs to be understood in relation to the notion of speculative realism; that is to say a philosophy
interested in the 'real' processes of matter, which defends a realist epistemology
(Bryant et al. 2011). According to Lozano, the Deleuzo-Guattarian philosophy
can bring about a novel understanding of the materiality of finance. Therefore,
Lozano argues that the Deleuzian philosophy provides an 'ontology' of finance
(2013a 2013b). In particular, Lozano claims to read Deleuze's *Difference and
Repetition* as 'heterodox political economy' (2013a).

Lozano explains that there is an ontological difference between traditional
finance and new forms of innovative finance:

> The first part of the problem begins with an ontological transformation
> of the financial asset. More specifically it concerns the progressive differ-
> entiation of two new classes of financial assets from out generic finance,
> but whose ontological composition is radically different from the kinds of
> assets which have historically populated financial markets: namely, there is
> the synthetic asset . . . and there is the securitized asset, which is a product
> of the process of securitization.
>
> (2013a)

According to Lozano, synthetic and securitized assets are ontologically different from shares or bonds, that is traditional forms of financial assets. This
means that synthetic assets have a being which is qualitatively different from the
being of a share or a bond. Accordingly, the credit default swaps and the collateralized debt obligations correspond to synthetic assets (Lozano 2013a). I can
hypothesize that Lozano's argument comes from the fact that synthetic assets
seem more disconnected from material reality than traditional securities such as
shares or bonds, which are related to specific and clearly defined companies or
entities, even though synthetic assets are very important within the framework
of financialization.

In an article, William Vlcek (2010) provides an analysis of a specific financial
method that is related to Lozano's analysis of finance. Vlcek describes informal
networks of financial networks in the Arab world. According to Vlcek, specific
informal financial networks, called 'hawala' in the Arab world, systematically circumvent state regulation, in particular in the context of the war on terror (Vlcek
2010). Informal financial networks avoid the arborescent logic of state regulation
through a 'rhizomatic logic'. Vlcek uses the notion of rhizome developed in the
first plateau of *A Thousand Plateaus* (1987). The rhizomatic logic is ontologically
creative and is marked by qualitative multiplicities. By contrast, the arborescent
logic is marked by quantitative multiplicities.

As far as Vlcek is concerned, the rhizomatic logic of informal finance in the
Arab world is creative. Accordingly, informal finance is said to produce a new
being. The reasoning of Vlcek on a limited object corresponds to Lozano's
more ambitious and broader ontological understanding of finance. However,
for Lozano, only recent financial innovations such as synthetic or securitized

assets like derivatives are creative, as opposed to traditional financial assets such as shares or bonds. Vlcek's specific argument concerning informal finance in the Arab world therefore also contradicts Lozano's point on the difference between simple and complex securities. Vlcek argues that a simple and traditional form of financial operation is ontologically creative, whereas Lozano argues that only complex financial assets are ontologically creative.

Similarly, Hillier and Van Wezemael (2008) provide a Deleuzian take on finance, which is pro-market. Hillier and Van Wezemael analyse a case of 'Private Finance initative for the construction of Throckley Middle School in Newcastle upon Tyne' (2008). Hiller and Van Wezemael try to find the reason why the project failed in 2005. The Deleuzian concept of assemblage is operated by Hillier and Van Wezemael: 'Throckley Middle School is therefore not only a "given place", but an assemblage as well as an element of other assemblages: of practices, of socio-technologies, of rules and regulations, of humans and non-humans' (2008: 158–159).

It should be noted that the use of concept of assemblage by Hillier and Van Wezemael (2008) is connected to the sociology of Latour and actor network theory. This is demonstrated by the use of categories such as 'humans and non-humans' (Hillier and Van Wezemael 2008: 158) and 'actant', which correspond to the vocabulary of actor network theory (Hillier and Van Wezemael 2008: 161). Hillier and Van Wezemael therefore consider private finance and its impacts on Throckley Middle School as a series of networks between non-human and human actants (Latour 2005). According to Hillier and Van Wezemael, the actor network theory is entirely compatible with the philosophy of Deleuze and Guattari. By contrast, I would argue that the Deleuzo-Guattarian notion of assemblage devotes more attention to processes of material transformation with the notions of territorialization and deterritorialization.

Hillier and Van Wezemael reject the idea that capitalism is an alienating system per se: 'We support arguments that the capitalist system should not be regarded as a totality' (2008: 178). Accordingly, for Hillier and Van Wezemael, it would only be possible to analyse local assemblages and how they relate to finance or private finance, as opposed to criticizing capitalism as a whole. Hillier and Van Wezemael's Deleuzian analysis of private finance relativizes the power of finance as an instrument of exploitation. For Hillier and Van Wezemael, private finance can be positive, ontologically speaking, and be part of rhizomatic logics. Acording to Hillier and Wezemael, the Deleuzian analysis of finance is therefore pro-market.

Furthermore, Neu et al. (2009) provide a Deleuzian reading of accounting, which is connected to finance. Arguably, the Deleuzian reading of accounting by Neu et al. (2009) is related to the liberal interpretation of Deleuze and Guattari. Neu et al develop a number of Deleuzo-Guattarian concepts such as assemblage, bodies without organs or territory in order to conceptualize accounting (2009: 319). More precisely, Neu at al. present a case study in El Salvador about 'international development lending' (2009: 319). The study by Neu et al. is empirical (2009). Furthermore, Neu at al. (2009: 321) combine a

Deleuzo-Guattarian approach with Latour's actor network theory, in particular with the notion of 'actant' – a category also used by Hillier and Van Wezemael (2008).

Neu et al., like Lozano (2013a, 2013 b), Hillier and Van Wezemael (2008) and Vleck (2010), argue that capitalism can be ontologically productive and creative:

> Like capitalism itself, which is a complex mixture of creativity (capitalism is, after all, wildly creative) and the creation of demands oriented towards infantile pleasure-seeking, this tension between becoming something new and truly life-enhancing and becoming something new and simply taken-for-granted always exists within both international organizations and the professional discipline of accounting.
>
> (Neu et al. 2009: 346)

According to Neu et al. (2009), capitalism does not constitute a system inherently based on exploitation. Similarly, finance and accounting in a capitalist context are not particularly considered as instruments of capitalist exploitation. Neu et al. (2009) use a Deleuzo-Guattarian conceptualization, which they combine with actor network theory in order to describe the human and non-human processes of accounting, as opposed to criticizing them. Neu et al. (2009) do not confront the issue of capitalist relations of power. The position of Neu et al. (2009) is very similar to that of Hillier and Van Wezemael (2008) on these issues. Neu et al. (2009) operate a Deleuzo-Guattarian methodology to construct an ontological and material description of a specific financial process: accounting. In sum, for Neu et al. the Deleuzo-Guattarian philosophy provides a more sophisticated instrument of analysing the workings of capitalism or specific financial processes.

The Deleuzo-Guattarian take on finance by Neu et al. (2009), like the positions of Hillier and Van Wezemael (2008), Vlcek (2010) and Lozano (2013a, 2013b), is related to a pro-market celebration of finance. Lozano (2013a, 2013b) provides the most ambitious and overtly philosophical project in terms of reading of finance, whereas Vlcek (2010) and Hillier and Van Wezmael (2008) operate a Deleuzo-Guattarian analysis of a specific area of finance. However, all these authors use the philosophy of Deleuze and Guattari to provide an ontological description of the creativity of finance, which celebrates its power. I, however, do not subscribe to this position and would suggest that a Deleuzian engagement with finance should be revolutionary and that the power of finance should be resisted.

It can be noted that Armstrong et al. (2012), in passing, conduct a Deleuzian analysis of finance from the point of view ethics. Armstrong et al. reflect on: 'responsible innovation in finance' (2012). Armstrong et al. therefore argue that finance can produce innovations with 'precaution' (2012). This, then, could be connected to the Deleuzian interpretation of Spinozist ethics. In others words, the pro-market Deleuzo-Guattarian reading of finance adopts a mainly onto-logical approach. By contrast, the Deleuzo- Guattarian ethics is not much used.

Critical Deleuzo-Guattarian literature in finance studies

Other approaches operate a Deleuzo-Guattarian analysis of finance from a more critical perspective. My own revolutionary take on Deleuze and Guattari and financialization is closer to this scholarship, which is more interdisciplinary than the pro-market literature above. These critical analyses of finance will be engaged with below.

Jameson carries out a Deleuzo-Guattarian analysis of the issue of finance in contemporary capitalism (1997), which is critical both about financialization and capitalism. Jameson connects the analyses of Arrighi on World-Systems Theory with the philosophy of Deleuze and Guattari. According to Jameson:

> There is a deterritorialization in which capital shifts to other and more profitable forms of production, often enough in new geographical regions. Then there is the grimmer conjuncture, in which the capital of an entire center or region abandons production altogether in order to seek maximization in nonproductive spaces, which as we have seen are those of speculation, the money market, and finance capital in general.
>
> (1997: 260)

Jameson uses the Deleuzian concept of 'deterritorialization' to analyse contemporary capitalism (1997: 260). According to Jameson, contemporary financialized capitalism is marked by a double deterritorialization. The first is said to be characterized by the offshoring of production from former industrial centres to the periphery, where labour is cheaper, and the second is constituted by finance. According to Jameson, finance is characterized by 'speculation' in postmodern capitalism (1997: 260).

Similarly, finance capital is described as abstract and non-productive: 'Globalization is rather a kind of cyberspace in which money capital has reached its ultimate dematerialization' (Jameson 1997: 260). In other words, for Jameson finance is self- referential as postmodern culture (1991). Accordingly, in a financialized capitalism, it becomes increasingly difficult to distinguish between production and speculation. Jameson's Deleuzian analysis is therefore very close to Baudrillard's notions of hyperreality and simulation (1995). Jameson, however, does not develop a revolutionary politics against financialization.

Steven Shaviro (2010) provides a Deleuzian critical reading of finance. Shaviro draws mainly on the *Postscript on the Societies of Control* (1992a). Additionally, he provides an explanation of the Deleuzian notion of control:

> Where the disciplinary society "molds the individuality" of each person, the control society addresses us instead as what Deleuze calls dividuals . . . That is to say, our identities are multiple, and they are continually being decomposed and recomposed, on various levels, through the modulation of numerous parameters.
>
> (2010: 1)

According to Shaviro, societies of control are characterized by the end of disciplinary capitalism with its Fordist mechanisms. Accordingly, control is thought to correspond to a new form of capitalism described as: 'open, fluid, and rhizomatic', as opposed to rigid and arborescent (Shaviro 2010: 2). I would argue that control is fluid but not rhizomatic, as it exercises power. In fact, the rhizomatic logic escapes power relations.

Furthermore, for Shaviro, societies of control are connected to the rise of neoliberalism. Accordingly, neoliberalism could be characterized by a number of phenomena: the 'transition from the welfare state to the neoliberal state', the transition 'from Fordism to post-Fordism', the transition 'from Taylorism to Toyotaism', the transition from 'formal subsumption to real subsumption of labor under capital' and the transition from 'industrial capital . . . to finance capital' (Shaviro 2010: 3).

Societies of control could be characterized by a logic of 'debt', which permeates subjectivity: 'The financialization of human life means that market competition, with its calculus of credit and debt, is forcibly built into all situations, and made into a necessary precondition for all potential actions' (Shaviro 2010: 8). Accordingly, for Shaviro, 'predatory capitalism' as an economic system is characterized by debt and a fundamental instability (2010: 8). Shaviro connects debt with the 'neoliberal market' (2010: 8) and not specifically with finance. In sum, Shaviro operates the Deleuzian concept of society of control to provide an understanding of neoliberalism. To be fair, Shaviro's project in this short text seemed mainly programmatic and speculative. Clearly, Shaviro operates a critical Deleuzian reading of finance.

Eugen Holland, in his essay 'Deleuze & Guattari and Minor Marxism', incidentally deals with the question of finance from a Deleuzian perspective (2013). According to Holland, the philosophy of Deleuze and Guattari in *Anti-Oedipus*, *A Thousand Plateaus* and *What Is Philosophy?* is defined by 'minor Marxism' (2013: 2). Minor Marxism is characterized by a critical transformation of orthodox Marxism through poststructuralist theory. In particular, the minor Marxism of Deleuze and Guattari is marked by a specific conceptualization of the question of the role of finance in the capitalist system (Holland 2013: 2). Holland describes finance capital as 'fictitious capital' (2013: 11). Additionally, Holland argues that finance capital is characterized by an 'unprecedented mobilization of the virtual' (2013: 13).

According to Holland, the dominance of finance capital over industrial capital corresponds to a 'deterritorialization' of capitalism (2013: 13). The financialization of capitalism could therefore be characterized by a further deterritorialization of capitalism through fictitious capital. According to Holland, fictitious capital is related to the Deleuzian concept of virtual. Holland's idea that financialization of contemporary capitalism is related to the increased importance of the virtual and of the fictitious over the real and the industrial is related to a certain extent to Baudrillard's concept of simulation (1995). Holland's critical analysis of finance does not, however, provide a reflection on a revolutionary politics of resisting finance.

Forslund and Bay develop the notion of critical finance studies (2009). They advocate the creation of a specific and interdisciplinary field of finance studies, which would criticize finance and its influence on contemporary capitalism. Forslund and Bay operate the philosophy of Deleuze and Guattari to define critical finance studies:

> Philosophy can teach us how to create financial concepts that will permit us to comprehend finance differently; ethics will give us the opportunity to study how to turn finance "back against itself so as to summon forth a new earth, a new people".
>
> (2009: 289)

According to Forslund and Bay, critical finance studies should create philosophical concepts of finance. Deleuze and Guattari defined philosophy as a 'creation of concepts' (1994: 8). Forslund and Bay connect the creation of concepts to a political approach because it should summon forth a new earth; that is to say a new and more egalitarian political system. Critical finance studies should be politically critical about the power of finance in the context of contemporary capitalism.

In another article Bay, in line with Deleuzo-Guattarian philosophy, explicitly relates financial markets to a form of creativity: 'financial derivation, far from being simply a hyperbolic tool of speculation, is an economic geno-practice, the productive play, the mobility itself of economy, its inventive . . . line of flight on which new "economies" are engendered' (2012: 30). In other words, every financial market is constituted by a line of flight that marks an ontological creation. The concept of line of flight is a Deleuzo-Guattarian concept first presented in *Anti-Oedipus* (1977), and one that is extensively used, for example in *Kafka: For a Minor Literature* (1986) and *A Thousand Plateaus* (1987). Essentially, a line of flight constitutes the deterritorialization of a specific territory.

Bay also uses the Deleuzo-Guattarian concept of 'event' in relation to contemporary finance (Bay 2012: 52). According to Bay, finance is constituted by events that are disconnected from the actual sphere of commodities and production. In fact, the definition of finance could be: 'exchange without exchange, exchange for the sake of exchange, exchange where nothing is exchanged except the exchange' (Bay 2012: 52).

Therefore, finance can be at the same time 'abstract and creative' (Bay 2012: 52). The Deleuzian analysis of finance carried out by Bay is related to Baudrillard's concept of simulation, because financial exchanges are disconnected from the 'real' sphere of commodities (1995).

In *Critical Finance Studies: An Interdisciplinary Manifesto*, Bay and Schinckus provide an analysis of finance that draws partly on the philosophy of Deleuze and Guattari and partly on Simmel (2012: 1). In fact, Bay and Schinckus quote Deleuze's *What Is a Dispostif?* along with Foucault and Agamben to describe finance as an 'apparatus' (Deleuze 1992b). Finance, then, is seen as non-productive either from the ontological or from the economic perspective, because it operates a capture of future ontological processes or labour.

Additionally, Bay and Schinckus repeat the Deleuzo-Guattarian conclusion that finance is characterized by a 'purely monetary self-relation as an event, the sense-event of finance' (2012: 4), which entails that finance is a speculative sphere disconnected from the 'real' sphere of production. Accordingly, finance could be marked by a monetary circulation unconnected with commodities. From this perspective, the argument of Bay and Schinckus (2012) is close to Baudrillard's concept of simulation (1995).

Bay and Schinckus also use the Deleuzo-Guatarian concept of 'assemblage' to describe the financial processes in contemporary capitalism. According to Bay and Schinckus, the financial assemblage could be 'creative' and 'inventive' (2012: 4). This idea of finance as a creative assemblage contradicts the view that finance is an apparatus that operates a capture of the creativity of other domains. *Critical Finance Studies: An Interdisciplinary Manifesto* provides a critical Deleuzo-Guattarian analysis of finance.

Lightfoot and Lilley provided a critical analysis of Policy Analysis Market (2007). Policy Analysis Market consisted of financial instruments that were supposed to be 'Prediction Markets' (Lightfoot and Lilley 2007: 84). Lightfoot and Lilley drew on Baudrillard's concept of 'simulation' to critically analyse Policy Analysis Markets (2007: 95). Lightfoot and Lilley articulated the concept of simulation with the Deleuzian notion of 'fold' (2007: 89). According to Lightfoot and Lilley, the fold connects the virtuality of finance and its actuality (2007: 89). In particular, derivatives and Policy Analysis Markets constitute a 'simulated future of an ordered, predicted, singular real' (Lightfoot and Lilley 2007: 96).

Ertürk et al. provide a different Deleuzo-Guattarian analysis of finance (2013). Ertürk et al. are critical of 'financial devices' and 'financial elites' (2013: 336). Furthermore, Ertürk et al. tackle the issue of 'financial innovation' (2013: 336). Ertürk et al. operate a Deleuzo-Guattarian critique of finance:

> In the Deleuzian usage, device can refer to a political plan or contrivance which involves disguise, deception, opportunism and force, quite different from its Callonian usage . . . to draw out the implication that device could be part of a much more explicitly political analysis of the problems of the present-day capitalism.
>
> (2013: 336–337)

In other words, Ertürk et al. (2013) provide a Deleuzo-Guattarian critique of financial processes as well as a critique of social studies of finance and of the approaches to finance that are related to actor network theory. Financiers use financial devices as 'weapons' in a social war (Ertürk et al. 2013: 337). Ertürk et al. (2010, 2013) operate the Deleuzian concept of war machine to analyse the functioning of financial devices as weapons in the context of a class struggle. In particular, Ertürk et al. provide a Deleuzo-Guattarian critique of financial devices as war machine using the specific example of 'hedge funds' (2013: 340). Hedge funds become weapons through a specific assemblage of financiers, technical instruments and social stratifications. In other words, financiers acting as the warriors consciously operate specific financial weapons such as 'high frequency trading' (Ertürk et al. 2013: 341).

In conclusion, the critical Deleuzo-Guattarian literature in finance studies provides a number of positions that partly overlap. A first position considers finance to be ontologically productive, even though it has a negative impact on the economy (Bay 2012; Forslund and Bay 2009; Shaviro 2010). A second position associates a Deleuzian analysis of finance with Baudrillard's concept of simulation (Bay 2012; Bay and Schinckus 2012; Holland 2013; Jameson 1997; Lightfoot and Lilley 2007). A third position operates a critical analysis of finance with the Deleuzian concept of war machine (Ertürk et al. 2013). All these authors operate critical and interesting descriptions of finance and capitalism. I sympathize with their scholarship, even though it is not directly connected to the project of this book, which is more about financialization than finance.

Conclusion

In this chapter, I have operated three main tasks. First, I explained how Foucault, on the one hand, and Deleuze and Guattari, on the other, anticipated financialization with concepts such as human capital, neoliberal governmentality or machinic enslavement and societies of control. Foucault and Deleuze and Guattari were, however, unable to fully understand financialization because of historical reasons. I therefore needed to integrate the literature on financialization, which I analysed in the previous chapter (Bonefeld and Holloway 1995b; Bryan and Rafferty 2006; Bryan et al. 2009; Duménil and Lévy 2011; Harvey 2005; Lazzarato 2009, 2012; McNally 2009; Martin et al. 2008; Martin 2002, 2007; Mirowski 2009, 2013). Second, I criticized the Marxian politics of the financialization literature, in particular the notions of class politics and of revolutionary subject. I operated this critique with the poststructuralist philosophies of Foucault and of Deleuze and Guattari. Third, I engaged with the literature on finance that draws on Deleuze and Guattari. I criticized part of the literature that uses Deleuze and Guattari to celebrate finance and capitalism, and sympathized with the part that is critical of finance.

In the next chapter, I shall explore a revolutionary response to financialization, which will draw on the oeuvre of Deleuze and Guattari. This will be operated through a positive dialogue between the Marxian literature on financialization and the revolutionary interpretation of Deleuze and Guattari.

7 Resisting financialization

Introduction

In the first part of this book, I analysed the reception accorded to Deleuze and Guattari. In the second part, I examined financialization drawing on Marxian literature. I then endeavoured to show that Deleuze and Guattari on the one hand, and Foucault on the other anticipated financialization, even though they had produced their analyses in the 1970s and 1980s. Nevertheless, Deleuze and Guattari as well as Foucault were critical about the politics of Marxian literature on financialization, which was grounded on the notions of revolutionary subject and class politics.

In this final chapter, I shall analyse resistance and financialization, that is resistance to financialization. The chapter will be mainly speculative as the literature connecting Deleuze and resistance to financialization is very scarce and lacks substantial engagement with the political economy of financialization (Nail 2013). Generally speaking, I wish to put in place a fruitful dialogue between Marxian literature on financialization and Deleuze, as opposed to only criticizing Marxism from the perspective of Deleuze and Guattari or Foucault. This, then, is very similar to Thoburn's notion of 'resonance' between Deleuze and Marx (2003: 1). The Deleuzo-Guattarian perspective, which I shall pursue in this chapter, will correspond to the revolutionary interpretation of Deleuze and Guattari that was developed in the first part.

My goal in this final chapter is fairly modest since I should like to elaborate upon a Deleuzo-Guattarian politics of resistance to financialization. I do not pretend to provide the only sensible Deleuzo-Guattarian politics of resistance to financialization. On the contrary, I shall merely try to set an analysis in motion that will need to be improved by future research. My elaboration upon a Deleuzo-Guattarian politics of resistance to financialization will seek to avoid two opposite flaws of philosophical engagement with politics: 'speculative leftism' (Bosteels 2005; Nail 2013) and the notion of 'blueprint' (Lenin 1969). According to speculative leftism, political philosophy should not try to inform the fundamental spontaneity of revolutionary practices, whereas according to *What Is to Be Done?* (1969), for instance, political philosophy should provide a detailed methodology for revolution.

My analysis of a Deleuzo-Guattarian politics will seek to articulate philosophical concepts and specific recent political practices connected to resisting financialization. I shall draw on two recent examples in order to make two main points. First, I shall argue negatively that resisting financialization from a Deleuzo-Guattarian perspective cannot operate within the framework of a social democratic politics. This point will be grounded on the analysis of French president François Hollande's response to financialization, which I shall argue was a failed social democratic project of resistance to the power of finance (2012a: 5). Second, I shall argue positively that resisting financialization from a Deleuzo-Guattarian perspective implies affective horizontal politics, which I shall elaborate drawing on an analysis of the Occupy Wall Street movement.

I shall argue that Hollande's social democratic project to regulate finance failed because it was mainly a Fordist project that could not work in a post-Fordist financialized environment. Hollande sought to regulate finance within the French national state, even though flows of capital can cross international borders (Holloway 1994). Second, I shall argue that Hollande's social democratic politics would have entailed an increase of the striation connected to representative politics. In particular, the implementation of a Fordist regulation of international flows of capital could have implied a paranoid reterritorialization on the French national state.

The Occupy Wall Street movement is often primarily described in terms of a problematic lack of representation of oppressed groups (Graeber 2013; Tormey 2012). Oppressed groups are voiceless because representative democracy does not represent them: 'OWS is one kind of resistance that "represents" in its post-representativity the response of those at the margin of wealthy countries of the metropolitan centre' (Tormey 2012: 135). Even though I would partly subscribe to this analysis of Occupy Wall Street, I would argue that Occupy Wall Street was also a movement of resistance to financialization, and this for at least three reasons. First, it symbolically identified finance as its main enemy through both its name and occupation of Zuccotti Park, a location situated in the very geographical centre of global finance. After all, it was not by chance that Lower Manhattan, that is to say New York's financial district, was chosen, and not, for instance, the United Nations district. Second, many people in the Occupy Wall Street movement emphasized the question of debt – a central feature of financialization – as a specific form of control and oppression in particular on the We Are the 99 Percent blog (2014). Third, Occupy Wall Street gave birth to Strike Debt!, which provides practical forms of resistance to financialization through 'debt struggle' (Caffentzis 2013a: 6).

Financialization is a complex process that characterizes contemporary capitalism through a number of features such as the explosion of international financial flows, of derivatives (Bryan and Rafferty 2006), the financialization of subjectivity (Martin 2002), or the increase in the exploitation of labour (Bryan et. al. 2009) through finance's 'calculative competition' (Harvie 2008b: 31). Financialization is central to contemporary capitalism since the collapse of the Bretton Woods Financial system and Fordism. Financialization is so pervasive, however, that it seems extremely complicated to resist its power. In fact, resisting international flows of capital and derivatives seems much more complicated than it was to organize a strike in a 1960s car factory in Detroit or Turin.

The most obvious subjective experience of financialization is debt: student debt, mortgage or private debt. Therefore, 'debt struggle' can be considered a form of resistance to financialization, and more broadly to capitalism (Caffentzis 2013a: 6). Cancelling debt can be seen as a strategic objective to resist financialization. Achieving such a political objective would correspond to challenging the very existence of capitalism, as its current neoliberal regime of accumulation is based on debt (McNally 2009). The aim of this chapter will therefore be to reflect how a Deleuzo–Guattarian politics could induce resistance to debt as well as to other features of financialization.

However, as the autonomist Marxist and the open Marxist literatures argue, debt is a particularly subtle form of control because it is an instrument of discipline for labour as well as a form of displacement of conflict between capital and labour (De Angelis 2001; Holloway 2010). In other words, debt concurrently intensifies and displaces conflict because capital gives future surplus value to workers through cheap credit, but at the same time capital needs to increase exploitation in order to extract additional surplus value to pay off its debt: 'The fictional world of credit thus softens the asperities of the disciplines of abstract labour, but also extends and deepens them' (Holloway 2010: 184).

Deleuzo–Guattarian critique of a social democratic response to financialization

By a social democratic response to financialization, I mean a politics based upon organizing a political party representing the interests of the majority of the people, winning general elections and finally, successfully implementing a regulation of financialization. In sum, social democracy assumes that it can regulate the 'flows' of finance (Deleuze and Guattari 1987: 462) I shall argue in this section that this political strategy is currently neither operational nor desirable from the perspective of a revolutionary interpretation of Deleuze and Guattari.

The failure of social democratic resistance to financialization

I shall ground my critique of a social democratic regulation of finance on the analysis of the politics of French President François Hollande.[1] As I have argued, drawing on the Marxian literature on financialization, financialization is a global process. Therefore, France as any other country in the global economy is financialized. France is subjected to international flows of capital through its stock market, the CAC 40, of which 46.4 per cent was owned by foreign investors on 31 December 2005 (Poulain 2006: 39). Similarly, France's currency (the euro) is traded daily on the Forex. The major French banks had to be bailed out by the French government in October of 2008 without reverting to any nationalizations for a total of 360 billion euros after the bankruptcy of Lehman Brothers on 15 September 2008 during the financial crisis of 2007–2008 (Samuel 2008). This shows that French banks were connected to the global finance. Finally, the French government's fiscal policy is impacted by international flows of capital through trading on French sovereign bonds, which causes fiscal austerity (Haugh et. al. 2009). The French state therefore appears to have a very limited leeway in relation to financialization.

Finance was a very important theme during the French presidential election of May 2012, and François Hollande, the candidate of the social democratic left, won the election partly because of the pledges he made on this issue. First, finance was substantially debated as it was considered to be the major cause of the economic crisis that had begun in 2008. Second, the importance of finance was debated as it was considered to be the main reason for the eurozone crisis through the European sovereign bond crisis. In the French context, the media often adopted a xenophobic attitude with regard to the European sovereign bonds crisis by depicting it as an aggression of Anglo-Saxon speculators against the European social model (Gatinois et al. 2010).

The pledges of the presidential candidate Hollande

Before the presidential election, Hollande provided a detailed outline of his programme in a speech delivered in Le Bourget on 22 January 2012. The speech was very important because it was the first time Hollande outlined how he would deal with the economic and financial crisis if he were elected president. Finance was clearly addressed:

> Before I talk about my project, I will tell you something. In the battle that we are going to fight, I am going to tell you who is my enemy, my real enemy. He has no name, no face, no party, and he will not stand for an election. Therefore, he will not be elected, and yet it is he who rules. This enemy is the world of finance.
>
> (Hollande 2012a: 5; my translation)

As far as Hollande was concerned, finance as a system needed to be politically combatted. Consequently, the financial crisis was not analysed as the outcome of the actions of a series of unethical financiers in the context of a healthy financial system. The word 'enemy' used by Hollande showed his recognition of conflictuality between the interests of finance and those of the majority of the population. Hollande also demonstrated his historical understanding of the systematic power of finance:

> In full view of us all, within 20 years, finance has taken control of the economy, of society and even of our lives. Now, it is possible in less than a second to move extravagant sums of money and even to threaten states. This power has become an empire.
>
> (2012a: 5; my translation)

Hollande demonstrated his understanding of the fact that financialization of global capitalism had started well before the financial crisis of 2007–2008. Interestingly, Hollande recognized that the power of finance was not only about economic matters; it was also about exercising control over people's lives. This analysis was very close to that of Martin, who argued that there is financialization of 'daily life', for example through the development of the practice of 'day trading' (2002: 46). Similarly, Hollande's speech mentioned the word 'empire' referring to finance. This resonates with the autonomist Marxist works by Hardt and Negri and their conceptualization of the concept of 'empire' (2000). However, according to Hardt and Negri, 'empire' does not specifically correspond to the issue of the power of finance, but rather to a form of decentralized and universal power in the context of post-Fordist capitalism (2000: xv). Arguably, financialization operates more as a process through the circulation of international flows of capital through bonds, shares and derivatives. However, financialization as Hardt and Negri's 'empire' operates within the framework of real subsumption through debt, in particular through subprime mortgage derivatives.

In other words, from the perspective of Hollande, finance consisted of a structured system that challenged national economies and governments: 'Now, it is possible . . . even to threaten states' (Hollande 2012a: 5; my translation). The idea was that there was a contrast between the sovereignty of countries and their governments and international flows of finance that escaped national regulation. Hollande therefore made it clear that his priority was to deal with the excessive power of finance as he had argued in his speech in Le Bourget on 22 January 2012. His written 'presidential project', which was published on 30 January 2012, provided a series of measures meant to fulfil the task of confronting finance through social democratic regulation (own translation) (Hollande 2012b).

First, in the First Proposal of his 'presidential project', Hollande promised to create a state owned bank that would finance the economy, as opposed to the financial sector that would mainly speculate:

> I will create a Bank of Public Investment. Through regional funds, I will favour the development of small and medium enterprises, and provide support to high potential sectors and the ecological and energetic transformation of industry. I will allow the regional governments, which are very important centres of our economy, to buy equity in the corporations that are strategically important for local development and the competitiveness of France. Some of this funding will be made available for the third sector.
>
> (Hollande 2012b: 6; my translation)

Hollande's idea was to foster development of the French economy through public funding as opposed to money provided by finance, which would only fund speculative activities. The creation of this Bank of Public Investment would therefore have been a challenge for the major French banks involved in the subprime crisis and bailed out by the French government (Samuel 2008).

Second, the 'presidential programme' of Hollande with its Proposal Seven provided another measure specifically addressed to the financialization of the French economy:

> I will separate the activities of banks that are useful for investment and employment from their speculative operations. I will prohibit French banks from exercising activities in tax havens. It will no longer be possible to use toxic financial products that make speculators wealthy and are dangerous for the economy.
>
> (Hollande 2012b: 11; my translation)

Hollande displayed an intention to fight the financialization of French banks. He proposed to reduce the power of finance through the implementation of a new form of Glass–Steagall Act that would prevent retail banks from investing the money of their customers in investment banks activities. The fact that the major French retail banks had been investing in financial markets and, in particular, in subprime derivatives was the main reason why the French government was forced to bail them out (Samuel 2008).

Also, Hollande proposed to increase tax on banks without specifically targeting their financial profits based on speculative activities so as to prevent them from using tax havens. It was not clear though whether Hollande was referring to French banks or all banks operating in France or in a business relationship with a French organization. Hollande only associated some activities of finance and banking with speculation, as though it were possible to separate healthy from unhealthy finance. Actually, within the framework of financialized capitalism, flows of finance capital perform the task of intensifying competition between forms of capital, in particular through derivatives (Bryan and Rafferty 2006).

Eventually, other measures in Hollande's Proposal Seven were aimed not only at banks but also more generally at finance. First, Hollande advocated a Tobin tax, which consisted of a small tax on every financial operation (Hollande 2012b: 11). Even though announcing a Tobin tax was clearly ambitious and might perhaps have limited the power of finance, Hollande did not specify how the tax would be implemented. For instance, it was not clear whether the tax would be raised on a French or on the European Union or eurozone level. This was a major issue, because a Tobin tax on the French level would not have had the same efficiency as a Tobin tax on the level of the European Union. Hollande's Proposal Seven recommends curbing the bonuses of CEOs and traders (2012b: 11). This was a way of responding to public outrage at huge bonuses payments in the context of a major crisis (Gatinois et al. 2010).

Third, in Proposal Eleven of his 'presidential project', Hollande provided for a series of measures to tackle the power of finance on a European level:

> I will propose to our partners a pact of responsibility, of governance and of growth so as to put an end to the crisis and the spiral of austerity that is worsening. I will start a re-negotiation of the European treaty, which

was the outcome of the agreement of 9 December 2011, by encouraging growth and employment. Similarly, the role of the European Central Bank will be changed and based on these proposals. I will recommend issuing Eurobonds.

(2012b: 13)

This clearly corresponded to a Keynesian paradigm. Essentially, Hollande's Proposal Eleven implied stimulating the economy through public funding. The idea consisted of providing huge sums of public investment through bonds that would be traded on financial markets.

This Keynesian stimulation was intended to operate on the European Union or eurozone level with the help of the European Central Bank. Accordingly, the economic stimulation provided by the eurobonds could have restored prosperity and growth and put an end to the crisis. However, the Keynesian project presupposed that the eurobonds would not be the subject of speculation by financial markets. Furthermore, Hollande's Proposal involved further European integration and federalism since issuing eurobonds required European economic and fiscal governance.

Despite some inconsistencies, the social democratic political programme of Hollande was an aggressive Keynesian project that planned to reduce the power of finance, in particular through the implementation of a Tobin tax and the separation between investment banks and retail banks, which was inspired by the Glass–Steagall Act of the New Deal in 1933. Hollande's social democratic programme involved a regulation of the flows of financialization. As a result, this aggressive discourse scared pro-business media. In particular, *The Economist* called the French President 'the rather dangerous Mr Hollande' (2012b).

Deleuzo-Guattarian analysis of the failure of the social democratic response

Hollande failed to apply his social democratic politics of regulation of financialization. The French media blamed lobbying by French banks (Parienté 2013) and the opposition of Angela Merkel on the issue of eurobonds (*The Economist* 2012a). I shall, however, try to provide a Deleuzo-Guattarian analysis of the failure of social democratic politics of resistance to financialization. Arguably, the failure of Hollande's social democratic politics to regulate financialization has more to do with social democratic politics per se than with the size of France, or with the fact that social democratic politics were not properly implemented by Hollande.

The strategy of Hollande to overcome the power of finance and resist it can be described as a Fordist and Keynesian project according to which finance should be controlled by state interventionism. In other words, the mental structures of Hollande continue to correspond to a Fordist society. Fordist capitalism implies that industrial capitalism is dominant and that financial capital has a limited role. In this kind of capitalism, which existed from 1945 to the 1970s, the state had a major function in controlling and supervising the economy. Typically, the French economy operated through soft planning (Hobsbawm 1994: 273). The Fordist economy corresponds to what after Foucault Deleuze describes as a 'disciplinary society', which is organized around closed institutions (Deleuze 1992a: 3). Production is mainly national and material, with commodities such as cars or television sets industrially produced (Hobsbawm 1994: 263). Deleuze and Guattari describe the role of the state in a capitalist system marked by Fordism as follows:

> The capitalist State is the regulator of decoded flows as such, insofar as they are caught up in the axiomatic of capital . . . The capitalist State completes the becoming-concrete so fully that, in another sense, it alone represents a veritable rupture with this becoming, a break with it, in contrast to the other forms that were established on the ruins of the Urstaat.
>
> (1977: 252)

Hollande's analysis, which was based on a Fordist understanding of capitalism, did not work. In fact, Hollande's regulatory projects aimed at implementing State control upon finance. The opposition between Hollande and Merkel on the eurobonds issue (*The Economist* 2012a) was particularly interesting. Part of the French press saw the issue as part of a traditional conflict between the two nations. This, then, would have been the opposition between two nationalisms (Todd 2013). In reality, the opposition showed that nations, states and their power of regulation were no longer efficient in our contemporary financialized world (Holloway 1994). Nations have become tradable assets on financial markets and derivatives markets, namely the different sovereign bonds markets. The Fordist and Keynesian paradigms no longer work because capital can cross borders and escape the sovereignty of states (Negri 2008: 237).

Hollande, as president of France, a relatively powerful country, believed he would be able to exercise power upon finance, and in particular investment banks. He did not, however, see that the contemporary French state did not have the same regulatory power in relation to capitalism as it used to in the context of Fordist capitalism. During the Fordist age of capitalism, the regulatory power of finance was characterized by the Bretton Woods financial system, which essentially allowed each state to limit the power of finance within its national boundaries (Bryan and Rafferty, 2006: 112). All things being equal, the eurobonds idea was an attempt to circumvent the lack of power of states on the national level through the creation of a kind of European super state. Therefore, the eurobonds project was the most ambitious measure imagined by Hollande to resist the power of finance.

In reality, capital through financialization operates beyond nations and the boundaries of states. The notion of Integrated World Capitalism, which was coined by Guattari, therefore corresponds to the appropriate level of analysis (Guattari and Negri 1990: 47). Financialization is a global process, not a national one. This issue was also addressed by Hardt and Negri, whose concept of 'empire' insists on the post-national functioning of contemporary capitalism (2000:xv). Finance has performed a permanent commensuration of all the assets that constitute the economy since the 1970s through the incredible development of derivatives, which has brought about an intensification of competition in particular for labour (Bryan and Rafferty 2006: 176).

This corresponds to Deleuze's argument in the *Postscript on the Societies of Control*, suggesting that capitalism functions as if it were a single corporation with shares (1992a: 4). Financialization through derivatives is able to provide a considerable increase in competition. Consequently, the only thing that the French government and Hollande can do in the financialized Integrated World Capitalism is to foster the competitiveness of the different financialized assets that happen to be situated in France through neoliberal policies such as austerity and wage cuts, as opposed to implementing a coherent national economic policy (Holloway 1994). The internationalization of capital through international flows of finance capital has thus reduced the power of the national state to regulate finance.

In other words, social democratic politics against financialization would be grounded on an interventionist and Keynesian regulation such as the one put in place after the Second World War through the Bretton Woods financial system. In our financialized context marked by post-Fordism and societies of control, however, this is no longer economically feasible because national states no longer have the power to easily regulate international flows of capital. It is quite possible that, had Hollande resisted the banks' and Merkel's lobbying, financial flows would have fled the French economy which would have caused a deepening of the economic crisis. Perhaps France would have been expelled from the eurozone, which would have created a major political crisis as well as a devaluation of the French Franc or the French euro, a default on French sovereign debt and, possibly, a bank run in France.

A second Deleuzo-Guattarian critique of social democratic regulatory politics of finance can be applied to the question of representative democracy. I argue that a social democratic regulation of financialization through the state would entail a stratification of subjectivity. In other words, regulating finance through state interventionism would involve exerting vertical power upon subjectivities, which could be negative. For instance, it could entail a brutal reterritorialization of the state through the closure of national borders so as to control international flows of capital.

As I have argued in the case of Hollande, social democracy implies that finance can be regulated through state action and that state action can be mastered through a parliamentary system and party politics. A parliamentary system and party politics entail a number of points: first, that a political party can actually represent the general will of a certain category of citizens, the working class for instance for social democratic politics; second, that a political party can implement a policy in parliament through deliberative democracy, which represents the general will of a category of citizens.

Representative democracy is based on the mainstream political philosophy of the Enlightenment, in particular on the theorization of the articulation between the people, reason and the political will. In fact, the case is made that it is only through representation that an anarchic multitude of individuals with different passions and interests can be transformed into a rational people with a general will (Rousseau 2002). In other words, political philosophy, which grounds social democratic politics, argues that democracy can only be operated through representation. Technically, the functioning of representation is grounded on the idea of a contract between the represented and the representatives (Locke 2003; Rousseau 2002). Obviously, political philosophies that advocate direct democracy would disagree, in particular the anarchist tradition (Crowder 1991).

However, for Deleuze and Guattari, representation performs a capture of desiring machines because it proceeds through recording. Representation captures the lines of flight of desiring machines and stabilizes them into paranoid poles. Instead, we have before us a system of three terms, where this conclusion becomes completely illegitimate. Distinctions must be made: the repressing representation, which performs the repression; the repressed representative, on which the repression actually comes to bear; the displaced represented, which gives a falsified apparent image that is meant to trap desire (Deleuze and Guattari 1977: 115).

A critique of representative democracy can be operated in light of the Deleuzo- Guattarian critique of psychoanalysis. Psychoanalysis is criticized in *Anti-Oedipus* because it proceeds to a 'theatre' of the unconscious, which would in fact produce a repression of the desiring machine through a capture of desire. In contrast, Deleuze and Guattari argue that the unconscious operates like a factory. Therefore, they construct the concept of desiring machines so as to describe the functioning of the unconscious and of desire. The representation implies a violence of the representative upon the represented. Additionally, the representative constructs an imaginary image of the represented, which corresponds to a form of symbolic violence: 'the representation reduces the representative to what is blocked in this system' (Deleuze and Guattari 1977: 165).

The political system of representative democracy cannot be considered really democratic from a Deleuzo-Guattarian perspective because it is grounded on a relationship of power between the represented and the representatives. The representatives, that is the members of parliament, cannot rationally talk on behalf of the citizens they are meant to represent according to the contractualist philosophy of representative democracy (Locke 2003; Rousseau 2002). On the contrary, the representatives exert a relationship of power on the represented, and so their main objective is not democracy, but rather to reproduce these power relationships.

Furthermore, the Deleuzo-Guattarian critique of representative democracy corresponds to a critique of the mainstream political philosophy of the Enlightenment. In fact, the representatives do not operate the general will of the people through deliberative procedures since they exert a relationship of power upon the represented. The contract through which the represented alienate their sovereignty to the representative is not a democratic and rational procedure, but only the result of an asymmetric relationship of power (Rousseau 2002). In fact, the rational and democratic politics theorized by Rousseau or other theorists of the mainstream political philosophy of the Enlightenment conceal asymmetric relationships of power and a confiscation of revolutionary lines of flights by the representatives of the people.

Additionally, the repression of the representative upon the represented produces a 'displaced represented, which gives a distorted apparent image that is meant to trap desire' (Deleuze and Guattari 1977: 115). The symbolic violence of the representation operates a displacement of the represented. In particular, revolutionary desire is trapped into party politics and its logic of social categories and interests. By way of example, the revolutionary desire of students and workers in May '68 was represented by trade unions bargaining for higher wages at the Grenelle agreements. The revolutionary, which by definition escapes representation, is therefore forced into a representation, for instance a social democratic party.

Representative democracy is arguably linked to the exercising of state power. Social democracy thus consists of a specific way of exercising state power:

> A very general pole of the State, "social democracy," can be defined by this tendency to add, invent axioms in relation to spheres of investment and sources of profit: the question is not that of freedom and constraint, nor of centralism and decentralization, but of the manner in which one masters the flows.
>
> (Deleuze and Guattari 1987: 462)

Social democracy in relation to financialization can therefore be understood as the project to master the flows of finance through state power. This specific form of state power could imply paranoid reterritorialization of subjectivity on the nation against international flows of finance capital. The initial objective to exert democratically state power in order to regulate finance could lead to nationalist reterritorializations and national antagonisms, for instance between France and its traditional tax havens such as Switzerland or Luxembourg.

Finally, according to Deleuze and Guattari, state power is always despotic and implies the operating of extraordinary violence upon society:

> modern capitalist and socialist States take on the characteristic features of the primordial despotic State. As for democracies, how could one fail to recognize in them the despot who has become colder and more hypocritical, more calculating, since he must himself count and code instead of overcoding the accounts? . . . the despotic State is the abstraction that is realized.
>
> (1977: 220)

Social democracy therefore only proposes a milder form of the exercising of power by the despotic state.

Resisting financialization through horizontal politics

Unlike social democratic politics of regulation of financialization, I argue that Deleuzo- Guattarian politics of resistance to financialization should be understood within the framework of horizontal politics. Occupy Wall Street therefore constitutes an interesting case for reflecting on Deleuzo-Guattarian resistance to financialization, because it was a social movement that emphasized horizontal politics and clearly targeted financialization, because of its symbolic name and the geographical location of Zuccotti park close to Wall Street. Second, many people in Occupy Wall Street emphasized the question of debt, which is central to financialization (Caffentzis 2013a, 2013b). In particular, many students who had student debts and many people who had medical debts talked about it on the We Are the 99 Percent blog (2014). Finally, Occupy Wall Street contributed to the emergence of Strike Debt! and activism related to debt struggle. A horizontal politics involves more autonomous forms of subjectivity that avoid the brutal statist reterritorialization of social democracy.

Many horizontalist political experiments have emerged in Latin America these last 20 years. The Zapatista movement was able to develop forms of horizontal politics in Mexico as early as 1994. It was able to confront financial markets, at least momentarily, because the 1994 uprising contributed to capital flight:

> Capital was frightened away by the zapatistas, but it was fleeing from the combination of the insubordination and non-subordination of labour in Mexico: its flight expressed the unity of the antagonism of labour (overt and latent) to capital. It "re-composed" labour, brought together resistances to capital that had appeared to be separate.
>
> (Holloway 2000: 173)

Similarly, in Argentina after the crisis of 2001, some groups were able to operate forms of horizontal politics and self-management (Colectivo Situaciones 2003). Arguably, horizontal politics emerged as a form of collective and affective response to the traumatic economic and financial crisis of December 2001 (Sitrin 2007: 47). However, despite the interest generated by these experiments, which created 'spaces of liberty' (Guattari and Negri 1990), it should be noted that Argentina was reterritorialized as a populist state in the 2000s with Néstor Kirchner and later Cristina de Kirchner's Peronism through a control of international flows of finance (Grigera 2013).

Additionally, horizontal politics in Latin America were often connected to spacialization of self-management through the actual control of spaces of autonomy that would escape the power of the state and of capital:

> territorialization of those involved: Indians, farm-workers and popular urban sectors. However, the logic of territory is very different from that of the social movement. While one acts in accordance with the demands of the state, the other is "living space" – characterized by the capacity to integrally

produce and reproduce the daily lives of its members in a totality that is not unified but rather diverse and heterogeneous.

(Zibechi 2008)

These forms of territorialization of autonomy (Zibechi 2012) imply some form of material interaction with the environment and permanent occupation, as performed in Chiapas by the Zapatista movement.

It could be argued that Occupy Wall Street corresponds to this form of territorialization exemplified by the Zapatista movement. I would argue, however, that occupying a camp temporarily cannot be compared to self-managing whole areas of Chiapas for more than 20 years. The main reason is probably connected to a problem of state repression. After all, what the New York Police Department was able to do in Zuccotti Park the Mexican army was unable to achieve in Chiapas; that is, taking control of a 'space of freedom' (Guattari and Negri 1990). The horizontal politics of Occupy Wall Street are therefore probably less durable and material than the horizontal politics of the Zapatista movement in Chiapas. Nonetheless, I subscribe to the fact that the occupation technique implied maybe more durable forms of politics than migration between the summits of the global justice movement. Zuccotti Park could be associated with a 'temporary autonomous zone' (Bey 1991).

Occupy Wall Street started on 17 September 2011 (Schmitt et al. 2011: 2). A number of activists demonstrated in the Financial District of New York and occupied Zuccotti Park at Liberty Plaza. This square was just a few hundred metres away from the New York Stock Exchange. On 17 September 2011, the protesters gathered for an 'occupation of Wall Street' (Schmitt et al. 2011: 2). The protesters were able to occupy Zuccotti Park at night, despite police presence (Schmitt et al. 2011: 3). The camp occupying Zuccotti Park was not evicted by the NYPD before 15 November. The objective of the protestors and the activists who occupied Zuccotti Park was therefore to combat the power of finance symbolized by Wall Street.

Wall Street and the Financial District are the centre of power of American finance because the New York Stock Exchange is based there as well as the headquarters of many important investment banks such as Goldman Sachs, J. P Morgan and Morgan Stanley, all of which were involved in the financial crisis of 2007–2008. The Chicago Board of Trade in which derivatives are traded is another important financial centre of power. Arguably, Wall Street is the centre of world finance (Arrighi 1994: 14). Consequently, setting up a protest camp in Lower Manhattan entails confronting the power of finance on the global scale. Furthermore, the slogan 'We are the 99%' was a symbol of the struggle of Occupy Wall Street against the power of finance and its role in increasing inequalities, which brought about an extreme accumulation of wealth for 1 per cent of the population.

Occupy Wall Street operated through a permanent camp as well as through other actions including protest marches and demonstrations in New York City. For instance, 700 protesters connected to Occupy Wall Street were arrested by the New York Police Department on Brooklyn Bridge on 1 October 2011.

However, camp life and how it was organized was crucially important. The General Assembly was an essential part of it (Taylor and Greif 2011: 22). Thousands of people gathered and communicated through a series of signs and techniques such as repeating the message of the speaker in waves. This happened in particular when Slavoj Žižek gave a speech at Zuccotti Park on 9 October 2011 (Taylor 2011a: 65). The General Assembly was able to take decisions and was not only a place for discussion and debate. Notably, the General Assembly was able to determine a declaration with demands on 29 September 2011.

Furthermore, new technologies and social networks were used extensively by Occupy Wall Street. In particular, blogging was a way to share experiences and thoughts for many activists or individuals who wanted to support Occupy Wall Street. On the We are the 99 Percent blog thousands of people posted photographs of themselves with text explaining why they belonged to the 99 per cent and often complaining about student debt or medical debt (2014). Similarly, the sessions of the General Assembly were streamed on the internet. Arguably, YouTube and Twitter were also important elements for spreading and organizing Occupy Wall Street (Thorson et al. 2013: 421).

The Occupy Wall Street movement was characterized by a refusal of traditional forms of leadership and authority. Many famous critics and intellectuals including Naomi Klein, Žižek and Reverend Jesse Jackson approached Zuccotti Park and Occupy Wall Street. However, even though they were allowed to address the General Assembly, they did not become leaders of Occupy Wall Street or even official speakers. This implied a rupture with the tradition of the civil rights movement of the 1960s and its charismatic leader, Martin Luther King. Similarly, Occupy Wall Street did not explicitly join an established left-wing political party or trade union. In particular, Occupy Wall Street did not try to connect with the Democratic party or the AFL-CIO, or even with more radical organizations such as the Industrial Workers of the World, Trotskyist or communist groups. Arguably, the Occupy Wall Street movement kept away from traditional forms of politics, even though it occasionally supported industrial actions organized by trade unions such as the general strike in Oakland on 2 November 2011 (Taylor 2011b: 139).

An essential feature of Occupy Wall Street was its ability to spread to a significant number of American cities as well as to cities in other parts of the world. Occupy movements took place in Oakland, Boston, London, Paris and Brussels. Arguably, all these movements used the technique of the camp in a central square, the 'We are the 99%' slogan, as well as other Occupy Wall Street features, though with differences. It can be argued that the Occupy movement had a direct global impact on resisting financialization.

Some authors criticized Occupy Wall Street for its lack of institutionalization and dismissed it (Kreiss and Turfekci 2013: 166; Mirowski 2013). Furthermore, a discussion emerged between scholars who supported the Occupy Wall Street movement. On the one hand, anarchists tended to laud the decision making-process of Occupy Wall Street. In particular, the anthropologist David Graeber argued that the Occupy Wall Street movement was anarchistic (2011b) and produced a number of arguments to substantiate his analysis of Occupy Wall Street.

First, Graeber pointed to 'the refusal to recognise the legitimacy of existing political institutions' by Occupy Wall Street (2011b). This entailed a critique of the existing functioning of representative democracy in America. Second, Graeber argued that Occupy Wall Street was characterized by 'the refusal to accept the legitimacy of the existing legal order' (2011b). In particular, Occupy Wall Street occupied a public space without permission. Third, Graeber argued that Occupy Wall Street was marked by 'the refusal to create an internal hierarchy, but instead to create a form of consensus-based direct democracy' (2011b). This referred to the refusal of leadership and the democratic practices of the General Assembly.

Fourth, Graeber argued that Occupy Wall Street was characterized by 'the embrace of prefigurative politics' (2011b). This implied that the Zuccotti Park camp was a kind of small anarchist society operating though freedom and equality. In other words, the deliberative process of operating a consensus is related to the performative action of creating an anarchistic moment. Graeber's position is therefore more closely related to the idea of the process and the experience of the Occupy Wall Street movement, and less so to the durability of the movement and its capacity to achieve strategic objectives.

Unlike Graeber, others considered that the Occupy Wall Street movement could spawn new forms of organizations. A controversy occurred between these two interpretations and, not surprisingly, there was opposition between the views of anarchists and communists. Jodi Dean argued that the Occupy Wall Street movement was 'pointing toward the possibility of a new party' (2013). In actual fact, Occupy Wall Street was a movement that could bring about an organizational alternative to the problematic Leninist militarized conception of the political party. According to Dean, this party needed to be 'communist', namely with the totalized strategic objective to transcend capitalism and create an egalitarian society (2013).

Dean's point was based on psychoanalytical reasoning. First, the Occupy Wall Street movement corresponded to the creation of a 'division'; that is, strong disagreement with the hegemonic ideology that claimed finance was good for the majority of the population (Dean 2011: 88). Second, according to Dean, the Occupy Wall Street movement could be the point of departure of a communist party, that is to say 'collective desire for collectivity' (2012: 20). In other words, the Occupy Wall Street movement needed the party so as to avoid organizational problems connected to anarchism, which would be based primarily on the articulation of individual desire to reach consensus.

Similarly, Žižek argued that it was important for the Occupy Wall Street movement to durably tackle the question of the 'commons' (2011: 69). Therefore, according to Žižek it was necessary for the Occupy Wall Street movement to generate change in contemporary financialized capitalism. Otherwise, the Occupy Wall Street movement would be no more than a 'carnival' (Žižek 2011: 68). In the Middle Ages, carnival was the only moment in the year when the population was allowed to symbolically challenge the secular and religious powers. The social function of carnival was to allow people for a brief moment to symbolically criticize the social order to ensure that it could be maintained the rest of the year.

Arguably, two main views emerged in relation to the Occupy Wall Street movement. An anarchistic view focused on the decision-making process and the horizontal practices of Occupy Wall Street, whereas the communist view insisted more
on the urgency for the left to create a new form of communist party. Both these
views could be drawn upon to elaborate a politics of resistance to financialization.

Occupy Wall Street and Deleuzo-Guattarian resistance: itinerant politics

I shall provide a Deleuzo-Guattarian understanding of Occupy Wall Street,
which is different from these interpretations. The anarchist interpretation of
Occupy Wall Street is based on a leaderless form of politics such as Deleuzo-
Guattarian politics. Nevertheless, its advocacy of a rational form of democracy
through consensus and deliberation is not related to the Deleuzo-Guattarian
emphasis on a politics of affects. Likewise, the insistence on the organization
of a 'new party' in the communist interpretation (Dean 2013) is not related to
my Deleuzo-Guattarian understanding of resisting financialization. In order to
develop a form of Deleuzo-Guattarian politics of resistance to financialization
and debt, I shall draw on the concepts of 'itinerant' politics and 'event'.

The notion of 'itinerance' is developed in *A Thousand Plateaus*:

> Not that the division of labor in nomad science is any less thorough; it is
> different. We know of the problems States have always had with journey-
> men's associations, or *compagnonnages*, the nomadic or itinerant bodies of the
> type formed by masons, carpenters, smiths, etc.
>
> (Deleuze and Guattari 1987: 368)

Itinerance is associated with 'minor science', as opposed to 'royal science'. Itinerance corresponds to the practice of metallurgy, which is nomadic and based
on the mastering of matter. Itinerance opposes the power of the state and its
reterritorialization. Consequently, itinerant politics corresponds to politics that
do not rely on a vanguard party and its hierarchical organization. Accordingly,
the Leninist party replicates the hierarchical bureaucracy of the state because it
wants to exercise state power.

Furthermore, the idea of itinerant politics can be associated with the notion of
'relay' that was developed by Deleuze as an alternative to the Leninist model of
the organization in the early 1970s (Deleuze and Foucault 1977). Radical politics
was considered as a series of 'relays' between limited and situated theoretical and
practical experiences:

> We must set up lateral affiliations and an entire system of networks and
> popular bases; and this is especially difficult. In any case, we no longer define
> reality as a continuation of politics in the traditional sense of competition
> and the distribution of power, through the so-called representative agencies
> of the Communist Party or the General Workers Union.
>
> (Deleuze and Foucault 1977: 212)

Deleuze provided the example of this conception of politics as a series of relays with the Prison Information Group (Dosse 2010: 310). The Prison Information Group allowed for a productive collaboration between prisoners and intellectuals through leaderless practice. In the same fashion the different Occupy Wall Street movements in different cities could be understood as a series of relays of leaderless resistance against financialization.

Similarly, Pignarre and Stengers drew on the question of 'itinerant' politics, which they associated with circulation between different situated practices (2011: 123). Each relay or each situated experience implied a moment of collective creation (Pignarre and Stengers 2011: 123). Consequently, there could be 'itinerant' politics consisting of different or perhaps even heterogeneous struggles. Situated feminist experience could be relayed into situated postcolonial experience, for instance. Yet, this idea of 'itinerant' politics could bring about a transcending of financialization through an intensification of the itinerary and the multiplication of relays.

The Occupy Wall Street movement can be considered as belonging to itinerant politics. First, the Occupy Wall Street movement through its horizontality and its leaderless practice refused the party's hierarchy. Similarly, power circulated in the Occupy Wall Street movement since it was not organized in top-down relationship between leader and followers. Additionally, the horizontal practice of the Occupy Wall Street movement was characterized by creativity. For instance, conversations in the camp between different people coming from different backgrounds generated moments of creation. The usage of blogs to talk about personal experiences about debt was another creative form (We Are the 99 Percent 2014). Similarly, the slogan 'We are the 99%' was the collective creation of the Occupy Wall Street movement.

Guattari, however, during a journey to Brazil in the early 1980s, expressed a slightly different view in relation to Lula and the Workers' Party on the question of leadership:

> The question, therefore, is not whether we should organize or not, but whether or not we are reproducing the modes of dominant subjectivation in any of our daily activities, including militancy in organizations. It is in these terms that the "function of autonomy" must be considered. It is expressed on a micropolitical level, which has nothing to do with anarchy, or with democratic centralism.
>
> (Guattari and Rolnik 2008: 44)

It seems that a party or a leader can operate as a relay for micropolitics as long as this corresponds to no more than relative reterritorialization – and not to brutal restratification – which allows spaces of autonomy to be created:

> Part of Guattari's interest lay in seeing how micropolitical changes in sensibility and subjectivity could find support in a focal point provided by the charismatic figure of an outsider relayed by the mass media – Lula – and be

given a certain consistency through the formation of the young Workers' Party (PT).

(Nunes and Trott 2008: 40)

This argument also corresponds to Guattari's refusal of the dualism between anarchic spontaneism and rigid centralism. Every political situation is an assemblage that needs to be analysed according to its specific situation. Nonetheless, this point is rather limited and does not contradict Deleuze and Guattari's critique of Leninism. It implies that specific forms of organization can be useful as long as they do not destroy the lines of flight of a specific situation, which a rigid top down leadership would entail.

The ability of Occupy Wall Street to spread to the rest of the United States and the world was another characteristic of itinerant politics. Occupy Oakland or Occupy Montréal did not obey to the orders of an international hierarchy with a strong leadership and a blueprint for political action or revolution. In contrast, they spontaneously and creatively set up camps and decided which actions they wanted to carry out. In particular, Occupy Oakland organized a general strike on 2 November 2011 (Taylor 2011b: 139) without taking orders from a centralized leadership. A general strike can be seen as a form of resistance to financialization as it disrupts the process of intensification of competition operated by the 'competitive calculation' of financialization (Harvie 2008b: 31). The Occupy movement spread without totalized and hierarchized planning, but rather according to the internal and horizontal logic of the social movement. Nonetheless, the Occupy movement was also able to demonstrate solidarity, in particular against the brutal behaviour and arbitrary arrests of the police (Taylor 2011b: 141).

The movement Strike Debt! can be seen as a relay of the situated emancipatory practices started by the Occupy Wall Street. Strike Debt! sets a direct challenge to financialization, and hence arguably to capitalism. Strike Debt! promotes the rolling jubilee which involves the purchasing and cancelling of debt. Actually, it is an extremely powerful and revolutionary tool with potential itinerant and viral effects as it is possible to cancel huge amounts of debt for very limited investment: 'You can buy a $1,000 debt for $50 . . . That's why demand at this point for amend to the debt system, which has become so generalized within the working class, is an extremely important and volatile demand' (Caffentzis 2013a: 12). In other words, the rolling jubilee is potentially a revolutionary tool as it can coordinate debtors extremely rapidly and 'transform the power relationships' of financialized capitalism (Caffentzis 2013a: 12).

Occupy Wall Street and Deleuzo-Guattarian resistance: the event

I shall argue that Occupy Wall Street can be understood as an event from the perspective of a revolutionary interpretation of Deleuze and Guattari. It is possible to draw a rupturalist theory of the revolutionary event from Deleuze and

Guattari's standpoint. Deleuze provides an elaborate definition of the event in *The Logic of Sense*:[2]

> Becoming unlimited comes to be the ideational and incorporeal event, with all of its characteristic reversals between future and past, active and passive, cause and effect, more and less, too much and not enough, already and not yet. The infinitely divisible event is always *both at once*. It is eternally that which has just happened and that which is about to happen, but never that which is happening (to cut too deeply and not enough) . . . Concerning the cause and the effect, events, *being always effects*, are better able to form among themselves functions of quasi-causes or relations of quasi-causality, which are always reversible (the wound and the scar).
>
> (Deleuze 1993b: 45)

The event cannot be understood within the framework of a traditional understanding of time with a past determining the present and the future. In particular, the traditional understanding of time implies that it is possible to operate probabilistic predictions about the future as long as it possible to have cognition about the past. By contrast, the event belongs to another form of time, which is eternal and belongs to the becoming.

This corresponds to the opposition between *chronos* and *aion* (Deleuze 2004: 77). *Aion* is the time of the event. Politically speaking, *chronos* corresponds to the regular and normal functioning of politics within the framework of financialization, whereas *aion* is related to the possibility of collective resistance against financialization, through Occupy Wall Street or Strike Debt! for instance.

The event, however, which corresponds to the becoming requires a 'counteractualization' (Deleuze 1993b: 80). This allows for the group involved in an event to become an 'actor of its own event' (Deleuze 1993b: 80). Events appear as virtuals within the repetition of being, namely financialization. Then the revolutionary event implies actualizing a virtual within capitalism through a counteractualization. From this point of view, any counteractualized event brings about rupturalist politics of resistance against financialization. Consequently, the event of revolution constitutes an eternal present:

> The question of the future of the revolution is a bad question because, insofar as it is asked, there are so many people who do not *become* revolutionaries, and this is exactly why it is done, to impede the question of the revolutionary-becoming of people, at every level, in every place.
>
> (Deleuze and Parnet 1987: 147)

Furthermore, the event understood in Deleuzian terms can be related to the concept of rhizome. The rhizomatic logic consists of an explosion of creativity that cannot be predicted in advance according to a bird's eye view of rationality (Deleuze and Guattari, 1987: 7). It is opposed to the arborescent logic, which provides complete cognition of a specific situation. In contrast, the rhizome operates through connections, which always exceed pre-existing structures.

Therefore, the event is at the same time a rupture within a rhizomatic logic and a moment of intensity; that is to say of pure becoming. Occupy Wall Street corresponded, politically, to both of these features. First, Occupy Wall Street operated a rhizomatic rupture in relation to financialization because it consisted of a creative and novel form of politics through resisting the power of capital. For instance, Occupy Wall Street invented the slogan 'We are the 99%'. Similarly, the transformation of Zuccotti Park into an occupation camp demanded a great deal of creativity. Second, Occupy Wall Street was an event as a form of pure intensity.

The idea of event as pure moment of intensity in a political context is well captured by the concept of 'moments of excess'; that is to say 'collective creativity that threatens to blow open the door of their societies' (The Free Association 2011: 31). In a moment of excess, a number of individuals are transformed into a political and collective intensity through the logic of the political event, for instance a demonstration, a riot, or a specific social movement like 'the struggle against the poll tax in the late 1980s/early 1990s' (The Free Association 2011: 33). This corresponds to the transformation of a subjected group into a group subject. A group of people is transformed into a 'pack' with similar intensive subjectivity (Deleuze and Guattari 1987: 29). By contrast, a group of people with a similar arborescent subjectivity consists of a 'mass' with a rigid leader (Deleuze and Guattari 1987: 33).

I would argue that the Deleuzian conception of the event is different from the Badiouan conception of the event. Badiou understands the event as a form of truth procedure within the framework of a rationalist philosophy (2001, 2005). There are artistic events, scientific events, events connected to love and political events. Therefore, Badiou operates a rationalistic and universalistic conceptualization of the political event, and it would probably be possible to understand Occupy Wall Street in this fashion. On the one hand, Deleuze agrees with Badiou because the event is a rupture with the state of things, that is financialized capitalism. However, the Deleuzian conception of the event is different from Badiou's because the event is also a moment of excess; that is to say of pure intensity according to an affective as opposed to a rationalist logic. People resisted financialization together in Zuccotti Park because they shared the same excessive subjectivity at a specific moment and not only because they agreed with some abstract principles with which a Badiouan truth procedure might be associated.

Conclusion

In this final chapter, I have tried to provide a speculative reflection on resistance to financialization from the perspective of a revolutionary interpretation of Deleuze and Guattari. I have tried to create a 'resonance' (Thoburn 2003: 1) between a revolutionary interpretation of Deleuze and Guattari and the Marxian literature on financialization.

This, however, was mainly an exploratory and necessarily limited attempt, and for two main reasons. First, the articulation of Deleuze and a form of politics of resistance to finance is a novel field that requires much further research. Second, Deleuzian philosophy does not provide any clear political programme, which could be implemented, as opposed to Leninist politics. Therefore, I have tried to develop a form of Deleuzian politics of resistance to financialization in relation to two recent political events: French President Hollande's failed social democratic response to financialization and Occupy Wall Street as a horizontal form of resistance to financialization.

In the first section, I criticized a social democratic response to financialization through an analysis of President Hollande's failed attempt to regulate financial markets in France. On the one hand, social democratic regulation of finance seems much more suited to a Fordist context, as opposed to the current post-Fordist context, which can be characterized with reference to the Deleuzian concept of societies of control. On the other hand, social democratic politics are grounded on representative democracy, whereas a Deleuzian revolutionary politics advocates a horizontal politics.

In the second section, I explored what could be referred to as a Deleuzo-Guattarian and revolutionary politics of resistance to financialization through an analysis of Occupy Wall Street. I argued that a Deleuzo-Guattarian and revolutionary politics could not be based on Leninism with its emphasis on rigid top-down leadership and organization. Also, the Leninist party is a form of closed institution operating through discipline within the framework of a Fordist context (Deleuze 1992a). Nevertheless, I argued that horizontal politics of resistance, based only on rational consensus through deliberation, would not correspond to a Deleuzo-Guattarian and revolutionary politics. By contrast, I argued that a Deleuzo-Guattarian and revolutionary politics would be grounded on shared affective subjectivity, as opposed to a rationalist understanding of politics (for instance, Badiou 2005; Rousseau 2002).

I suggested that a Deleuzo-Guattarian and revolutionary politics of resistance to financialization could be understood as centred around two concepts: itinerant politics and event. Itinerant politics imply a number of connections between heterogeneous and situated practices, which could generate a revolution through capillarity and without a totalized strategy (Deleuze and Foucault 1977). The Deleuzian event entails a creative rupture with the chronological and consequential logic of financialization and of the power of capital (Deleuze 2004). This corresponds to a logic of *aion* and becoming, as opposed to *chronos* and being (Deleuze 2004). Additionally, the Deleuzian event entails a form of collective intensity, which transforms subjectivity and can be described using the concept of 'moments of excess' (The Free Association 2011). I argued that such a moment of excess occurred at Zuccotti Park.

Finally, I would suggest that revolutionary politics of resistance to financialization have to confront debt, which for subjectivity is the most obvious materialization of finance, and I argue that Occupy Wall Street addressed the issue, for example through Strike Debt! (Caffentzis 2013a). A revolutionary

Deleuzo–Guattarian politics of resistance to financialization would therefore generate a 'jubilee' of debt; that is to say an immediate end to all existing debt (Graeber 2011b: 2). I would suggest that this revolutionary jubilee would be brought about through an itinerant politics and revolutionary events with, for example, the continuation of the line of flight of the Occupy Wall Street movement, and not through a totalized Leninist politics. Successfully resisting financialization would involve an important challenge to the power of capital, which increasingly today is grounded on debt.

Notes

1 There were other attempts to resist financialization, in particular in the United States with Obama. However, they were not as systematic as Hollande's clearly social democratic programme. Iceland is another interesting case involving an ambitious regulation of the financial sector. However, because of the size of Iceland, I decided to analyse the French example. More recently, the centrist Macron and – in a different way – the right-wing populist Trump have deepened financialization and neoliberalism.
2 I used this translation of *The Logic of Sense* in relation to the question of the event because it is more faithful to the French text.

Concluding comments

The question this book wanted to respond to was: 'How can a revolutionary interpretation of Deleuze and Guattari politicize financialization?' In order to respond to this question I have articulated two problematics. The first part of this work provided an analysis of the reception of Deleuze and Guattari by political philosophy and the second part consisted in an application of my revolutionary understanding of Deleuze and Guattari to financialization. This application of a revolutionary understanding of Deleuze and Guattari to financialization implied an engagement with the Marxian literature on financialization as well as an analysis of practical struggles such as the Occupy Wall Street movement.

My response to the question proposed the idea that it was possible to create a productive resonance (Thoburn 2003: 1) between a poststructuralist philosophy and a Marxian understanding of financialization. Even though I showed in Chapter 6 in particular that Deleuze and Guattari had been influenced by the oeuvre of Marx, I did not try to assert that Deleuze and Guattari corresponded entirely to Marxism. In contrast, I tried to articulate a fruitful dialogue between Deleuze and Guattari and Marxians, despite differences in particular on the problematization of a politics of resistance to financialization.

I argued drawing on a revolutionary interpretation of Deleuze and Guattari that resisting financialization could not be based on the notions of class politics and of revolutionary subject as these notions were more suited to Fordism. In contrast, through an analysis of the Occupy Wall Street movement I argued that a politics of resistance to financialization could only work with the Deleuzo-Guattarian notions of event and itinerant politics. This work contributes to a continuation of the debates between Deleuze and Guattari and Marx within the broader framework of the debates between poststructuralism and Marxism.

A brief wrap-up of the book might be useful at this stage before final comments and reflections. In the Introduction, I explained how I would construct a study of the reception of Deleuze and Guattari by political philosophy through in particular a careful textual analysis and a taking into account of political context. I argued that it was not possible to use the Deleuzian concept of buggery and the Deleuzo-Guattarian notion of cartography in order to perform this task. My study of the reception of Deleuze and Guattari was influenced in particular by Cleaver's analysis (2000) of the reception of *Capital*. Then I argued that I would apply this analysis of the reception of Deleuze and Guattari to the question of financialization, in particular as it is problematized by the Marxian literature. This allowed me to operate a non-naïve and situated application of a revolutionary interpretation of Deleuze and Guattari to financialization.

In the first part of the book, I demonstrated through a careful textual analysis that three main interpretations of the philosophy of Deleuze and Guattari existed. In other words, reading Deleuze and Guattari or interpreting Deleuze and Guattari was not a neutral and transparent action but was related to interpretative traditions and strategies. In Chapter 2, I analysed a first position that characterized the philosophy of Deleuze and Guattari as being elitist, that is to say a purely philosophical oeuvre reserved for an elite of professional philosophers. This interpretation implied a depoliticization of Deleuze and Guattari. Some authors, influenced in particular by Marxism, using this interpretative strategy criticized Deleuze and Guattari; some others, on the contrary, celebrated the Deleuzo-Guattarian oeuvre. In Chapter 3, I demonstrated that there was a liberal interpretation of the philosophy of Deleuze and Guattari that argued that the Deleuzo-Guattarian oeuvre was compatible with capitalism. Some authors used this interpretive strategy so as to articulate a poststructuralist version of the liberal philosophy, as though Deleuze and Guattari were more effective to defend the market than Locke or Adam Smith. Other authors used this interpretative strategy in order to discredit them as revolutionary thinkers or even thinkers for the left.

In Chapter 3, I argued that a revolutionary reception of Deleuze and Guattari existed that asserted that this oeuvre could be used so as to criticize and transcend capitalism. Some of these authors were Marxists, others were more anarchist and anti-Marxist. I supported this interpretation and the second part of this work was informed by this specific interpretation. To a certain extent, this interpretive tradition was the more faithful to Deleuze and Guattari as they claimed to have 'remained Marxists' (Deleuze and Negri 1995: 171).

In the second part of this book, I applied a revolutionary interpretation of Deleuze and Guattari to financialization. In Chapter 5, I explained that Deleuze and Guattari had not been able to fully understand financialization because they had died in 1992 and 1995, that is to say before, for instance the systemic crisis of 2007–2008. Therefore, I engaged with the Marxian literature on financialization so as to understand this phenomenon. In other words, I argued that a revolutionary interpretation of Deleuze and Guattari had to listen to the Marxian literature in order to understand financialization. I criticized as well social studies of finance because they did not take into account the relations of power implied by financialization, as opposed to the Marxian literature.

However, in Chapter 5, I explained that Deleuze and Guattari anticipated some of the analyses of the financialization literature through concepts like machinic enslavement or societies of control. Likewise, Foucault, who also provided poststructuralist reflection about capitalism, anticipated financialization with his work on neoliberal governmentality (2008). I argued that Deleuze and Guattari like Foucault shared a critique of the Marxist categories of class politics and revolutionary subject that are performed by the Marxian literature on financialization in order to articulate a resistance to financialization. Additionally, I engaged with different authors that drew on Deleuze and Guattari so as to study finance. I was critical of the authors who celebrated finance, whereas I was sympathetic to other authors who were critical about finance and capitalism.

I argued drawing on Deleuze and Guattari as well as Foucault that the categories of class politics and revolutionary subject provided by the Marxist political grammar are no longer effective in a financialized and post-Fordist context. Therefore, in Chapter 7, I provided a Deleuzo-Guattarian politics of resistance to financialization. I tried to avoid two 'speculative leftism' (Bosteels 2005). In order to do so, I analysed two practical political attempts to resist financialization: the failed social-democratic attempt of Hollande in France and the Occupy Wall Street movement. I criticized the Keynesian and statist approach of Holland to resist which could not work in a post-Fordist context. Then, I argued that the Occupy Wall Street movement corresponded to a Deleuzo-Guattarian politics of resistance to financialization through an event and an itinerant politics.

This work has a number of limitations. First, it has developed specific concepts of Deleuze and Guattari, as opposed to others. Other researchers could either improve my engagement with the notion of event and itinerant politics or decide to work on different concepts from the philosophy of Deleuze and Guattari. Second, I grounded this work on an emerging Marxian literature on financialization that is a contemporary and fluid phenomenon. Therefore, this work should be considered as a historically situated analysis of financialization that seeks to be discussed, continued or even refuted by other scholars, in particular if they reflect about resisting financialization. The literature on financialization has to adapt to the fluidity of its object, especially if it is critical.

If we can now return to the question to which this book has tried to respond ('How can a revolutionary interpretation of Deleuze and Guattari politicize financialization?'), I will try to articulate what constitutes the contribution of this book. The failure of Hollande's attempt to regulate finance as well as the incredible rise of real estate prices in Paris since 1997, which I talked about in the Introduction, are all part of the same conundrum. Contemporary capitalism is fundamentally characterized by financialization. Therefore, describing and understanding contemporary capitalism is necessarily connected to an analysis of financialization and how it is articulated to neoliberalism. This book operated an analysis of financialization through an engagement with an interdisciplinary Marxian literature. This is an important contribution of this book in terms of accumulation of knowledge in relation to the economy and its articulation with the rest of social and subjective life.

Second, this work has sought to identify a revolutionary resistant subjectivity that could confront financialization. This was operated through the novel conceptualization of subjectivity provided by Deleuze and Guattari as Marxism was unable to provide an effective politics of resistance to contemporary capitalism. I argued drawing on Deleuze and Guattari that resisting financialization would imply an 'event' and an 'itinerant politics'. I elaborated a Deleuzo-Guattarian politics of resistance through an analysis of Occupy Wall Street. I argued that a Deleuzo-Guattarian conceptualization of resistance could replace Leninist politics which was more appropriate to Fordist capitalism. This is another important contribution of this book in terms of articulation of an anti-capitalist politics of resistance based on Deleuze and Guattari.

Third, this work has provided an analysis of the reception of Deleuze and Guattari by political philosophy. I demonstrated that the political philosophy of Deleuze and Guattari was interpreted differently by political philosophy, in particular through an elitist understanding, a liberal understanding and a revolutionary understanding. This showed that reading the political philosophy of Deleuze and Guattari was always a situated practice that is connected to a number of political decisions and that there is no epistemic neutrality in relation to reading philosophy. This is another important contribution of this book.

In this work, first, my approach was always connected to providing the context of the arguments and the texts I was engaging with. Second, I always sought to be faithful to the sense of the arguments and the texts I was engaging with. Third, I selected texts and arguments according to a political strategy, that is to say providing a revolutionary politics of resistance to financialization. In a way, I read 'politically' Deleuze and Guattari and the Marxian literature on financialization (Cleaver 2000).

References

Adamson, M. (2009) 'The financialization of student life: five propositions on student debt', *Polygraph*, 2, pp. 107–120.

Althusser, L. (1971) 'Ideology and ideological state apparatuses', in *Lenin and Philosophy and Other Essays*, pp. 126–187. London: Monthly Review Press.

Althusser, L. and Balibar, E. (1997) *Reading Capital*. London: Verso.

Alliez, E. (2003) 'Ontology and logography', in P. Patton and J. Protevi (eds) *Between Deleuze and Derrida*, pp. 84–97. London: Continuum.

Alliez, E., Colebrook, C, Hallward, P., Thoburn, N. and Gilbert, J. (2010) 'Politics? A round-table', *New Formations*, 68(Spring), pp. 143–187.

Alliez, E. and Goffey, A. (eds) (2011) *The Guattari Effect*. London: Continuum.

Armstrong, M., Cornut, G., Delacôte, S., Lenglet, M., Millo, Y., Muniesa, F., Pointier, A. and Tadjeddine, Y. (2012) 'Towards a practical approach to responsible innovation in finance: New Product Committees revisited', *Journal of Financial Regulation and Compliance*, 20(2), pp. 147–168.

Arrighi, G. (1994) *The Long Twentieth Century: Money, Power and the Origins of Our Times*. London: Verso.

Arrighi, G. (2007) *Adam Smith in Beijing: Lineages of the Twenty-First Century*. London: Verso.

Badiou, A. (1999) *Deleuze: The Clamor of Being*. Minneapolis: University of Minnesota Press.

Badiou, A. (2001) *Ethics: An Essay on the Understanding of Evil*. London: Verso.

Badiou, A. (2004) 'The Flux and the Party – In the Margins of Anti-Oedipus', *Polygraph*, 15–16, pp. 75–92.

Badiou, A. (2005) *Being and Event*. London: Continuum.

Badiou, A. (2009) *Logics of Worlds: Being and Event, Volume 2*. London: Continuum. Baiou, A. (2010) *The Communist Hypothesis*. London: Verso.

Badiou A. (2011) *Le Réveil de l'histoire: Circonstance, 6*. Paris: Lignes. Badiou, A. and Balmès, F. (1976) *De l'Idéologie*. Paris: Maspéro.

Balazs, E. (1968) *La Bureaucratie Céleste, Recherches sur l'Economie et la Société de la Chine Traditionnelle*. Paris: Gallimard.

Balibar, E. (1994) 'In search of the proletariat: the notion of class politics in Marx', in *Masses, Classes, Ideas: Studies on Politics and Philosophy before and after Marx*, pp. 125–149. London: Routledge.

Barret, C. (2014) 'Quataris check in to Paris Grand for €330m', *Financial Times*, 7 August. Available at: www.ft.com/cms/s/0/b427c6d0-1e10-11e4-bb68-00144feabdc0.html#axzz3Mahk6aBc (accessed 22 December 2014).

Baudrillard, J. (1995) *Simulacra and Simulation*. Ann Arbor: University of Michigan Press.

Bay, T. (2012) 'Chrematistic deviations', *Journal of Interdisciplinary Economics*, 24(1), pp. 29–54.

Bay, T. and Schinckus, C. (2012) 'Critical finance studies: an interdisciplinary manifesto', *Journal of Interdisciplinary Economics*, 24(1), p. 16.

Becker, G. S. and Elías, J. J. (2007) 'Introducing incentives in the market for live and cadaveric organ donations', *The Journal of Economic Perspectives*, 21(3), pp. 3–24.

Bernstein, E. (1961) *Evolutionary Socialism: A Criticism and Affirmation*. New York: Random House.

Beverungen, A., Dunne, S. and Hoedemaekers, C. (2009) 'The university of finance', *Ephemera Theory & Politics in Organization*, 9(4), pp. 261–270.

Bey, H. (1991) *T.A.Z.: The Temporary Autonomous Zone, Ontological Anarchy, Poetic Terrorism*. Brooklyn: Autonomedia.

Black, F. and Scholes, M. (1973) 'The pricing of options and corporate liabilities', *Journal of Political Economics*, 81(3), pp. 637–654.

Blomberg, J., Kjellberg, H. and Winroth, K. (2012) *Marketing Shares, Sharing Markets: Experts in Investment Banking*. New York: Palgrave.

Bogue, R. (1989) *Deleuze and Guattari*. London: Routledge.

Boltanski, L. and Chiapello, E. (2005) *The New Spirit of Capitalism*. London: Verso.

Bonefeld, W. (1995) 'Monetarism and Crisis', in W. Bonefeld and J. Holloway (eds) *Global National State and the Politics of Money*, pp. 35–68. London: Palgrave Macmillan.

Bonefeld, W. and Holloway, J. (1995a) 'Conclusion: money and class struggle', in W. Bonefeld and J. Holloway (eds) *Global National State and the Politics of Money*, pp. 210–223. London: Palgrave Macmillan.

Bonefeld, W. and Holloway, J. (eds) (1995b) *Global National State and the Politics of Money*. London: Palgrave Macmillan.

Bonefeld, W. and Holloway, J. (1995c) 'Introduction: the politics of money' in W. Bonefeld and J. Holloway (eds) *Global National State and the Politics of Money*, pp. 1–6. London: Palgrave Macmillan.

Bosteels, B. (2005) 'The speculative left', *South Atlantic Quarterly*, 104(4), pp. 751–767.

Bosteels, B. (2011) *Badiou and Politics*. London: Duke University Press.

Bourdieu, P. and Passeron, J.-C. (1979) *The Inheritors: French Students and Their Relations to Culture*. Chicago: University of Chicago Press.

Braudel, F. (1995) *The Mediterranean and the Mediterranean World in the Age of Philip II. Vol 1*. London: University of California Press.

Brenner, R. (2006) *The Economics of Global Turbulence: The Advanced Capitalist Economies from Long Boom to Long Downturn*. London: Verso.

Breton, A. (1988) *Oeuvres Complètes*. Paris: Gallimard.

Brott, S. (2010) 'Deleuze and "The Intercessors"', *Log*, 18(Winter), pp. 135–141.

Bryan, D. and M. Rafferty (2006) *Capitalism with Derivatives: A Political Economy of Financial Derivatives, Capital and Class*. New York: Palgrave Macmillan.

Bryan, D. and Rafferty, M. (2009) 'Homemade financial crisis', *Ephemera Theory & Politics in Organization*, 9(2), pp. 357–362.

Bryan, R., Martin, R. and Rafferty, M. (2009) 'Financialization and Marx: giving labor and capital a financial makeover', *Review of Radical Political Economics*, 41(4), pp. 458–472.

Bryant, L. Srnicek, N. and Harman, G. (2011) *The Speculative Turn: Continental Materialism and Realism*. Melbourne: Re.press.

Buchanan, I. (2008) *Deleuze and Guattari's Anti-Oedipus*. London: Continuum.

Butler, J. (1987) *Subjects of Desire: Hegelian Reflections in Twentieth-Century France*. New York: Columbia University Press.

Caffentzis, G. (1999) 'On the notion of a crisis of social reproduction: a theoretical review', in M. Dalla Costa and G. F. Dalla Costa (eds) *Women, Development, and Labor of Reproduction: Struggles and Movements*, pp. 153–188. Trenton: Africa World Press.

Caffentzis, G. (2002) 'Neoliberalism in Africa, apocalyptic failures and business as usual practices', *Alternatives. Turkish Journal of International Relations*, 1(3), pp. 80–104.

Caffentzis, G. (2013a) *The Making of the Debt Resisters' Movement: From Occupy Wall Street to Strike Debt*. Creative Commons.

Caffentzis, G. (2013b) *In Letters of Blood and Fire: Work, Machines and the Crisis of Capitalism*. Oakland: Autonomedia.

Callon, M. (2007) 'What does it mean to say that economics is performative?', in D. MacKenzie, F. Muniesa, F. and L. Siu (eds) *Do Economists Make Markets? On the Performativity of Economics*, pp. 311–357. Princeton: Princeton University Press.

Christofferson, M. S. (2004) *French Intellectuals Against the Left: The Antitotalitarian Moment of the 1970s*. New York: Berghahn Books.

Cleaver, H. (2000) *Reading Capital Politically*. London: AK Press.

Clouscard, M. (1999) *Néo-Fascisme et Idéologie du Désir*. Bègles: Le Castor Astral.

Colectivo Situaciones (2003) 'On the researcher-militant', EIPCP. Available at: http://eipcp. net/transversal/0406/colectivosituaciones/en (accessed 12 May 2014).

Colwell, C. (1997) 'Deleuze and Foucault: series, event, genealogy', Theory & Event, 1997(2). Available at: https://muse.jhu.edu/journals/theory_and_event/v001/1.2colwell.html (accessed 17 December 2014).

Crowder, G. (1991) *Classical Anarchism: the Political Thought of Godwin, Proudhon, Bakunin, and Kropotkin*. Oxford: Clarendon Press.

Cusset, F. (2008) *French Theory, Foucault, Derrida, Deleuze & Cie and Transfers of Intellectual Life in the United States*. Minneapolis: University of Minnesota Press.

Dean, J. (2011) 'Claiming division, naming a wrong', in A. Taylor, K. Gessen, editors from n+1, Dissent, Triple Canopy and the New Inquiry (eds) *Occupy: Scenes from Occupied America*, pp. 87–92. London: Verso.

Dean, J. (2012) *The Communist Horizon*. London: Verso.

Dean, J. (2013) 'Occupy Wall Street: after the anarchist moment', *Socialist Register*, 49, pp. 52–62.

De Angelis, M. (2001) 'Global capital, abstract labour, and the fractal panopticon', *The Commoner*, 2001(1), pp. 1–19.

De Angelis, M. (2003) 'Neoliberal governance, reproduction and accumulation', *The Commoner*, 2003(Spring/Summer), pp. 1–28.

De Beaupuy, F. (2013) 'Paris luxury property lures overseas rich as French flee taxes', *Bloomberg*, 15 October 2013. Available at: www.bloomberg.com/news/2013-10-14/paris-luxury-property-lures-overseas-rich-as-french-flee-taxes.html (accessed 18 October 2014).

De Brunhoff, S. (1967) *La Monnaie Chez Marx*. Paris: Editions Sociales.

De Brunhoff, S. (1977) *L'Offre de Monnaie, Critique d'un Concept*. Paris: Maspero.

De Landa, M. (2004) 'Deleuzian interrogations: a conversation with Manuel De Landa, John Protevi and Torkild Thanem', *Tamara*, 3(4), pp. 65–86.

De Landa, M. (2010) *Deleuze: History and Science*. New York: Atropos Press. Deleuze, G. (1972) *Proust and Signs*. New York: George Braziller.

Deleuze, G. (1983) *Nietzsche and Philosophy*. New York: Columbia University Press.

Deleuze, G. (1984). *Kant's Critical Philosophy: The Doctrine of the Faculties*. Minneapolis: University of Minnesota Press.

Deleuze, G. (1988a) *Bergsonism*. New York: Zone Books.

Deleuze, G. (1988b) *Foucault*. Minneapolis: University of Minnesota Press.

Deleuze, G. (1988c) *Spinoza: Practical Philosophy*. San Francisco: City Lights.

Deleuze, G. (1989) *"Coldness and Cruelty" in Masochism*. New York: Zone Books.

Deleuze, G. (1990) *Expressionism in Philosophy: Spinoza*. New York: Zone Books.

Deleuze, G. (1991) *Empiricism and Subjectivity: An Essay on Hume's Theory of Human Nature.* New York: Columbia University Press.

Deleuze, G. (1992a) 'Postscript on the societies of control', October, 59(Winter), pp. 3–7.

Deleuze, G. (1992b) 'What is a dispositif?', in T. J. Armstrong (ed.) *Michel Foucault Philosopher*, pp. 159–168. New York: Routledge.

Deleuze, G. (1993a) *The Fold: Leibniz and the Baroque.* Minneapolis: University of Minnesota Press.

Deleuze, G. (1993b) *The Deleuze Reader.* New York: Columbia University Press.

Deleuze, G. (1994) *Difference and Repetition.* New York: Columbia University Press. Deleuze, G. (1995) 'Letters to a harsh critic', in *Negotiations: 1972–1990*, pp. 3–12. New York: Columbia University Press.

Deleuze, G. (2004) *The Logic of Sense.* London: Continuum.

Deleuze, G. and Augst, B. (1998) 'On the new philosophers and a more general problem', *Discourse*, 20(3), pp. 37–43.

Deleuze, G., Descamps, C., Eribon, D., and Maggiori, R. (1995) 'On a thousand plateaus', in G. Deleuze, *Negotiations: 1972–1990*, pp. 25–34. New York: Columbia University Press.

Deleuze, G. and Eribon, D. (1995) 'Life as a work of art', in G. Deleuze, *Negotiations: 1972–1990*, pp. 94–101. New York: Columbia University Press.

Deleuze, G. and Foucault, M. (1977) 'Intellectuals and power', in F. Bouchard (ed.) *Foucault, Language, Counter-Memory, Practice*, pp. 205–217. Ithaca: Cornell University Press.

Deleuze, G. and Guattari, F. (1977) *Anti-Oedipus: Capitalism and Schizophrenia.* New York: Viking Press.

Deleuze, G. and Guattari, F. (1986) *Kafka: Toward a Minor Literature.* Minneapolis: University of Minnesota Press.

Deleuze, G. and F. Guattari (1987) *A Thousand Plateaus: Capitalism and Schizophrenia.* Minneapolis: University of Minnesota Press.

Deleuze, G. and F. Guattari (1994) *What Is Philosophy?* New York: Columbia University Press.

Deleuze, G. and Guattari, F. (1995) 'On anti-Oedipus', in G. Deleuze, *Negotiations: 1972–1990*, pp. 13–24. New York: Columbia University Press.

Deleuze, G. and Negri, T. (1995) 'Control and becoming', in G. Deleuze, *Negotiations: 1972–1990*, pp. 169–176. New York: Columbia University Press.

Deleuze, G. and Parnet, C. (1987) 'Many politics', in *Dialogues II*, pp. 124–128. London: Athlone Press.

Derrida, J. (1997) *Of Grammatology.* Baltimore: Johns Hopkins University Press. Dosse, F. (1997) *The History of Structuralism: The Sign Sets. 1967–Present.* Minneapolis: University of Minnesota Press.

Dosse, F. (2010) *Gilles Deleuze & Félix Guattari Intersecting Lives.* New York: Columbia University Press.

Dosse, F. (2012) 'Deleuze and structuralism', in D. W. Smith and H. Somers-Hall (eds) *The Cambridge Companion to Deleuze*, pp. 126–150. Cambridge: Cambridge University Press.

Dowling, E. and Harvie, D. (2014) 'Harnessing the social: state, crisis and (big) society', *Sociology*, 48(5), pp. 869–886.

Duménil, G. and Lévy, D. (2005) 'Costs and benefits of neoliberalism: a class analysis', in G. A. Epstein (ed.) *Financialization and the World Economy*, pp. 17–33. Northampton: Edward Elgar.

Duménil, G. and Lévy, D. (2011) *The Crisis of Neoliberalism.* London: Harvard University Press.

Epstein G. A. (ed.) (2005) *Financialization and the World Economy.* Northampton: Edward Elgar.

Ertürk, I., Leaver, A. and Williams, K. (2010) 'Hedge funds as "war machine": making the positions work', *New Political Economy*, 15(1), pp. 9–28.

Ertürk, I., Froud, J., Johal, S., Leaver, A. and Williams, K. (2013) '(How) do devices matter in finance?', *Journal of Cultural Economics*, 6(3), pp. 336–352.

Fama, E. (1965) 'The behavior of stock market prices', *Journal of Business*, 38(1), pp. 34–105.

Feder, E. K. (2010) 'Power/knowledge', in D. Taylor (ed.) *Michel Foucault: Key Concepts*, pp. 55–68. Durham: Acumen.

Ferry, L. and Renaut, A. (1990) *French Philosophy of the Sixties: An Essay on Antihumanism*. Amherst: University of Massachusetts Press.

Fisher, M. (2009) *Capitalist Realism: Is There No Alternative?* Winchester: Zero Books.

Forslund, D. and Bay, T. (2009) 'The eve of critical finance studies', *Ephemera: Theory & Politics in Organization*, 9(4), pp. 285–299.

Foucault, M. (1977a) *Discipline and Punish: The Birth of Prison*. London: Penguin.

Foucault, M. (1977b) 'Preface', in G. Deleuze and F. Guattari, *Anti-Oedipus: Capitalism and Schizophrenia*, pp. xi–xiv. New York: Viking Press.

Foucault, M. (1978) *The Will to Knowledge: The History of Sexuality, Vol 1*. London: Penguin.

Foucault, M. (1989) *The Order of Things*. London: Verso.

Foucault, M. (1998a) 'Nietzsche, genealogy, history', in *Essential Works of M. Foucault: Volume 2: Aesthetics, Method and Epistemology*, pp. 369–391. New York: The New Press.

Foucault, M. (1998b) 'Theatrum philosophicum', in *Essential Works of M. Foucault: Volume 2: Aesthetic, Method, and Epistemology*, pp. 343–368. New York: The New Press.

Foucault, M. (2002) *The Archaeology of Knowledge*. London: Routledge.

Foucault, M. (2006) *Madness and Civilization: A History of Insanity in the Age of Reason*. London: Routledge.

Foucault, M. (2007) *Security, Territory, Population*. New York: Palgrave Macmillan.

Foucault, M. (2008) *The Birth of Biopolitics*. New York: Palgrave Macmillan.

Froud, J. and Williams, K. (2000a) 'Restructuring for shareholder value and its implications for labour', *Cambridge Journal of Economics*, 24(6), pp. 771–798.

Froud, J. and Williams, K. (2000b) 'Shareholder value and financialisation consultancy promises, management moves', *Economy and Society*, 29(1), pp. 80–110.

Garo, I. (2008) 'Molecular revolutions', in I. Buchanan I. and N. Thoburn (eds) *Deleuze and Politics*, pp. 54–73. Edinburgh: Edinburgh University Press.

Garo, I. (2011a) *Foucault, Deleuze, Althusser & Marx – La Politique dans la Philosophie*. Paris: Démopolis.

Garo, I. (2011b) *Marx et l'Invention Historique*. Paris: Syllepse.

Garo, I. (2012) 'Infâme dialectique'. Isabelle Garo's website. Available at: http://isabelle.garo.free.fr/chantier/Infame_dialectique.html (accessed 9 May 2012).

Gatinois, C., Michel, A. and Vergès, M. (2010) 'Rumeurs, paris irrationnels: les spéculateurs attisent l'affolement des marchés', *Le Monde*, 9 February 2010. Available at: www.lemonde.fr/europe/article/2010/02/09/rumeurs-paris-irrationnels-les- speculateurs-attisent-l-affolement-des-marches_1303028_3214.html (accessed 28 August 2013).

Genosko, G. (2012) 'Deleuze and Guattari: Guattareuze & Co', in D. W. Smith and H. Somers-Hall (eds) *The Cambridge Companion to Deleuze*, pp. 151–169. Cambridge: Cambridge University Press.

Graeber, D. (2011a) *Debt: The First 5000 Years*. Brooklyn: Melville House.

Graeber, D. (2011b) 'Occupy Wall Street's anarchist roots: the "Occupy" movement is one of several in American history to be based on anarchist principles', *Al Jazeera*, 30 November 2011. Available at: www.aljazeera.com/indepth/opinion/2011/11/2011112872835904508.html (accessed 28 April 2014).

Graeber, D. (2013) *The Democracy Project: A History, a Crisis, a Movement*. New York: Spiegel & Grau.

Grigera, J. (2013) *Argentina Después De La Convertibilidad (2002–2011)*. Buenos Aires: Imago Mundi.

Gros, F. (1995) 'Le Foucault de Deleuze: une fiction métaphysique', *Philosophie*, 47 (September), pp. 53–63.

Grosz, E. (1985) 'Feminism, representation and politics', *On the Beach*, 9(1985), pp. 14–19.

Grosz, E. (1993) 'A thousand tiny sexes: feminism and rhizomatics,' *Topoi: An International Review of Philosophy*, 12(2), pp. 167–179.

Grosz, E. (2000) 'Deleuze's Bergson: duration, the virtual and a politics of the future', in C. Colebrook and I. Buchanan (eds) *Deleuze and Feminist Theory*, pp. 214–234. Edinburgh: Edinburgh University Press.

Guattari, F. (1996) 'Postmodernism and ethical abdication', in G. Genosko (ed.) *The Guattari Reader*, pp. 114–117. Cambridge: Blackwell.

Guattari, F. (2000) *The Three Ecologies*. London: The Athlone Press.

Guattari, F. and Alliez, E. (1996) 'Capitalistic systems, structures and processes', in G. Genosko (ed.) *The Guattari Reader*, pp. 233–247. Cambridge: Blackwell.

Guattari, F. and Negri, T. (1990) *Communist Like Us*. New York: Semiotext(e).

Guattari, F. and Rolnik, S. (2008) *Molecular Revolution in Brazil*. Cambridge: MIT Press.

Gutting, G. (2001) *French Philosophy in the Twentieth Century*. Cambridge: Cambridge University.

Hallward, P. (2006) *Out of this World: Deleuze and the Philosophy of Creation*. London: Verso.

Haraway, D. (1991) 'A cyborg manifesto: science, technology, and socialist- feminism in the late twentieth century', in *Simians, Cyborgs, and Women: The Reinvention of Nature*, pp. 149–181. New York: Routledge.

Hardt, M. and Negri, T. (2000) *Empire*. London: Harvard University Press.

Hardt, M. and Negri, T. (2004) *Multitude: War and Democracy in the Age of Empire*. New York: Penguin.

Hardt, M. and Negri, T. (2009) *Commonwealth*. London: Harvard University Press.

Harvey, D. (2005) *A Brief History of Neolibralism*. Oxford: Oxford University Press.

Harvey, D. (2012) *Rebel Cities: From the Right to the City to the Urban Revolution*. London: Verso.

Harvie, D. (2008a) 'Review of Dick Bryan and Michael Rafferty, *Capitalism with Derivatives: A Political Economy of Financial Derivatives, Capital and Class* (Palgrave Macmillan: Basingstoke and New York, 2006)', *Economic Issues*, 13(2), pp. 73–75.

Harvie, D. (2008b) 'The measure of a monster: capital, class, competition and finance', *Turbulence*, 4, pp. 29–31.

Haugh, D., Ollivaud, P. and Turner, D. (2009), 'What drives sovereign risk premiums? An analysis of recent evidence from the euro area', *OECD Economics Department Working Papers*, 718, pp. 2–24.

Hillier, J. and Van Wezemael, J. (2008) '"Empty, swept and garnished": the public finance initiative case of Throckley Middle School', *Space and Polity*, 12(2), pp. 157–181.

Hobsbawm, E. (1994) *The Age of Extremes: The Short Twentieth Century 1914–1991*. London: Michael Joseph.

Holland, E. W. (2012) 'Deleuze and psychonalysis', in D. W. Smith and H. Somers-Hall (eds) *The Cambridge Companion to Deleuze*, pp. 306–336. Cambridge: Cambridge University Press.

Holland, E. W. (2013) 'Deleuze & Guattari and Minor Marxism', *The Selected Works of Eugene W Holland*. Available at: http://works.bepress.com/eugene_w_holland/3 (accessed 22 September 2013).

Hollande, F. (2012a) *Discours de François Hollande au Meeting du Bourget le 22 Janvier 2012*. Available at: www.ps19.org/. . ./Discours-de-François-Hollande-au- meeting-du-Bourget. pdf (accessed 28 August 2013).

Hollande, F. (2012b) *Mes 60 Engagements pour la France*. Available at: www.parti- socialiste. fr/. . ./les-60-engagements-pour-la-france-de-francois-hollande.pdf (accessed 28 August 2013).

Holloway, J. (1994) 'Global capital and the national state', *Capital & Class,* 18, pp. 23–49.

Holloway, J. (1995) 'The abyss opens: the rise and fall of Keynesianism', in W. Bonefeld and J. Holloway (eds) *Global National State and the Politics of Money*, pp. 7–34. London: Palgrave Macmillan.

Holloway, J. (2000) 'Zapata in Wall Street', in W. Bonefeld and K. Psychopedus (eds) *Politics of Change*, pp. 173–196. London: Palgrave Macmillan.

Holloway, J. (2010) *Crack Capitalism*. New York: Pluto Press.

Howard, P. N. and Muzammil, M. H. (2011) 'The upheavals in Egypt and Tunisia: the role of digital media', *Journal of Democracy*, 22(3), pp. 35–48.

Hughes, J. (2009) *Reader's Guides: Deleuze's Difference and Repetition*. London: Continuum.

Irigaray, L. (1985) *This Sex Which Is Not One*. Ithaca: Cornell University Press. James, W. (2005) *Understanding Poststructuralism*. Acumen: Durham.

Jameson, F. (1991) *Postmodernism: The Cultural Logic of Late Capitalism*. Durham: Duke University Press.

Jameson, F. (1997) 'Culture and finance capital', *Critical Inquiry*, 24(1), pp. 246–265.

Jameson, F. (2007) *Archaeology of the Future: The Desire Called Utopia and Other Science Fictions*. London: Verso.

Jardine, A. (1984) 'Woman in limbo: Deleuze and his br(others)', *Substance*, 13(3–4), pp. 46–60.

Jardine, A. (1985) *Gynesis: Configurations of Woman and Modernity*. Ithaca: Cornell University Press.

Johnson S. (2005) 'Gender relations, empowerment and microcredit: moving forward from a lost decade', *European Journal of Development Research*, 17(2), pp. 224–248.

Khalfa, J. (2003) *Introduction to the Philosophy of Gilles Deleuze*. London: Continuum.

Kreiss, D. and Turfekci, Z. (2013) 'Occupying the political: Occupy Wall Street, collective action, and the rediscovery of pragmatic politics', *Cultural Studies – Critical Methodologies,* 13(3), pp. 163–167.

Krippner, G. (2005) 'The financialization of the American economy', *Socio-Economic Review*, 3, pp. 173–208.

Lambert, G. (2006) *Who's Afraid of Deleuze and Guattari? An Introduction to Political Pragmatics*. London: Continuum.

Lapavitsas, C. (2011) 'Theorizing financialization', *Work Employment and Society*, 25(4), pp. 611–626.

Latour, B. (2005) *Reassembling the Social: An Introduction to Actor-Network-Theory*. Oxford: Oxford University Press.

Lazzarato, M. (2008) 'Mai 68, la "critique artiste" et la révolution néolibérale', *La Revue Internationale des Livres et des Idées*, 2008(7), p. 30. Available at: www.revuedeslivres.net/articles. php?idArt=271 (accessed 5 February 2011).

Lazzarato, M. (2009) 'Neoliberalism in action inequality, insecurity and the reconstitution of the social', *Theory, Culture & Society*, 26(6), pp. 109–133.

Lazzarato, M. (2012) *The Making of the Indebted Man: An Essay on the Neoliberal Condition*. Los Angeles: Semiotext(e).

Lawlor, L. (2012) 'Phenomenology and metaphysics, and chaos: on the fragility of the event in Deleuze', in D. W. Smith and H. Somers-Hall (eds) *The Cambridge Companion to Deleuze*, pp. 103–125. Cambridge: Cambridge University Press.

Lenin, V. I. (1937) *The State and Revolution*. London: Lawrence & Wishart.

Lenin, V. I. (1969) *What is to Be Done? Burning Questions of Our Movement.* New York: International Publishers.

Lenin, V. I. (1977) *Collected Works, Volumes 1, 2, 3.* London: Lawrence & Wishart. Lenin, V. I. (1999) *Imperialism: The Highest Stage of Capitalism.* Chippendale: Resistance Books.

Lévy, B.-H. (1979) *Barbarism with a Human Face.* New York: HarperCollins.

Lewis, M. (2010) *The Big Short: Inside the Doomsday Machine.* New York: W. W. Norton & Company.

Lightfoot, G. and Lilley, S. (2007) 'The glass beads of global war: dealing, death and the policy analysis market', *Critical Perspectives on International Business*, 3(1), pp. 83–100.

Locke, J. (2003) *Two Treatises of Government and A Letter Concerning Toleration.* London: Yale University Press.

Lozano, B. (2013a) 'Why even do heterodox political finance with Deleuze?', Speculative Materialism blog. Available at: http://speculativematerialism.com/why- even-do-heterodox-political-finance-with-deleuze/ (accessed 23 September 2013).

Lozano, B. (2013b) 'Deleuze's guidebook to synthetic finance', Speculative Materialism blog. Available at: http://speculativematerialism.com/category/deleuzes- guidebook-to-synthetic-finance/ (accessed 23 September 2013).

Luxemburg, R. (1971) *The Accumulation of Capital.* London: Routledge.

MacKenzie, D. (2006) *An Engine, not a Camera: How Financial Models Shape Markets.* Cambridge: The MIT Press.

MacKenzie, D. (2009) *Material Markets: How Economic Agents Are Constructed.* New York: Oxford University Press.

Mackenzie, D. and Millo, Y. (2003) 'Negotiating a market, performing theory: the historical sociology of a financial derivatives exchange', *American Journal of Sociology*, 109(1), pp. 107–145.

McNally, D. (2009) 'From financial crisis to world-slump: accumulation, financialisation, and the global slowdown', *Historical Materialism*, 17, pp. 35–83.

Mandarini, M. (2005) 'Antagonism, contradiction, time: conflict and organization in Antonio Negri', *Sociological Review*, 53(1), pp. 192–214.

Marazzi, C. (2011) *The Violence of Financial Capital.* London: Semiotext(e).

Martin, R. (2002) *Financialization of Daily Life.* Philadelphia: Temple University Press.

Martin, R. (2007) *An Empire of Indifference: American War and the Financial Logic of Risk Management.* London: Duke University Press.

Martin, R., Rafferty, M. and Bryan, R. (2008) 'Financialization, risk and labour', *Competition and Change: The Journal of Global Political Economy*, 12(2), pp. 121–133.

Marx, K. and Engels, F. (1969) *Selected Works, Volume One.* Moscow: Progress Publishers.

Marx, K. (1970) 'Critique of the Gotha Program', in K. Marx and F. Engels, *Selected Works, Volume Three*, pp. 13–30. Moscow: Progress Publishers.

Marx, K. (1976) *Capital: A Critique of Political Economy, Volume 1.* London: Penguin. Massumi, B. (1992) *A User's Guide to Capitalism and Schizophrenia: Deviations from Deleuze and Guattari.* London: MIT Press.

Mengue, P. (2003) *Deleuze et la Question de la Démocratie.* Paris: L'Harmattan. Mirowski, P (2009) 'Defining neoliberalism' in P. Mirowski and P. Plehwe (eds) *The Road from Mont Pèlerin: The Making of the Neoliberal Thought Collective*, pp. 417–455. Cambridge: Harvard University Press.

Mirowski, P. (2013) *Never Let a Serious Crisis Go to Waste: How Neoliberalism Survived the Financial Meltdown.* London: Verso.

Mohun, S. (2006) 'Distributive shares in the US economy, 1964–2001', *Cambridge Journal of Economics*, 30(3), pp. 347–370.

Morgan, J. and Olsen, W. (2011) 'Aspiration problems for the Indian rural poor: research on self-help groups and micro-finance', *Capital & Class*, 35(2), pp. 189–212.

Nail, T. (2013) 'Deleuze, Occupy, and the actuality of revolution', *Theory and Event*, 16(1), pp. 20–35.

Negri, T. (2008) *Good Bye Mister Socialism*. London: Seven Stories Press.

Negri, T. (2011) 'Gilles-felix', in E. Alliez and A. Goffey (eds) *The Guattari Effect*, pp. 156–171. London: Continuum.

Neu, D., Everett, J. and Rahaman, A. S. (2009) 'Accounting assemblages, desire, and the body without organs: a case study of international development lending in Latin America', *Accounting, Auditing & Accountability Journal*, 22(3), pp. 319–350.

Nietzsche, F. (1994) *On the Genealogy of Morality*. Cambridge: Cambridge University Press.

Nunes, R. (2010) 'Politics in the middle: for a political interpretation of the dualisms in Deleuze and Guattari', *Deleuze Studies*, 4(Supplement), pp. 104–126.

Nunes, R. and Trott, B. (2008) '"There is no scope for futurology; history will decide": Félix Guattari on molecular revolution', *Turbulence*, 4, pp. 38–47.

Obstfeld, M., and Taylor, A. M. (2004) *Global Capital Markets: Integration, Crisis and Growth*. Cambridge: Cambridge University Press.

Oksala, J. (2010) 'Freedom and bodies', in D. Taylor (ed.) *Michel Foucault: Key Concepts*, pp. 85–97. Durham: Acumen.

Olkowski, D. (2000) 'Body, knowledge and becoming-woman: morpho-logic in Deleuze and Irigaray', in C. Colebrook and I. Buchanan, *Deleuze and Feminist Theory*, pp. 86–109. Edinburgh: Edinburgh University Press.

Parienté, J. (2013) 'De la décision "historique" à la mesure "excessive": comment Moscovici a changé d'avis sur l'ex-taxe Tobin', *Le Monde*, 12 July. Available at: www.lemonde.fr/ decryptages/article/2013/07/12/de-la-decision-historique-a-la-mesure-excessive-comment-moscovici-a-change-d-avis-sur-l-ex-taxe-tobin_3446850_1668393.html (accessed 28 August 2013).

Patton, P. (2000) *Deleuze and the Political*. London: Routledge.

Patton, P. (2003) 'Future politics', in P. Patton and J. Protevi (eds) *Between Deleuze and Derrida*, pp. 14–29. London: Continuum.

Patton, P. (2004) 'Power and right in Nietzsche and Foucault,' *International Studies in Philosophy*, XXXVI(3), pp. 43–61.

Patton, P. (2005) 'Deleuze and democratic politics', in L. Tønder and L. Thomassen, (eds) *Radical Democracy: Politics between Abundance and Lack*, pp. 50–67. Manchester: Manchester University Press.

Patton, P. (2007) 'Derrida, politics and democracy to come', *Philosophy Compass*, 2(6), pp. 766–780.

Patton, P. and Protevi, J. (2003) 'Introduction', in P. Patton and J. Protevi (eds) *Between Deleuze and Derrida*, pp. 1–14. London: Continuum.

Pignarre, P. and Stengers, I. (2011) *Capitalist Sorcery: Breaking the Spell*. New York: Palgrave Macmillan.

Pollin, R. (2007) 'Resurrection of the rentier', *New Left Review*, II(46), pp. 140–153.

Poulain, J.G. (2006) 'La détention du capital des sociétés françaises du CAC 40 à la fin 2005', *Bulletin de la Banque de France*, 149, pp. 39–41.

Preda, A. (2009) *Framing Finance*. London: University of Chicago Press.

Rancière, J. (2007) *Hatred of Democracy*. London: Verso.

Rancière, J. (2009) 'Critique de la critique du "spectacle"', *La Revue Internationale des Livres et des Idées*, 12(2009), pp. 46–52. Available at: www.revuedeslivres.net/articles.php?idArt=360 (accessed 5 February 2011).

Read, J. (2003) *The Micro-Politics of Capital.* Albany: State University of New York Press.

Read, J. (2009) 'The fetish is always actual, revolution is always virtual: from noology to noopolitics', *Deleuze Studies*, 3(Supplement), pp. 78–101.

Rousseau, J.-J. (2002) *The Social Contract, and The First and Second Discourses.* New Haven: Yale University Press.

Samuel, H. (2008) 'Banking bail-out: France unveils €360bn package', *Telegraph*, 13 October 2010. Available at: www.telegraph.co.uk/finance/financialcrisis/3190311/Banking-bail-out-France-unveils-360bn-package.html (accessed 8 September 2013).

Schiller, R. (2013) *Finance and the Good Society.* Oxford: Princeton University Press.

Schmitt, E., Taylor, A. and Greif, M. (2011) 'Scenes from an Occupation', in A. Taylor, K. Gessen, editors from n+1, Dissent, Triple Canopy and the New Inquiry (eds) *Occupy: Scenes from Occupied America*, pp. 1–6. London: Verso.

Schwab, G. (ed.) (2007) *Deleuze, Derrida, Psychoanalysis.* New York: Colombia University Press.

Sedghi, A. and Shepherd, J. (2011) 'Tuition fees 2012: what are the universities charging?', *Guardian*, 23 June 2011. Available at: www.theguardian.com/news/datablog/2011/mar/25/higher-education- universityfunding (accessed 30 January 2014).

Shaviro, S. (2010) 'The "bitter necessity" of debt: neoliberal finance and the society of control'. Available at: www.shaviro.com/Othertexts/Debt.pdf (accessed 6 May 2013).

Sibertin-Blanc, G. (2006) *Politique et Clinique: Recherche sur la Philosophie Pratique de Gilles Deleuze.* Available at: http://documents.univlille3.fr/files/pub/www/recherche/theses/SIBERTIN_BLANC_G UILLAUME.pdf (accessed 18 January 2013).

Sibertin-Blanc, G. (2009) 'Politicising Deleuzian thought, or, minority's position within Marxism', *Deleuze Studies*, 3(Supplement), pp. 119–137.

Sitrin, M. (2007) 'Ruptures in imagination: horizontalism, autogestion and affective politics in Argentina', *Policy & Practice – A Development Education Review*, 5, pp. 43–53.

SMIC (2014) 'SMIC: + 1,1 % au 1er Janvier 2014'. Available at: www.service-public.fr/actualites/00812.html (accessed 5 August 2014).

Sokal, A. and Bricmont, J. (2004) *Intellectual Impostures.* London: Profile.

Sørensen, B. M. (2005) 'Immaculate defecation: Gilles Deleuze and Félix Guattari in organization theory', in C. Jones and R. Munro (eds) *Contemporary Organization Theory*, pp. 120–133. Oxford: Blackwell.

Steinherr, A. (2000) *Derivatives: The Wild Beast of Finance. A Path to Effective Globalisation.* New York: Wiley.

Stengers, I. (2011) 'Relaying a war machine?', in E. Alliez and A. Goffey (eds) *The Guattari Effect*, pp. 134–155. London: Continuum.

Stephanson, A. and Jameson, F. (1989) 'Regarding postmodernism – a conversation with Fredric Jameson', *Social Text*, 21(July/August), pp. 3–30.

Stivale, C. J. (1984) 'The literary element in "Mille Plateaux": the new cartography of Deleuze and Guattari', *Substance*, 13(3–4), pp. 20–34.

Stivale, C. J. (ed.) (2011) *Key Concepts: Gilles Deleuze.* Durham: Acumen.

Strike Debt!, Occupy Wall Street (2012) *The Debt Resistors' Operations Manual.* New York: Common Notions.

Tampio, N. (2009) 'Assemblages and the multitude: Deleuze, Hardt, Negri, and the postmodern left', *European Journal of Political Theory*, 8(3), pp. 383–400.

Taylor, A. (2011a) 'Scenes from an Occupation', in A. Taylor, K. Gessen, editors from n+1, Dissent, Triple Canopy and the New Inquiry (eds) *Occupy: Scenes from Occupied America*, pp. 63–65. London: Verso.

Taylor, D. (2014) 'Uncertain ontologies', *Foucault Studies*, 2014(17), pp. 117–133.

Taylor, M. (2006) *From Pinochet to the Third Way: Neoliberalism and Social Transformation in Chile.* London: Pluto Press.

Taylor, S. (2011b) 'Scenes from Occupied Oakland', in A. Taylor, K. Gessen, editors from n+1, Dissent, Triple Canopy and the New Inquiry (eds) *Occupy: Scenes from Occupied America,* pp. 134–145. London: Verso.

Taylor, A. and Greif, M. (2011) 'Scenes from an Occupation', in A. Taylor, K. Gessen, editors from n+1, Dissent, Triple Canopy and the New Inquiry (eds) *Occupy: Scenes from Occupied America,* pp. 19–22. London: Verso.

The Economist (2012a) 'The feeling's mutual Mr Hollande and Mrs Merkel are clashing over Eurobonds, and more', *The Economist,* 26 May 2012. Available at: www.economist.com/node/21555917 (accessed 28 August 2013).

The Economist (2012b) 'The rather dangerous Mister Hollande', *The Economist,* 28 April 2012. Available at: www.economist.com/node/21553446 (accessed 28 August 2013).

The Free Association (2011) *Moments of Excess: Movements, Protest and Everyday Life.* Oakland: PM Press.

The Invisible Committee (2007) *The Coming Insurrection.* Paris: La Fabrique.

Thoburn, N. (2003) *Marx, Deleuze and Politics.* London: Routledge.

Thorson, K., Driscoll, K., Ekdale, B., Edgerly, S., Thompson, L. G., Schrock, A., Swartz, L., Vraga, E. K. and Wells, C. (2013) 'YouTube, Twitter and the Occupy movement: connecting content and circulation practices', *Information, Communication & Society,* 16(3), pp. 421–450.

Tiqqun (2011) *This Is Not a Program.* London: Semiotext(e).

Todd, E. (2013) 'Goodbye Hollande!', *Marianne,* 12 May. Available at: www.marianne.net/Goodbye-Hollande%C2%A0_a228622.html (accessed 28 August 2013).

Tormey, S. (2012) 'Occupy Wall Street: from representation to post-representation', *Journal of Critical Globalisation Studies,* 5, pp. 132–137.

Tournier, M. (1972) *Vendredi, ou, Les limbes du Pacifique.* Paris: Gallimard.

Turbulence Collective (2009) 'Life in limbo?', *Turbulence: Ideas for Movement,* 5, pp. 3–7.

Vlcek, W. (2010) 'Alongside global political economy – a rhizome of informal finance', *Journal of International Relations and Development,* 13(4), pp. 429–451.

Wade, R. (2008) 'Financial regime change?', *New Left Review,* II(53), pp. 5–21.

Watson, J. (2009) *Guattari's Diagrammatic Thought Writing between Lacan and Deleuze.* London: Continuum.

We Are the 99 Percent (2014). Available at: http://wearethe99percent.tumblr.com/ (accessed 28 April 2014).

Williams, J. (2003) *Gilles Deleuze's Difference and Repetition: A Critical Introduction and Guide.* Edinburgh: Edinburgh University Press.

Williams, J. (2005) *Understanding Poststructuralism.* Durham: Acumen.

Zibechi, R. (2008) 'The revolution of 1968: when those from below said enough!', *Americas Program.* Available at: www.cipamericas.org/archives/662#_ftn10 (accessed 12 May 2014).

Zibechi, R. (2010) *Dispersing Power: Social Movement as Anti-State Forces.* Oakland: AK Press.

Zibechi, R. (2012) *Territories in Resistance: A Cartography of Latin American Social Movements.* Oakland: AK Press,

Žižek, S. and Douzinas, C. (eds.) (2010) *The Idea of Communism.* London: Verso.

Žižek, S. (1989) *The Sublime Object of Ideology.* London: Verso.

Žižek, S. (ed.) (1994) *Mapping Ideology.* London: Verso.

Žižek, S. (2004) *Organs Without Bodies.* London: Routledge.

Žižek, S. (2011) 'Don't fall in love with yourselves', in A. Taylor, K. Gessen, editors from n+1, Dissent, Triple Canopy and the New Inquiry (eds) *Occupy: Scenes from Occupied America,* pp. 66–70. London: Verso.

Index

actor network: 122–123, 153–154, 158; *see also* Latour, B.

Althusser, L.: 4, 13–14, 35, 60–61, 87; *see also* symptomatology

Alliez, E.: 6, 39–41, 57, 73, 96, 98, 140; *see also* autonomism; Marxism

anarchism: 18, 27, 39–40, 45, 51, 57, 80–83, 85–86, 96, 98–99, 135, 173–175, 177, 183; multitude 169; *see also* Bey, H.; Graeber, D.; Massumi, B.

Annales School: *see also* Braudel; geophilosophy

analytic philosophy 44, 50

anti-capitalism: 17–18, 30, 32, 37, 61, 72, 75, 82, 93–94, 185; *see also* anarchism; Marxism

arborescent: 27, 31, 54, 92, 94, 152, 156, 178–179; *see also* rhizomatic

archaeology: 4–5, 132, 147; *see also* Foucault, M.; structuralism

Arrighi, G.: 106–107, 155, 172; *see also* world-systems theory

assemblage: 11, 33–34, 36, 38, 51, 54–56, 59, 63, 73–74, 89–90, 142, 148, 150, 153, 158; *see also* De Landa, M.; Deleuze, G.; Guattari, F.; Neu, D.; social studies of finance

autonomism: 18, 30–31, 76, 81–87, 89, 91, 96–99, 108, 125–126, 128, 131, 143, 162, 164, 171–172, 176; *see also* Alliez, E.; Bey, H.; Caffentzis, G.; Guattari, F.; Hardt, M.; horizontal politics; Lazzarato, M.; multitude; Negri, T.; The Invisible Committee; Tronti, M.; Read, J.; Thoburn, N.

Badiou, A.: 8, 10, 13, 15, 17, 23–32, 37–38, 42, 48, 60, 91, 179–180; *see also* communism; Maoism; Marxism; subject

Balibar, E.: 4, 83; *see also* Althusser, L.; Marxism

Baudrillard, J.: 155–159; *see also* critical Deleuzo-Guattarian literature in finance studies; Postmodernism; poststructuralism

Becker, G. S.: 115, 137; *see also* Foucault, M.; Mirowski, P.; neoliberalism

Bergson, H. 31, 39, 52, 62, 66

Bernstein, E.: 126; *see also* social democracy

Bey, H.: 172; see also anarchism; autonomism; Occupy Wall Street

body without organs: 34, 41, 141–142; *see also* Deleuze, G.; Guattari, F.

Boltanski, L.: 17, 49, 67–72, 75; *see also* Chiapello, E.; May '68; new spirit of capitalism

Bonefeld, W.: 1, 103, 106–107, 125, 127, 129–130, 146, 150, 159; *see also* financialization; Fordism; Holloway, J.; Keynesianism; open Marxism; political economy

Bosteels, B.: 15, 24, 27–28, 102, 160; speculative leftism 184; *see also* Badiou, A.; Maoism

Bourdieu, P.: 10, 67; 1995 social movement 30; higher education 119; *see also* class; culture

Braudel, F.: 35, 51; *see also* Annales School; geophilosophy

Brenner, R.: 106–107; *see also* financialization; political economy

Bricmont, J.: critique of poststructuralism 2, 93; *see also* Sokal, A.

Bryan, D.: 3, 15, 18, 103–105, 110–113, 124, 129–131, 146, 152, 159, 161, 165, 168; *see also* derivatives; financialization; Keynesianism; Rafferty, M.

buggery: methodology 6–7; 182; *see also* Deleuze, G.; Guattari, F.

177, 180–185; *see also* Deleuze, G. and
Guattari, F.

Derrida, J.: 4–6, 50, 53, 70, 87; *see also*
deconstruction

derivatives: 3, 18, 104, 110–113, 126, 138,
146, 158, 161–162, 164–165, 167–168,
172; *see also* Bryan, D.; financialization;
Rafferty, M.

desiring machines: 23, 34–35, 54–55, 63,
88, 90–91, 94, 141–142, 148, 169; *see also*
Deleuze, G.; Guattari, F.

deterritorialization: 45, 55–56, 59, 84,
89, 92–93, 97, 99, 127, 141–143,
145–146, 148, 153, 155, 156; *see also*
reterritorialization; territorialization

discipline: 5, 27, 39–41, 55, 58, 80, 90, 92, 103,
107, 112, 119–120, 126–127, 132–134,
137, 140, 145, 147, 151, 154–158, 162, 167,
180; *see also* Foucault, M.

domination: 54, 77, 97–98, 118, 127; *see also*
Tiqqun

Dosse, F.: 2, 4–5, 9–10, 15, 23, 27, 29–31,
45, 59, 72, 130, 176; *see also* Deleuze, G.;
Guattari, F.

Duménil, G.: 103, 106, 125, 128–131, 146,
150, 159; *see also* financialization; Lévy,
D.; neoliberalism

empire: 57, 84, 87, 91, 98, 131, 140, 143,
163–164, 168; *see also* Hardt, M.; Negri,
T.; post-Fordism

Engels, F.: 103, 114, 126; *see also* Marx, K.

episteme: 4–5, 147; *see also* Foucault, M.

event: 15–16, 19, 25–29, 31, 56, 63, 71,
102, 133, 144, 147, 149, 157–158, 175,
177–182, 184; *see also* Occupy Wall
Street; revolution

fascism: 29, 80, 148; *see also* Deleuze, G.;
Guattari, F.

feminism: 23–24, 45–48, 79–80, 176; *see also*
Butler, J.; Grosz, E.; Irigaray, L.; Jardine, A.

Ferry, L. 43

finance: 1–3, 18–19, 101–106, 108, 110–111,
113–115, 117–129, 133, 138–141, 151–159,
161–168, 170–172, 174, 180, 183–184;
see also finance studies; financial crisis;
financialization; Marxism; political economy

finance studies: 3, 151, 155, 157–158; *see also*
finance; financialization

financial crisis: 1, 103, 113, 163–164; *see also*
finance; finance studies; financialization;
Marxism; political economy

financialization: 1–3, 8–9, 14–19, 21, 76, 97,
99, 130–133, 135, 137–141, 145–146,
150–151, 155–156, 159–168, 170–171,
173, 182–184; revolution 175–181; history
101–104; analysis 105–122; politics
123–129; *see also* finance; finance studies;
financial crisis; Marxism; political economy

Fisher, M. 1

Fordism: 3, 14, 67, 70, 103, 106–107, 118,
120–122, 143–145, 151, 156, 161, 166–167,
180, 182; *see also* financialization;
post-Fordism

Foucault, M.: methodology 4–6; 15–16,
18–19, 47, 50, 54–55, 61, 81, 86–87,
89–90, 97–98, 102, 104, 108, 110,
129–138, 145–151, 157, 159–160,
167–175, 180, 183–184; *see also* Deleuze,
G.; poststructuralism

Freud, S.: 34, 37, 63, 144; *see also*
psychoanalysis

Froud, J. 3, 113

Garo, I.; 17, 49, 60–64, 66, 72, 74, 90, 96,
147; *see also* Marxism

genealogy: 4–5, 117, 132; see Foucault, M.;
Nietzsche, F.

geophilosophy: 51; *see also* Deleuze, G.

governmentality: 15–16, 18, 134–137, 146,
159, 184; *see also* Foucault, M.

Graeber, D.: 15, 19, 128, 161, 173–174, 183;
see also anarchism; Occupy Wall Street

Grosz, E.: 17, 23, 45–48; *see also* feminism

Guattari, F.: *A Thousand Plateaus* 2, 4–5, 7–8,
10–12, 14–16, 23, 25, 27, 31–36, 47–48,
51–54, 59–60, 63, 77, 79, 86, 91, 94,
102–103, 130, 138–140, 142–144, 146, 148,
150, 152, 162, 170, 175, 178–179; *Anti-
Oedipus* 2, 4–5, 10–12, 14–16, 23, 29,
31–37, 51, 55–56, 58–60, 62–63, 79, 84,
86–87, 89, 94, 103, 130–132, 138–142,
145–150, 157, 167, 169–170; *What is
Philosophy?* 4–5, 9, 14, 16, 23, 25, 31–37,
50–51, 55, 58–59, 61, 77, 80, 83, 91, 94, 104,
106, 150, 157; *see also* assemblage; Deleuze,
G.; Deleuzo-Guattarian; desiring machine;
molar; molecular; Negri, T.; schizophrenic

Hallward, P.: 8, 13, 17, 23–24, 37–42,
47–48, 97; *see also* Badiou, A.; Deleuze,
G., Guattari, F.

Hardt, M.: 10, 57–58, 76, 84, 86, 94, 98,
131, 147, 164, 168; *see also* Negri, T.;
post-Fordism

For Product Safety Concerns and Information please contact our EU
representative GPSR@taylorandfrancis.com
Taylor & Francis Verlag GmbH, Kaufingerstraße 24, 80331 München, Germany

www.ingramcontent.com/pod-product-compliance
Ingram Content Group UK Ltd.
Pitfield, Milton Keynes, MK11 3LW, UK
UKHW020954180425
457613UK00019B/682